the
low cholesterol
cookbook

MABEL CAVAIANI

Introduction by Joseph T. Crockett, M. D.

Contemporary Books, Inc.
Chicago

To my husband Chuck,
for whose sake I started collecting and
developing low cholesterol recipes.

contents

acknowledgments

I would like to thank the following for their professional help and encouragement in the development and writing of this book:

Larry G. Ballantine, Ph.D.
Marion Bollman, R.D., Former Chief of the Menu Planning Division, U.S. Army Food Service Center, Chicago, Illinois
Beatrice Eskew, R.N., Gainsville, Missouri
Jessie Johnston, Home Economist
Dorothy Kennedy, Home Economist, U.S. Department of Commerce, National Marine Fisheries Service
Frances Lee, R.D., M.S., Former Chief of the Experimental Kitchen, U.S. Army Natick Laboratories
Edith Robinson, R.D., M.S., Nutritionist, Northwestern University Heart Attack Prevention Program, for reading and evaluating each chapter as I finished it and for her faith in my ability to put it all down on paper.
Vernon W. Schick, M.D. for advice and suggestions
Elizabeth Wedman, R.D., for her invaluable help with the chapter on instant dry milk and other editorial comments
Mr. and Mrs. William Maplesden and their family for testing and evaluating many of the recipes in this book

I would like to thank the following organizations for background information and resources used in this book: The American Heart Association, The Chicago Heart Association and The American Dietetic Association.

introduction

With the current stress on the importance of cholesterol and its effect on the cardio-vascular system, Mrs. Cavaiani's *Low Cholesterol Cookbook* is very timely and appropriate.

Persons who go on diets are forced to change their normal food patterns and generally feel deprived of the security they find in their accustomed foods. I firmly believe that no long-term diet can be successful unless the diet is emotionally acceptable to the patient and is composed of familiar foods served in a tasteful and attractive manner. Modification of the patient's usual diet is often necessary, but it should not be to the exclusion of all of their cultural dietary habits. It is important for the cook in the family to learn how to adapt familiar recipes to fit the restrictions of the specified diet. Consultation with a doctor or dietitian can often be most helpful in accomplishing these changes.

If the doctor recommends a low cholesterol diet for a patient, it is generally wise to suggest the use of the diet for his children as well, with certain modifications. The wife should thoroughly understand the basic principles and preparation of the diet and the children should also understand the need for the diet for themselves as well as their parents. Quite often, unfortunately, the wife is given a diet and very sketchy instructions with no specific directions and very few recipes. It is difficult to change the cooking habits of a lifetime and often the diet goes by the wayside, not because it is too difficult to prepare but because she isn't really aware of the basic principles involved.

Mrs. Cavaiani, I am happy to say, has done an excellent job in compiling and writing a good basic low cholesterol diet cookbook that can be used for housewives and cooks for their day to day cooking. It explains what substitutions are necessary and how to go about making them. It is based on the guidelines established by the American Heart Association and makes it very simple to follow those guidelines. It is a cookbook, not a diet manual, as she is careful to explain. Basic guidelines should be provided by the doctor. This cookbook shows how to use those guidelines to provide delicious meals for all of the family without deviating from the low cholesterol diet.

I have known Mabel Cavaiani since I was in medical school and she was just out of college. I remember the good meals she used to prepare in the small kitchenette of her first one-room apartment and I am happy to know she has used her professional background and interest in foods to prepare these low cholesterol recipes, which she is sharing with you. Incidentally, her husband Chuck has thrived on the recipes.

I shall not go into the arguments for and against the low cholesterol diet. Let it be sufficient to say I thoroughly support the principles of the low cholesterol diet as established by the American Heart Association and I hope you will read every page of this book since it explains those principles in a clear, concise and often amusing manner.

Joseph T. Crockett, M.D.
L.F.A.P.A.

preface

This is a cookbook, not a diet manual. It is a collection of recipes developed for the use of all of us who keep a "low cholesterol kitchen." It includes recipes and suggestions that you can use secure in the knowledge that they follow the basic guidelines established for a fat controlled, low cholesterol diet by the American Heart Association. I hope that it will help to explain the methods of food preparation necessary to a low cholesterol diet. No one book could contain *all* the recipes suitable for a low cholesterol diet; however, these recipes will serve as an introduction to the great variety of recipes you can use, and show you how to adapt many of the recipes you are using now to a low cholesterol diet.

When the doctor put your husband on a low cholesterol diet, I'm sure you thought that the future was going to be pretty horrible. But don't push the panic button — it really isn't as bad as all that. He wasn't condemning your husband to a life of dull and unappetizing "diet food." A low cholesterol diet can include such goodies as roast sirloin of beef, baked potatoes, tossed salads, hot breads, and apple pie! In fact, there are many and varied recipes that you can use and still follow the basic guidelines of the diet. I'm sure that you will find as you read through this book — and please do read through it, because all sorts of facts are scattered throughout — that many of your old favorites are included. An ingredient or two may be changed, but the basic product is the same.

When our doctor told my husband that it would be advisable for him to follow a low cholesterol diet, I, as a dietitian, was discouraged to discover how few recipes were available for my use. I decided right then to collect recipes that I could use for him and the rest of my family, and I was delighted to discover that the recipes I collected were so good that everyone in the family enjoyed them. I really didn't need to prepare one recipe for him and another for the rest of us. In fact, I found that, after we tried the low cholesterol cooking, we really preferred it. Now I am convinced that a low cholesterol diet is a good way of life for most people. It keeps my husband healthier and happier, and I'm sure that it will do the same for yours. I'm also sure that you will agree with me, after you have used it for a time, that you wouldn't go back to loads of butter, cream, and fat meat even if your doctor approved.

It is generally agreed that any woman whose husband must follow a low cholesterol diet is wise to use it as a guide in planning meals for her whole family. It encourages her children to follow a pattern that will become a habit with them, and this habit will probably help to prevent future heart attacks for them. The low cholesterol diet is not a short term project. It should generally be followed indefinitely. However, I'm happy to be able to tell you that you will find that it is an exceedingly simple adjustment to make. It is based on the substitution of polyunsaturated fats for saturated fats in the diet. To be more explicit, the American Heart Association explains it as follows:

Saturated animal fats are found in beef, lamb, pork, and ham; in butter, cream, and whole milk; and in cheese made from cream and whole milk.

Saturated vegetable fats are found in many solid and hydrogenated shortenings and in coconut oil, cocoa butter, and palm oil. Palm oil is used in commercially prepared cookies, pie fillings, and non-dairy milk and cream substitutes.

Polyunsaturated fats, which are recommended in this diet, are usually liquid oils of vegetable origin such as corn, cottonseed, safflower, sesame seed, soybean, and sunflower seed oils. They tend to lower the level of cholesterol in the blood by helping to eliminate excess newly formed cholesterol. Olive oil and peanut oil are also vegetable products but they are low in unsaturated fats and neither raise nor lower blood cholesterol. They may be used for flavor occasionally, but they do not take the place of the polyunsaturated fats. Your daily use of salad dressings, cooking fats, and margarines should emphasize the use of the polyunsaturated vegetable oils for their cholesterol lowering effects.

Chicken, turkey, fish, and lean veal are low in total fats and are recommended for your use in daily meal planning.

Hydrogenation changes liquid fats to solid fats, and hydrogenated foods should be avoided or used in moderation; but most margarines and shortenings that contain partially hydrogenated oils also contain acceptable amounts of polyunsaturates.

Most men cherish their masculine image. They take a dim view of anything that might call attention to the fact that they can no longer consume vast quantities of bacon and eggs and roast prime ribs of beef. (Of course, we know that a lot of their trouble is caused by these same eating habits, but it really isn't very tactful to talk about that right now.) However, there is no reason that you can't plan the same sort of meals they have been having, with a few modifications, and still stay within the diet restrictions established by your doctor. (The recipes in this book are for a low cholesterol diet. However, you must follow the guidelines that the doctor gives you. If your husband must lose weight, you should stick to the low calorie recipes with less fat in them until he has lost the required amount of weight.) In fact, no one needs to call attention to the fact that your husband is following a diet. Of course, if your husband likes to talk about his diet, let him go right ahead. You can just sit back and take the compliments about what good meals you have been serving in line with his diet.

One of the most important aspects of this new way of life is your own attitude. *The first thing* for you to do is to decide upon a positive approach to the problem. It is much easier for everyone concerned if you assume that this new method of cooking and planning menus is going to be interesting and rewarding — and, believe me, it *is* going to be rewarding for you. There are few rewards in life greater than seeing your husband healthy and happy. It is ever so much better to tell your family that you have a wonderful new recipe for homemade bread or roast beef than to apologize for the fact that it isn't the same recipe you had used previously. These new recipes that you will be using should not be judged against your old ones. These are new recipes, and should be judged on their own merits.

The second thing for you to do is to get rid of any lard, butter, cream, or other animal fats that you now have in your cupboard or refrigerator. Some people feel that you should serve butter and cream to guests, but I feel that it is your husband's home and should be managed for *his* well-being. I serve my guests margarine because that is what is best for my husband, and I feel that they certainly can use the margarine while they are in our home. You don't need to be offensive about it; just don't serve anything else, and if your guests say anything, just tell them very sweetly why you are doing it and go on to another subject. Who knows? They may be on the same diet and appreciate the fact that you are serving foods that they can eat also!

The third thing for you to do is to see to it that your cupboards, refrigerator, and freezer contain only the foods that are authorized for the diet. Of course, if other members of your family are on other special diets, then by all means go ahead and stock their needs, but it is much simpler to have only the things that are approved for this diet in the house. If you go to prepare a recipe and the only foods available are approved foods, it will certainly assure your using the right ones. The ingredients in this book all conform to the guidelines established by the American Heart Association for a fat controlled low cholesterol diet. If you want to use a recipe not in this book, you can check it out with the following guidelines from the American Heart Association:

MEAT, POULTRY, FISH, DRIED BEANS, PEAS, NUTS, AND EGGS

Recommended:

In most of your meat meals for the week: chicken, turkey, veal, fish.

In no more than five meals per week: beef, lamb, pork, ham.

High in vegetable protein and may be used in place of meat, occasionally: kidney beans, lima beans, baked beans, lentils, chick peas (garbanzos), split peas.

Egg whites as desired.

Avoid or use sparingly:

Duck, goose.

Shrimp are low in fat but high in cholesterol; use a 4 oz. serving not more than once a week.

Heavily marbled and fatty meats: spareribs, mutton, frankfurters, sausages, fatty hamburgers, bacon, luncheon meats.

Organ meats are very high in cholesterol (since liver is so high in vitamins and iron it may be served in one 4 oz. serving per week): liver, kidneys, heart, sweetbreads.

Egg yolks: limit three per week.

Cakes, batters, sauces and other food containing egg yolks.

VEGETABLES AND FRUITS

Recommended:

One serving every day should be a source of vitamin C: broccoli, raw cabbage, tomatoes, berries, cantaloupe, grapefruit, mango, melon, oranges, papaya, strawberries, tangerines.

One serving should be a source of vitamin A: dark green leafy or yellow vegetables or fruits, broccoli, carrots, chard, chicory, escarole, greens, peas, rutabagas, string beans, sweet potatoes and yams, watercress, winter squash, yellow corn, apricots, cantaloupe, mango, papaya.

Other vegetables and fruits are very nutritious and should be eaten in addition to the recommended daily allowance of high Vitamin C and A vegetables.

Avoid or use sparingly:

Olives and avocados are very high in fat calories and should be used sparingly.

BREAD AND CEREALS (whole grain, enriched or restored)

Recommended:

Breads made with a minimum of saturated fat: white enriched, whole wheat, English muffins, French bread, Italian bread, oatmeal bread, pumpernickel, rye.

Biscuits, muffins, griddle cakes made at home using an allowed oil as shortening.

Cereal (hot and cold), rice, melba toast, matzo, pretzels.

Pasta, macaroni, noodles (except egg noodles), spaghetti.

Avoid or use sparingly:

Butter rolls, commercial biscuits, muffins, donuts, sweet rolls, cakes, crackers, egg bread, cheese bread, commercial mixes using dried eggs and whole milk.

MILK PRODUCTS

Recommended:

Milk products that are low in dairy fats: fortified skimmed (nonfat) milk and fortified skimmed milk powder, low fat milk. (The label on the container should show that the milk is fortified with vitamins A and D. The word fortified is not enough.)

Buttermilk, yogurt, evaporated milk and cocoa made from skimmed milk or low fat milk.

Cheeses made from skimmed or partially skimmed milk such as cottage cheese (preferably uncreamed): farmer's, baker's, or hoop cheese, mozzarella and sapsago cheese made with partially skimmed milk.

Avoid or use sparingly:

Whole milk and whole milk products: chocolate milk, canned whole milk, ice cream, all creams including half and half, whipped cream, whole milk yogurt.

Nondairy cream substitutes, which usually contain coconut oil.

Cheeses made from cream or whole milk.

Butter.

FATS AND OILS

Recommended:

Margarines, liquid oil shortenings, salad dressings, and mayonnaise containing any of the following polyunsaturated vegetable oils: corn oil, cottonseed oil, safflower oil, sesame seed oil, soybean oil, sunflower seed oil.

Margarines and other products high in polyunsaturates can usually be identified by their label, which lists a recommended liquid vegetable oil as the first ingredient and one or more partially hydrogenated vegetable oils as additional ingredients. (Diet margarines are low in calories because they are low in fat. Therefore, it takes twice as much diet margarine to supply the polyunsaturates contained in a recommended margarine.)

Avoid or use sparingly:

Solid fats and shortenings: butter, lard, salt pork fat, meat fat, completely hydrogenated margarines and vegetable shortenings.

Peanut oil and olive oil may be used occasionally for flavor, but they are low in polyunsaturates and do not take the place of the recommended oils.

DESSERTS, BEVERAGES, SNACKS, CONDIMENTS

Acceptable — low in calories or no calories:
Fresh fruit and fruit canned without sugar, tea or coffee (no cream), cocoa powder, water ices, gelatin, fruit whips, puddings made with nonfat milk, sweets and bottled drinks made with artificial sweeteners, vinegar, mustard, catsup, herbs and spices.

Acceptable — high in calories:
Frozen or canned fruit with sugar added, jelly, jam, marmalade, honey, pure sugar candy such as gum drops, hard candy, mint patties (not chocolate), imitation ice cream made with safflower oil, cakes, pies, cookies, and puddings made with a polyunsaturated fat in place of solid shortening, angelfood cakes, nuts, especially walnuts, nonhydrogenated peanut butter, bottled drinks, fruit drinks, ice milk, sherbet, wine, beer, and whiskey.

Avoid or use sparingly:
Coconut and coconut oil, commercial cakes, pies, cookies, and mixes, frozen cream pies, commercially fried foods such as potato chips and other deep fried snacks, whole milk puddings, chocolate pudding (high in cocoa butter and therefore high in saturated fat), ice cream.

There are some good cholesterol free foods which have been developed by industry for use on a low cholesterol diet. Your local Heart Associaton can give you a list of them and help you learn which are available in your area. These include liquid egg substitutes, cholesterol free cheese and vegetable protein meat substitutes.

Liquid egg substitutes are not used in recipes in this book but may be used freely on a low cholesterol diet. They may be used in your own recipes as directed by information on the container. You may also substitute them using three tablespoons per egg white for egg whites in these recipes. Egg whites are generally less expensive than the liquid egg substitute, but there may be times when you prefer the liquid egg substitute, such as when you are making mayonnaise or French toast. My husband uses the liquid egg substitute and the cholesterol free cheese to make a great omelet, although I prefer to make an omelet using the liquid egg substitute along with onions, peppers and tomatoes for a Spanish omelet.

I would also like to point out that research has shown that an increased use of fiber seems to help lower the cholesterol count. Increasing fiber in the diet is really not all that difficult. Changing from white to whole wheat bread and adding a couple or three servings of fruits and vegetables a day will be enough to really help, and you should be doing that anyway.

High fiber also helps when you are trying to help your husband lose weight, since foods which are high in fiber are generally lower in calories than many of the processed foods in common use. High fiber foods take longer to chew. They are often more filling than other foods and tend to give a more satisfied feeling between meals.

As you can see from the above listing, there is really a great variety of foods still available to you for your menu planning. It is just a question of using the right ingredients and the right recipes. So cheerio, chin up, and remember the success or failure of your husband's diet depends on you and the food you offer him. And with these recipes you can offer him some wonderful meals!

chapter I

instant dry milk

Your doctor has probably suggested that you use skim milk in your battle against dairy fats. Probably, you discovered the skim milk available at the dairy counter is a weak, spiritless liquid that your husband uses only because it is the doctor's orders. I'm happy to say that this skim milk can be greatly improved by adding a quarter cup of instant nonfat dry milk to each quart. If your husband was in the Second World War, as mine was, he will probably give an anguished cry at the suggestion and refuse that horrible tasting stuff. Fortunately, the nonfat dry milk of today is greatly improved. It lost the sweetish caramel taste that used to mark it, and I defy anyone to notice it in your cooking. There are three forms of nonfat dry milk available now. However, the type generally available in stores is instant nonfat dry milk, which is the type used in this book. Not only is it the most available, it dissolves very easily in water or any other liquid and deserves the name instant.

There are many advantages to using instant dry milk: It costs just about half as much as the skim milk you find on the dairy counter. It is easy to store since it can be kept, unrefrigerated, in a large package. You can use it in its dry form for most cooking purposes. In fact, after you use it for some time you will wonder why no one told you about this convenience a long time ago.

Measures for instant dry milk vary from manufacturer to manufacturer. Therefore, read the directions on the package very carefully and use amounts as directed. I have used 3.2 ounces instant dry milk (or 1⅓ cups) to reconstitute a quart of liquid milk. Most manufacturers use this measure.

Since instant dry milk is whole milk with the fat and water removed, it may not act the way whole milk does in some recipes. Certain adjustments are necessary. The most important thing to remember is that there is a correct way to use it in each type of recipe. Generally speaking, you can use the directions on the package when substituting instant dry milk for whole or skim milk. However, when preparing cream sauces, puddings, and cream soups, it is best to increase the amount of instant dry milk by at least 50 percent. The table may be of help to you in figuring out how to substitute instant dry milk for whole milk in your recipes.

INSTANT DRY MILK CONVERSION TABLE

Instant Dry Milk	Water	Fluid Skim Milk
Regular Use		
⅓ cup	¾ cup	1 cup
⅔ cup	1¾ cups	2 cups
1 cup	2½ cups	3 cups
1⅓ cups	3½ cups	1 quart
Enriched Milk for Cream Sauces, Beverages, and Cream Soups		
½ cup	¾ cup	1 cup
1 cup	1¾ cups	2 cups
1½ cups	2½ cups	3 cups
2 cups	3¼ cups	1 quart

Note: If the package directions tell you to add butter to compensate for the loss of butterfat in the recipe, ignore them. Remember that getting rid of the butterfat in your husband's diet is the whole purpose for using instant dry milk in the first place.

Since instant dry milk can be added to many recipes in its dry form, without being reconstituted, it is really wonderful for baking. This means that many recipes you thought you could no longer use can be adapted to a low cholesterol diet by using instant dry milk and vegetable oil. If your husband enjoys a hot muffin for breakfast you could use the Basic Muffin recipe, or any of its variations — as long as you remember not to add anything containing a saturated fat.

And now that we have introduced you to the many advantages of instant dry milk in the low cholesterol diet and for general cooking, I would like to suggest that you use it for your whole family as well as for your husband. It will make your cooking so much simpler and will help to train your children to eat wisely and may prevent future heart trouble for them. Most of the recipes in this book that include milk specify instant dry milk. I'm sure you will find it so easy and advantageous to use that you will wonder again why someone didn't tell you about this wonderful stuff a long time ago.

If you are a dedicated bread baker, as I am — what else gives you the opportunity to work out all your frustrations by really beating something around? — you will love the convenience of instant dry milk for your bread baking. It is important in making some breads to scald the milk before using it. If you are using instant dry milk, you can skip that scalding step. However, don't forget that if the recipe calls for adding something to the hot milk, you should have the water hot enough to use instead of the scalded milk. The instant dry milk is added with the flour and the necessary amount of water is used as liquid. Using the instant dry milk is especially helpful in preparing a low cholesterol high protein diet for someone in your family, since you can increase the amount of protein and calcium in a very tasty way. Bread made with instant dry milk browns more evenly, the crust is more tender, and it seems to stay fresh longer. In fact, a great many bread recipes can be adapted for the diet by using instant dry milk, vegetable oil and yellow food coloring instead of the whole milk, butter, and eggs originally called for. And there is just something about homemade bread that makes your husband feel you really care and maybe this diet isn't so bad after all. The Fruit Bread recipe is popular with my family and friends, who never guess that it was adapted for a low cholesterol diet. It uses a lot of tricks to make it seem as though there are butter and eggs in it, but there really isn't a forbidden ingredient in it.

If your husband likes cream puddings but you have been forced to eliminate them from his diet because of the eggs and milk you might try one of the recipes adapted for Vanilla or Chocolate Cream Pudding. (Never use prepared puddings without reading the list of ingredients. Some of them are too rich in eggs and fat.) The Vanilla Cream Pudding uses yellow food coloring to give it a characteristic egg color. This is a really good pudding to use as a basis for all kinds of cream puddings and desserts. The recipe for Chocolate Cream Pudding has been adapted to use cocoa. Since cocoa has some thickening power of its own, less cornstarch is used.

Instant potatoes are a handy item; you can use them in many

ways to make a low cholesterol diet more interesting. They are much easier to prepare with instant dry milk, because you can combine these two dry ingredients and the seasonings, then add them all to the hot water. If your mixer has a metal bowl, the hot water can be put in and the mixing can be done in it; however, if the bowl of your mixer is glass, it is better to use a hand mixer and a metal bowl or pot for combining the hot water and dry ingredients.

Although proportions of water and potatoes may vary according to the brand of potatoes you use, the recipe for Instant Mashed Potatoes illustrates the easiest way to combine them. The same method can also be used successfully to prepare Instant Potato Soup.

The most important thing to remember when you are using instant dry milk in your recipes is that it should be added with the dry ingredients if possible. A simple way to do it is to take the basic recipe and figure out how much instant dry milk you will need to replace the milk in the recipe. Then decide whether the milk can be added to the dry ingredients or whether it first has to be reconstituted with water. In most cases you can add the instant milk to the other dry ingredients, then combine the water with the other liquids and continue as the recipe directs. You can even do this with meat loaf. Just add the instant dry milk with the meat and seasonings and use the correct amount of water for mixing the loaf.

Instant dry milk reconstitutes most easily in warm water. Just stir the instant dry milk into the warm water and it is ready to use for cooking. However, there are times when you do not want the milk to be warm. In that case, reconstitute the milk in cold water. You would use cold water if you were going to add the reconstituted milk to salad dressing, or, of course, to serve as a beverage. In order to understand the best method to use, I made a list for myself when I was first using it. It may be of help to you.

Instant dry milk may be used in the following ways:
1. Added to ingredients without reconstitution; as in meat loaf and instant mashed potatoes.
2. Mixed with dry ingredients; as in cakes, cookies, breads, and frosting.

3. Reconstituted in cold water and added; as for thinning salad dressings.
4. Reconstituted in warm water and combined with other ingredients before further cooking; as for gravies.
5. Reconstituted in warm water and added just before serving; as in some soups.
6. Combined with dry ingredients and water to make a thin liquid that is then added to boiling water; as in pudding and cocoa. (This method saves time and stirring because the food comes to a boil much faster).

Instant milk used as a beverage should be mixed with water, then chilled before it is served. One of the better known brands has envelopes that contain the right amount of instant dry milk to yield 1 quart of reconstituted milk. A friend of mine keeps some of these envelopes in her cupboard for her teenage son who thinks they are the greatest. He prepares the milk with ice cold water and then drinks it without further chilling. She appreciates the savings in money, as well as refrigerator space. If your husband prefers the taste of fresh milk, you could enrich the dairy counter skim milk with some instant dry milk, or you could mix up a quart of enriched instant dry milk and combine it with an equal amount of commercial skim milk. Instant dry milk can also be used to an advantage in preparing Hot Cocoa. (Cocoa should be used, not chocolate, to avoid the cocoa butter in chocolate.)

I think that whipping instant dry milk with gelatin is also one of the best methods, and it may be used for a great variety of desserts. It duplicates the creamy texture of a Bavarian Cream without including the forbidden whipped cream. It is so simple, yet so good, that I'm sure that your family will like it — and you can always serve it to friends who are dieting because it is so pretty and certainly lower in calories.

Instant dry milk may also be whipped and used as topping instead of whipped cream. It will never be as rich as whipped cream, but it does make a very good topping and will help to rescue your strawberry shortcake from the doldrums. Various brands of instant dry milk will have different yields but generally speaking you will get about three times as much whipped topping as the amount of water and instant dry milk combined. It helps to have the mixture, your bowl, and beater very cold. The whipped milk is not stable for too long a period; therefore, you should whip it as close to serving time as possible, then refrigerate it until ready to serve. If you take it out of the refrigerator again the next day and it is no longer light and fluffy, you can whip it up again. It will be satisfactory a second time. Chilled fruit juice may also be used instead of the ice water to give a pretty, flavorful topping.

Instant dry milk can also be used to prepare buttermilk if you need it for a recipe or if your husband likes to drink it. Some buttermilk is made without butterfat, but you can't be sure unless you check the list of ingredients on the container. If the brand that you have been using includes butterfat you can very easily make your own.

basic muffins

Yields 12 muffins

1 egg white	⅓ cup instant dry milk
¾ cup water	¼ cup sugar
¼ cup vegetable oil	1 tablespoon baking powder
2 cups all purpose flour	1 teaspoon salt

Beat egg white lightly with a fork. Stir water and oil into the egg white. Sift flour, instant dry milk, sugar, baking powder, and salt together into a bowl. Add egg mixture to flour mixture. Stir only until flour is moistened. Do not overmix. Fill oiled muffin tins ⅔ full of batter. Bake in a preheated hot oven (400°F) for 20 to 25 minutes or until golden brown. Loosen muffins from pans and serve them warm.

Variations
Nut Muffins: Add ½ cup chopped nuts to the dry ingredients.
Cranberry Muffins: Add ½ cup fresh cranberries to the egg mixture.
Orange Muffins: Put about 1 teaspoon orange marmalade on top of each muffin before you put them in the oven.
Spice Muffins: Add ¼ teaspoon each of ground cinnamon, cloves, and allspice with the dry ingredients.

fruit bread

Yields 3 loaves

1 cup warm water
1 tablespoon sugar
1 ounce compressed yeast
2 cups hot water
1 cup instant dry milk
1 cup sugar
¼ cup vegetable oil

¼ teaspoon yellow
　food coloring
1 cup chopped candied fruit
½ cup washed and drained
　light raisins
½ cup washed and drained
　dark raisins
10½ cups all purpose flour

Combine warm water, 1 tablespoon sugar, and compressed yeast. Allow yeast mixture to stand until it bubbles nicely, about 5 minutes. Put hot water into mixer bowl. Add instant dry milk, 1 cup sugar, oil, and yellow food coloring. Mix well. Add 1 cup flour and mix well. Add yeast mixture and beat well. Add 3 cups flour and beat well for about 5 minutes at medium speed or until it is too thick to beat in your mixer. (As the gluten develops, the batter will get thicker and harder to beat.) Remove the batter from the mixer and put it in a large bowl.

Add the fruit and raisins, stirring them into the batter. Continue to add flour and mix the dough until it leaves the sides of the bowl (about 4 to 5 cups of flour). Spread the remaining flour on a pastry board or work counter; turn the dough out onto the board; and knead well, using as much of the flour as necessary to make a light dough that is no longer sticky.

Return the dough to the bowl, grease the top of it lightly, and cover it. Let the dough rise in a warm place until it has doubled in volume. Punch it down, knead it for about 5 minutes, and return to the bowl. Let it rise again until it has doubled in volume. Turn the dough out onto a lightly floured pastry board, knead it lightly, and divide it into three portions. Round each portion into a ball, cover them with a cloth, and let them stand about 15 minutes. Shape each ball into a loaf, and put them into greased 9 x 5 x 3 inch loaf pans. Cover the pans lightly with a cloth and let the loaves rise again until doubled in volume. Bake in a preheated oven for 15 minutes at 400°F, then for 45 minutes at 350°F. Remove loaves from the oven and turn them out onto a wire rack. Brush them with melted margarine and allow them to cool. Frost them with powdered sugar frosting after cooled if desired.

vanilla cream pudding

Serves 4

½ cup water
1 cup instant dry milk
½ cup sugar
2½ tablespoons cornstarch
¼ teaspoon salt

1¼ cups water
3 drops yellow food
    coloring
1 tablespoon margarine
1 teaspoon vanilla

Combine ½ cup water with instant dry milk, sugar, cornstarch, and salt. Stir into a smooth liquid. Bring remaining water to a boil in a small saucepan. Add sugar mixture to boiling water. Stirring constantly, bring to boil again over low heat and cook for about 3 minutes. Remove from heat and add yellow food coloring, margarine, and vanilla. Stir lightly to mix well. Pour into dishes to cool.

chocolate cream pudding

Serves 4

½ cup water
1 cup instant dry milk
½ cup sugar
2¼ tablespoons cornstarch
2 tablespoons cocoa

¼ teaspoon salt
1¼ cups water
1 tablespoon margarine
1 teaspoon vanilla
1 tablespoon rum (optional)

Prepare pudding according to directions for the vanilla pudding, adding the cocoa with the sugar and cornstarch, and deleting the yellow food coloring.

This pudding is delicious with about a tablespoon of rum added with the vanilla.

instant mashed potatoes

Serves 4

1⅓ cups instant potatoes
⅓ cup instant dry milk
½ teaspoon salt

2 tablespoons margarine
1½ cups hot water
Paprika (optional)

The water should be hot but not boiling when used.

Combine instant potatoes, instant dry milk, and salt. Stir to mix well. Add margarine to hot water. Pour potato mixture into water, stirring with a fork until the potatoes are dissolved. Put into mixer bowl and beat 2 or 3 minutes at medium speed and 2 minutes at high speed. A little more water may be added if you like thinner mashed potatoes. Potatoes may be dusted with paprika before serving if desired.

This soup is a delicious hurry up dish for lunch on a cold day. No one will ever suspect you didn't spend the morning over a hot stove preparing it.

instant potato soup

Serves 4

½ cup finely chopped onions
¼ cup (½ stick) margarine
4 cups cold water
1¼ cups instant potatoes

1 cup instant dry milk
1 teaspoon salt
½ teaspoon white pepper

Sauté onions until lightly browned in margarine in a heavy saucepan. (A heavy saucepan will help you to keep the heat even and not burn the onions or scorch the soup.) Add water to onions, bring to a boil and cook 2 minutes. Combine instant potatoes, instant dry milk, salt and pepper. Stir lightly with a fork to mix well. Pour potato mixture into boiling water and onion mixture which has been removed from the heat. Stir with a fork until well mixed. Let soup stand about 5 minutes. Return to heat and bring to serving temperature. Do not allow soup to come to a boil because it will probably curdle if it does boil.

hot cocoa

Serves 6

¼ cup sugar
¼ cup cocoa
 1 cup instant dry milk
⅛ teaspoon salt

1 cup cold water
3 cups water
1 teaspoon vanilla
   Marshmallows (optional)

Combine sugar, cocoa, instant dry milk, and salt with 1 cup of the cold water. Stir to form a smooth liquid. Bring the remaining 3 cups of water to a boil. Turn the heat down and stir the cocoa mixture into the simmering water. Bring the cocoa back to serving temperature but do not boil. Add the vanilla and beat with a whisk until foamy. Pour into cups and serve. Marshmallows may be added if desired or it may be chilled and served as chocolate milk.

pineapple banana chiffon pie

Yield 1 9-inch pie

1 prebaked 9-inch pie shell
1 3-ounce package
   lemon gelatin
1 cup boiling water
1 cup drained, crushed
   pineapple

2 tablespoons lemon juice
   water, as necessary
⅓ cup instant dry milk
2 medium size bananas

Prepare a baked pie shell according to the directions in Chapter XI. Dissolve gelatin in boiling water. Drain pineapple well, reserving juice. Add lemon juice and enough water to pineapple juice to make 1 cup of liquid. Add liquid to gelatin and chill to a jelly-like consistency. Sprinkle instant dry milk over gelatin and beat at high speed until doubled in volume. Slice bananas and fold into gelatin. Pour gelatin and fruit mixture into pie shell and chill at least an hour before serving.

whipped instant dry milk

Yields 2½ to 3 cups

½ cup instant dry milk
¼ cup ice water

2 tablespoons lemon juice
¼ cup sugar

Combine instant dry milk and ice water in a chilled bowl and whip at high speed for about 4 minutes until soft peaks are formed. Add the lemon juice and continue to beat the mixture at high speed about 4 more minutes or until stiff. Fold the sugar into the mixture and refrigerate it until time to serve.

low fat buttermilk

Yields 1 quart buttermilk

1⅔ cups instant dry milk
3¼ cups water

½ cup buttermilk

Combine instant dry milk and water. Add buttermilk, stir lightly to mix and pour into a clean container. Allow milk to stand 8 hours or overnight at room temperature. Refrigerate until ready to use. (Buttermilk that you have prepared may also be used to start another batch of buttermilk.)

chapter II
appetizers and beverages

Cocktail parties can present many pitfalls for the unwary man who doesn't understand what is in all of those delicious little morsels. You don't want to hover over him, so it is a good idea to be sure he understands that liver paté, cheese balls, and dips with a sour cream or cream cheese base are forbidden. Most hostesses serve something for their calorie conscious friends such as carrot sticks, cherry tomatoes, or slices of smoked salmon or turkey. These are always permissible as well as assorted olives, which are high in calories but low in cholesterol. It is simplest if you are entertaining at home, where you can provide a variety of tidbits that he can enjoy with confidence. Miniature meat balls, spiced nuts, garlic olives, or miniature hamburgers or turkey sandwiches are only a few of the many items you can prepare. If you feel that the party is not complete without a paté, you can serve the salmon paté, which is low in cholesterol but high in acceptability.

Marinated beef chunks are a good contrast to the salmon paté if you want something with a little more texture and a more pronounced flavor. They can be served with a toothpick but that can be messy. It is better to save them for a small group where it is practical to provide each guest with a plate and fork.

When you are running a restaurant, it is a good idea to get along with all of your employees and hope that they will do the same. I had to work out the proportions for the recipe for Paprika Dip myself, but I got the list of the basic ingredients because of a disagreement in a Hungarian restaurant. When I complimented the waiter on the cheese, he told me what was in it because he was mad at the chef that day. I probably shouldn't have listened but my insatiable curiosity got the best of me — as it always does when a recipe is concerned — and I listened and remembered everything he told me. It is specially good for stuffing those little cherry tomatoes that look so good on an appetizer tray.

The Onion Dip and the Tunafish Dip are also good, although they are sort of standard. Still, on certain informal occasions a dip seems to add the right touch.

Many Italian stores carry antipasto packed in glass containers, which is always good since it is generally packed in olive oil and usually contains fish. If the antipasto is unavailable or you don't care for it, you can prepare your own marinated vegetables.

Remember that appetizers are to stimulate the appetite not depress it, so keep your servings small and colorful and not too rich. A light, not too sweet, fruit juice is good; and the old faithful tomato juice can be varied with many seasonings and herbs. You can serve hot bouillon or consomme laced with sherry on a cold day or something cool and icy on a hot day.

If you move into the dining room for your appetizer, you can branch out with a great variety of colorful and appetizing foods. Fruit cups come into their own here and you can vary them with the season. The fruit cups should be thoroughly chilled and can be garnished with a sprig of mint, a particularly fine strawberry, or a small scoop of sherbet. A teaspoon of Kirsch or Grand Marnier on each serving will greatly enhance the flavor of the fruit. A little champagne or ginger ale added to it just before it is served will give it an additional sparkle.

When melon is in season you can serve a very attractive melon cup or thin slices of honeydew melon with even thinner slices of lean ham. Cut the melon in half, remove the seeds, and slice the pieces about ¾ inch wide. Cut along the bottom of the melon near the rind but don't separate the melon from the rind. Put two slices of melon on a glass plate with two slices of ham at an angle, sprinkle the ham with coarsely ground pepper, and serve with a slice of lemon.

If your husband enjoys a shrimp or seafood cocktail on festive occasions, you can serve a fish cocktail instead of the seafood. Most of the flavor is in the sauce anyway. Use poached or steamed fish, serve it well chilled with a tasty sauce and bread sticks, and he'll love it. (Just remember to leave the fish in chunks for texture.)

Your husband's doctor will tell him how much and what kind of beverage is allowed in his diet. Black coffee is preferable to coffee with cream; in fact, cream is forbidden. If your husband insists he can't drink his coffee black, you can suggest he substitute double-strength reconstituted instant dry milk or dairy skim milk that has been enriched by the addition of ¼ to ½ cup of instant dry milk per quart. Artificial whiteners should be avoided unless you are very sure that they do not contain any saturated fats because many of them contain coconut oil. Regular evaporated and condensed milk should also be avoided because of their butterfat content, although evaporated skim milk is allowed. You might suggest that he use instant dry milk instead of the artificial coffee whiteners. The milk can be kept in a covered sugar bowl on the table or in one of those little glass dispensers for sugar. The instant dry milk can be stirred into hot coffee, which will dissolve the milk, or it can be mixed with instant coffee (according to the amount your husband likes), then the boiling water that dissolves the coffee will dissolve the milk as well.

Although alcoholic beverages do not contain cholesterol, they are high in calories and should be used sparingly if calories are important. Wine with soda or vodka with orange juice are comparatively low in calories and make a very good substitute for some of the stronger drinks. Some doctors feel that a glass of wine with dinner is a good idea, other doctors may forbid alcoholic beverages at any time.

Fruit juices are always acceptable and refreshing. They provide a good supply of vitamins and add color and zest to a meal or a snack. They may be used without restriction since there is no cholesterol in fruits or vegetables.

Chapter I includes a recipe for hot cocoa that may be chilled and used for chocolate milk. Other milk drinks may also be made with skim milk or reconstituted instant dry milk instead of whole milk or cream. It is not wise to use commercial chocolate milk since it generally contains butterfat.

Carbonated beverages may be used at your doctor's discretion, but they are generally allowed freely on a low cholesterol diet.

This is not the place for a bartender's guide nor a long list of cocktails or other drink recipes, but I do want to share with you one of the best hot drinks for a cold day I've ever found. It is for Hot Buttered Rum as made by a friend of ours, Robert Ihrig. Of course, we use margarine instead of butter and Bob and I don't agree on the amount of rum to use. I think that a cup of rum per gallon of cider is just about right — he thinks that a quart of rum per gallon of cider is right. However your tastes go I'm sure that you would like it in one of the versions.

salmon pepper paté

Yields about 2 cups

1 pound can red salmon	½ teaspoon onion powder
¾ cup (1½ sticks) margarine	½ teaspoon paprika
1 teaspoon lemon pepper or	¼ teaspoon monosodium
1 tablespoon lemon juice and	glutamate (MSG)
¼ teaspoon black pepper	

Drain salmon and remove bones and skin.

Cream margarine until light and fluffy in small bowl of mixer. Add salmon, lemon pepper, onion powder, paprika, and monosodium glutamate to creamed margarine and beat at medium speed until smooth. Scrape down bowl twice while combining margarine with other ingredients.

Grease a 2-cup mold or small bowl well with softened margarine and press paté into mold. Chill in refrigerator at least 3 hours before serving. Unmold and garnish with stuffed olives or pimiento strips. Serve with melba toast strips.

marinated beef chunks

Yields about 4 cups

¼ cup finely chopped fresh green peppers	4 cups cold, cubed, roasted or boiled beef

¼ cup finely chopped onions

1 cup of your favorite
   French or Italian
   dressing

Combiné all ingredients and marinate for 8 to 24 hours. Drain off excess dressing and serve in a glass bowl. (The glass bowl is because it looks prettier that way. It won't hurt it a bit to serve it in a ceramic or stainless steel bowl if you like it better that way.)

Veal or lamb may be substituted for the beef but pork or chicken don't work out as well.

Be sure that you have removed all visible fat from the meat and cooked it according to the directions in this book.

paprika dip

Yields about 2 cups

1 pound farmer's cheese
2 tablespoons grated onion
½ teaspoon garlic powder

1 tablespoon paprika
2 to 3 tablespoons
   evaporated skim milk

Combine all ingredients in a blender and mix lightly, or mix well with a spoon. You will get a lighter texture if you use the blender. If you want a firmer texture mix only with a spoon. Chill at least 24 hours before serving with rye krisp or melba toast.

onion dip

Yields about 1½ cups

1⅓ cups drained cottage
    cheese
½ cup water
2 tablespoons instant dry
   dry milk

2 tablespoons lemon juice
3 tablespoons dry onion
   soup mix

Combine cottage cheese, water, instant dry milk, and lemon juice in a blender and mix only until smooth. Add onion soup mixture, mix well, and refrigerate at least 8 hours. Serve with melba toast or rye krisp.

tunafish dip

Yields about 2 cups

½ cup (1 stick) margarine
1 12 ounce can drained
    tunafish
1 cup drained cottage
    cheese

1 tablespoon lemon juice
¼ teaspoon ground
    rosemary (optional)
¼ teaspoon white pepper

Cream margarine until light and fluffy in the small bowl of your mixer. Add tunafish, cottage cheese, lemon juice, rosemary, and pepper; beat at medium speed until smooth or mix in the blender. Chill at least 4 hours before serving.

Garlic powder or other seasonings may be substituted for the rosemary if desired.

marinated mushrooms

Yields about 2 cups

1 cup white vinegar
2 tablespoons vegetable oil
¼ teaspoon minced garlic
½ teaspoon ground sage

½ teaspoon ground thyme
½ teaspoon salt
1 tablespoon minced fresh
    parsley
1 pound sliced fresh
    mushrooms

Combine vinegar, oil, garlic, sage, thyme, salt, and parsley; mix well. Add mushrooms and cover. Refrigerate 2 to 3 days, stirring occasionally. Drain and serve well chilled.

pickled mushrooms and carrots

Yields about 3 cups

2 cups julienne fresh carrots	1 tablespoon mixed pickling spices
1 cup white vinegar	2 cups drained, canned button mushrooms
1 cup sugar	

Cook carrots in a minimum of water for about 10 minutes or until they are tender crisp. Drain well. Combine vinegar, sugar, and spices while carrots are cooking. Bring to a boil, add mushrooms and carrots. Return to a boil, remove from heat, and allow to cool. Refrigerate for 3 or 4 days. Drain and serve well chilled.

Mrs. Deane's pickled garden relish

Serves 6

½ small head of cauliflower	¾ cup wine vinegar
1 cup julienne fresh carrots	½ cup vegetable oil
1 cup celery, cut into 1-inch pieces	2 tablespoons sugar
¾ cup julienne fresh green peppers	1 teaspoon salt
4 ounces drained pimientos, cut into 1-inch pieces	½ teaspoon ground oregano
	¼ cup water
	3 ounces drained, pitted green olives

Separate cauliflower into flowerlets, then cut each flowerlet into slices about ¼ inch thick. Combine all ingredients in a large heavy frying pan and simmer, covered, for 5 minutes. Cool and refrigerate at least 24 hours. Drain well and serve well chilled.

Bob Ihrig's hot buttered rum

1 cup brown sugar
1 cup water
1 gallon apple cider

1 cup to 1 quart dark rum
1 pat margarine in each cup
   Nutmeg and cinnamon,
     ground

Combine sugar and water and bring to a boil. Reduce heat and simmer for 2 minutes. Add cider and bring to a simmer but don't boil it. Add rum to cider and remove from heat. Put a pat of margarine in each cup, add the hot cider and rum mixture, and serve with the spices in a shaker to be used as desired.

chapter III

soups

Soup is a versatile food. It can be a cup of consomme to start a meal or the main dish of the meal itself. Fortunately, soup fits very comfortably into a low cholesterol diet and a cup of soup can turn a routine meal into an occasion. My family loves soup and I'd hate to banish soup from our low cholesterol kitchen. Of course, we do have to give up sour cream garnish, egg dumplings, and soup made with cream and butter. But that is only a minor point since there are still so many good soups available to us. Beef or chicken bouillon cubes or powder may be used without restriction, and meat or poultry stocks may also be used once they have been chilled and the fat removed. Cream soups may be thickened with a white sauce made with oil or margarine, instant dry milk, and flour.

Noodles made with whole eggs should not be used unless you figure the egg yolks as part of your egg yolk allowance for the week. However, your favorite noodle or pasta recipe may be used if you substitute ¼ cup liquid egg substitute plus ½ teaspoon vegetable oil for each egg you delete. Pasta comes in so many different shapes that you can always find a special one for your soup.

Soda crackers, because of their saturated fat content, are likely to be restricted, but melba toast, bread sticks, croutons, toast, or Rye Krisp may be used with soup. Have you ever tried your favorite dry cereal with soup? My sister likes popcorn with her soup and that too is good. Even guests less dedicated to popcorn agree that it is a good combination with certain soups, such as split pea.

Your husband might also enjoy using some of those chopped imitation bacon bits, chopped chives, chopped onions, or chopped green peppers to top his bowl of soup.

Vegetable soup means all things to all people. It can be thickened with beans, potatoes, barley, or many other things. The vegetables can be large or small, or even pureed, but all countries and all nationalities have their favorite vegetable soups. As long as you have been careful to remove all the fat from the chilled stock or meat, you can use just about any combination of meats, poultry, or fish and vegetables that you prefer. I personally like a thick vegetable soup with chunks of meat in it. One of my friends once referred to it as a loose stew but that didn't stop her from eating a big second helping of it.

Vegetable soup seems to be best when it is made in a large batch in a big pot. By the time you add all the things you like best in a vegetable soup, you end up with several quarts of soup. Make vegetable soup every so often if only to clean out the refrigerator or freezer. It is so handy to pop small amounts of leftover vegetables, meats, good gravies, or broths into a special container in the freezer to be combined later with whatever you think it needs to be a really great soup. I tell everyone my freezer is the modern equivalent of the soup pot thrifty housewives used to simmer on the back of the stove.

A friend of mine who was kitchen manager in a large hospital in the Chicago area antagonized several people on the staff one time because she served such a good soup in the employees cafeteria and refused to give anyone the recipe for it. Later she told me, "How would they have reacted if I had told them that it was made from leftover chicken à la king, yesterday's turkey supreme, creamed peas and carrots, and some of those grilled onions we served with the steak at noon? Couldn't you just see their horrified expressions?"

The Vegetable Soup recipe is a good basic one, which you can vary to suit your own family's tastes. It yields a large amount for the normal family but freezes well and is good to have on hand for a quick meal. The vegetables may be varied but it is a good idea to use about the same total amount of vegetables. Canned vegetables may also be used if you don't have the frozen ones at the moment. The amount of salt you add to the soup will depend upon the strength of the broth and whether or not you use bouillon cubes. Bouillon cubes contain salt so be very scant with the salt when you are using them. Once you have finished the soup you can then season it to taste. However, if water is the base for your soup, the salt in the recipe should be about right.

Minestrone is a vegetable soup with beans, Italian seasoning and spaghetti, macaroni, or rice. As in a regular vegetable soup you can add or subtract vegetables from the recipe. It should always have Italian seasoning and spaghetti or rice in it. Minestrone is a heavy soup with infinite variations, all of them good. There is no standard recipe for it. The recipes vary from one region to another in Italy, and even from one home to another. It can be made with fat free stock, with bouillon cubes, or even without any meat base — using only vegetables — but it is best with meat stock and chunks of meat in it. The Minestrone recipe utilizes a meat stock and you can add chopped leftover meat as you see fit. Any type of pasta may be used; spaghetti, macaroni, or any of the fancier variations. It is a large recipe because like the Vegetable Soup it freezes well.

The proper way to prepare Minestrone is to cook the large pot of soup until it is ready. Then, remove the amount of soup that you plan to use at that time, add water if it is too thick, add the spaghetti to the boiling soup, and cook until the spaghetti is tender. In an Italian home this soup would be served with grated cheese, but since that is not part of a low cholesterol diet the cheese isn't mentioned in our recipe. If your husband inquires about the cheese, you can always tell him that it isn't in the recipe.

The Potato and Onion Soups are particularly good for a change of pace. They take far less time than the other vegetable soups.

If your husband likes split pea soup, you know that it's off his diet. You still can make it for him if you use a new method. Since the split peas contain starch they will combine with the fat from the ham bone to form the sort of heavy sauce that gives the soup its thickness and richness. However, this richness also keeps all of the fat in soup and this is what makes it forbidden on a low cholesterol diet.

Because you do want the flavor of the ham, cook the ham bone and ham until you have extracted all the flavor from it, then discard the bone. Cool the broth and remove the fat. Then finish your soup by adding the other ingredients. The Split Pea Soup recipe explains this method in greater detail.

This method for getting the flavor out of the ham without the fat can also be used in making bean or lentil soup. If you want to thicken the soup, you can always add some margarine along toward the end. This will combine with the starch in the soup to thicken and enrich it.

There is a good variety of dehydrated soups on the market. Many of them contain no saturated fat and may be used without restriction. Some of them contain a little hydrogenated fat but it is such a small amount that most doctors allow their use unless the diet is very restrictive. If you use them often, it might be wise to check with your husband's doctor regarding their use. Many of them form the basis for some wonderful recipes — it would be rough to have to give them up.

Cream soups are somewhat a problem because of certain ingredients in them. Many of them contain ingredients sautéed in butter and rich goodies such as cream or egg yolks. However, you can continue to use many of them by adapting them to your use. You can always use vegetable oil instead of butter for sautéing vegetables and instant dry milk and flour instead of egg yolks for thickening.

Before buying canned soups check the list of ingredients since they often contain saturated fats, although I was happy to find that one well known brand of cream of mushroom soup was made with vegetable oil. If you are accustomed to using canned soups in casseroles you might want to try one of the cream soups in this chapter. If you want a thick soup to use in a casserole do not add more flour to it, use less liquid or your casserole will not be as flavorful.

As anyone who has ever lived in or near a seaport knows, there are many wonderful soups and chowders made with fish. The people who live near the sea have learned to use all of the many varieties of fish available in their area. They often have unusual and interesting recipes and many of them are superb. Of course, if you live inland, you don't have access to the same variety of fish, but an astounding variety is now available in your local supermart. In this day of fast freezing techniques, there is no excuse for a lack of variety in the fish soups and chowders at your house. Not only can a low cholesterol dieter enjoy a great many fish chowders, you should make it a point to see that he does so. Although shellfish must be used sparingly, there is a great variety of fish and many recipes developed for their use. A good chowder needs no cream, though it is good that way; it can also be made with instant dry milk and margarine. Virginia White, a dietitian at the U.S. Army Natick Laboratories in Natick, Massachusetts, has lived all of her life in New England. Her fish recipes are wonderful. Virginia White's Fish Chowder uses instant dry milk and margarine, and I'm sure you will agree that it is excellent.

To avoid becoming involved in the battle of New England Chowder versus Manhattan Chowder, a recipe has been included for Manhattan Chowder lovers as well.

Salmon generally isn't thought of as a basis for a chowder, but it makes an excellent dish that is handy for unexpected occasions. It is a meal in itself. Served with salad, toast and fruit, it makes a delicious lunch or light supper. After all, you never know when Aunt Hattie is going to come over and it is much better than serving scrambled eggs or something that is rough on your husband's diet. With this recipe she needn't even know he is following a diet.

Fruit soup is not too well known but it is delicious hot or cold. If it is too sweet for you to enjoy for a first course it can always be served chilled for dessert. There are many different kinds of fruit soup; it can be varied depending upon the time of year and the fruits available. Frances Nielsen learned to make the fruit soup in this chapter from her mother-in-law when she and her husband Denny were first married.

vegetable soup

Yields 4 quarts

7 cups water or stock
3½ cups canned tomatoes and juice
4 beef bouillon cubes
1 cup chopped onions
1 cup thinly sliced carrots
1 cup diced raw potatoes
1 10-ounce package frozen peas
1 10-ounce package frozen baby lima beans
1 10-ounce package frozen green beans
1 tablespoon salt (if needed)
¼ teaspoon pepper
½ teaspoon ground oregano
½ teaspoon sweet basil leaves

Combine all the ingredients in a large heavy saucepan. Bring to a boil, reduce heat, and simmer about 1 hour or until vegetables are tender. If you have stock available you may not want to use the bouillon cubes. Any leftover meat would be a welcome addition; cut it up and add it to the soup at the beginning, then it will simmer with the vegetables for added flavor. If you use leftover chicken or turkey, it is best to use chicken bouillon cubes instead of the beef.

potato soup

Serves 4

2	cups diced fresh potatoes	2	cups hot water
½	cup chopped onions	⅛	teaspoon white pepper
2	cups water	1	teaspoon salt
¾	cup instant dry milk	¼	teaspoon monosodium glutamate (MSG)

Combine potatoes, onions, and 2 cups water in a heavy saucepan. Bring mixture to a boil, reduce the heat, and simmer it for about 20 minutes or until potatoes are soft. Stir instant milk into hot water. Remove soup from heat and stir milk into the soup. Add pepper, salt, and monosodium glutamate. Serve soup hot but do not bring it to a boil again after the milk is added.

minestrone soup

Yields 3½ quarts

1	cup navy or red beans	1	tablespoon salt
1	quart water	½	teaspoon pepper
1	cup finely chopped onions	½	teaspoon sweet basil leaves
3	tablespoons vegetable oil	2	teaspoons ground oregano
3	quarts stock	8	ounces frozen green beans
1	cup diced potatoes	2	tablespoons chopped parsley
1	cup shredded cabbage		

½ cup diced fresh green
    peppers
1 cup diced carrots
½ cup tomato paste

2 cups chopped leftover
    meat (optional)
4 ounces spaghetti, maca-
    roni or other pasta

Combine beans and 1 quart water. Bring to a boil and set aside for 1½ hours. Sauté onions in hot oil in heavy kettle, but do not let them brown. Add beans and all the remaining ingredients except spaghetti or macaroni. Bring to a boil, reduce heat and simmer for 2 to 2½ hours or until beans are soft. Add more water if necessary. Add spaghetti or macaroni and cook until tender. Serve hot.

onion soup

Yields 2 quarts

2 tablespoons (¼ stick)
    margarine
1 tablespoon vegetable oil
2 cups thinly sliced onions
6 cups boiling water or
    stock

6 beef bouillon cubes
2 teaspoons Worcester-
    shire sauce
¼ teaspoon monosodium
    glutamate (MSG)
Salt and pepper to taste

Heat margarine and oil in heavy saucepan. Add onions and sauté until onions are golden, stirring constantly. Dissolve bouillon cubes in hot water or stock and add gradually to the onions. (If you have a good rich stock you may not need the bouillon cubes.) Add Worcestershire sauce and simmer 5 minutes. Add monosodium glutamate and salt and pepper to taste. Serve hot.

split pea soup

Yields about 2 quarts

1 ham bone
3 quarts cold water

2 tablespoons chopped
    parsley

2 cups dried split peas
1 quart water
1 cup finely chopped onions
1½ cups chopped celery and
    tops

½ cup finely chopped
    carrots
Salt and pepper to taste
¼ cup (½ stick)
    margarine (optional)

Put ham bone in heavy saucepan and cover with 3 quarts of cold water. Bring to a boil, reduce heat, and simmer about 2 hours or until all bits of ham have left the bone. Remove bone and any bits of ham fat in the stock. Chill thoroughly to remove fat from the top of the stock.

While stock is chilling, cover split peas with 1 quart water in a large heavy saucepan. Bring to a boil and boil 2 minutes. Remove peas from heat and let stand 1 hour. Add ham stock and any bits of ham in it, onions, celery, parsley, and carrots. Bring to a boil, reduce the heat, and simmer soup for 2 to 2½ hours or until peas are tender and liquid has partially cooked away. Season to taste with salt and pepper. Add more water if you want a thinner soup. Add margarine and simmer about 5 minutes longer if a thicker soup is desired. Serve hot.

Imitation bacon bits may be sprinkled on the soup for a garnish if desired.

cream soup base

Yields 2 quarts

½ cup (1 stick) softened
    margarine
3 cups instant dry milk
½ cup all purpose flour

2 quarts water, stock, or
    vegetable water
Salt to taste
White pepper to taste

Combine margarine, instant dry milk, and flour. Mix well. Bring liquid to a boil in a heavy saucepan. Gradually add the flour and margarine mixture to the liquid, stirring constantly until it is thickened. Season to taste.

Variations

Vegetable Cream Soups: Add 2 cups chopped, cooked vegetables to 2 quarts hot cream soup base and serve immediately. Vegetables may be pureed or chopped finely. Single vegetables or a combination of vegetables may be used. Reheat soup if necessary.

Cream of Chicken Soup: Use chicken stock or bouillon to prepare soup base. Add 1 cup finely chopped chicken to 2 quarts hot soup base and serve immediately.

Cream of Mushroom Soup: Sauté 1 cup fresh or canned mushrooms in 2 tablespoons margarine or oil. (Use the mushroom juice as part of the liquid in the soup base if you use canned mushrooms.) Add to 2 quarts hot cream soup base and serve immediately.

Cream of Onion Soup: Sauté 1 cup finely chopped onions in 2 tablespoons margarine or oil. Add to 2 quarts hot cream soup base and serve immediately.

Virginia White's fish chowder

Serves 8

1½ pounds fish fillets (haddock, halibut or other white fish)
¾ cup diced raw potatoes
3 cups boiling water
⅓ cup finely chopped onions
⅓ cup diced fresh green peppers
⅓ cup (⅔ stick) margarine
⅓ cup all purpose flour

3 cups cold water
¾ cup instant dry milk
1 cup warm water
2 teaspoons salt
¼ teaspoon white pepper
¼ teaspoon monosodium glutamate (MSG)
Imitation bacon bits (optional)

Remove any skin or bones from the fish and cut it into cubes. Combine fish, potatoes, and boiling water. Simmer for about 20 minutes. Sauté onions and green peppers in margarine until onions are golden. Stir flour into onion mixture. Add 3 cups cold water and cook over low heat, stirring constantly, until smooth. Add undrained fish and potato mixture to onion mixture. Simmer for another 20 minutes. Stir instant dry milk into 1 cup warm water and add to soup just before you serve it. Add seasonings and serve hot. Soup may be garnished with bacon bits if desired.

Manhattan fish chowder

Serves 6

1 pound fish fillets or steaks
3 tablespoons vegetable oil
1 cup chopped onions
2 cups boiling water
2 cups canned tomatoes and juice
1 cup diced potatoes
½ cup diced carrots

½ cup chopped celery
¼ cup catsup
1 tablespoon Worcestershire sauce
1 teaspoon salt
¼ teaspoon pepper
¼ teaspoon ground thyme

Remove any skin or bones from fish and cut it into chunks. Sauté onions in hot oil in heavy saucepan until golden. Add water, tomatoes, potatoes, carrots, celery, catsup, Worcestershire sauce, salt, pepper and thyme. Simmer 45 minutes or until vegetables are tender. Add fish, cover and simmer another 15 or 20 minutes until fish flakes easily when tested with a fork. Serve hot.

salmon chowder

Serves 6

1 pound can red salmon
¾ cup chopped onions
½ cup chopped fresh green peppers

1 cup canned whole kernel corn
2 chicken bouillon cubes
1 cup hot water

2 tablespoons margarine	½ teaspoon salt
2 cups canned tomatoes and juice	⅛ teaspoon pepper
1 cup canned green beans	¼ teaspoon ground thyme
	½ cup instant dry potatoes

Drain salmon and reserve liquid. Discard skin and bones and break salmon into large pieces.

Sauté onions and green peppers in margarine in heavy saucepan until onions are golden. Add reserved salmon liquid, tomatoes, green beans, corn, chicken bouillon cubes, water, salt, pepper and thyme. Simmer for 15 minutes. Stir instant potatoes into chowder and simmer another 5 minutes. Add salmon pieces, stir to mix and serve hot.

Mrs. Nielsen's fruit soup

Serves 6

12 pitted prunes	2 lemon slices
¼ cup dark raisins	1 tablespoon grated orange rind
4 cups cold water	
¼ teaspoon ground cinnamon	1 cup canned peach slices or sliced fresh peaches
2 tablespoons grape jam	2 tablespoons cornstarch
	2 tablespoons cold water

Combine prunes, raisins, 4 cups cold water, cinnamon, grape jam, lemon slices and orange rind in a saucepan. Bring to a boil, reduce heat, and simmer 30 minutes. Remove lemon slices and add peach slices. Combine cornstarch and 2 tablespoons water and stir to form a smooth paste. Stir the smooth paste into the soup and simmer about 5 minutes or until clear and smooth. Serve warm or chilled.

chapter IV

meats

Planning an appetizing meat entree is probably the most difficult part of menu planning in the low cholesterol kitchen. Your husband is undoubtedly very fond of roast prime rib of beef, thick juicy steaks, spareribs and all the other high saturated fat dishes that are forbidden in a low cholesterol diet. In addition, the doctor may have told you to restrict the number of times you serve meat to him each week. Since you are going to take a positive attitude instead of a negative attitude toward his diet, the important thing is to explore just what meat items he *can* have and how to prepare them in the most satisfying manner. He can still enjoy quite a variety of meat dishes. Although it may be hard for him to realize now, he will probably reach a point where he will prefer the low fat recipes and find the others greasy and unattractive.

Specific cuts of meat with a lower fat content that are included in recipes in this book include the following:

Beef — round, rump roast, sirloin, tenderloin, and dried beef.

Pork — roast loin, center cut roasts or chops, tenderloin, lean ham, center cut ham steak, and canadian bacon.

Veal — round, rump roast, leg roast, sirloin, arm steak, and loin chop.

Lamb — sirloin roast, leg roast, and sirloin chops.

As you can see from the above, roasts may still be included in your menus. The most important difference is that now a lean cut of meat is selected and it is prepared in a way that will get rid of most of the remaining fat. The roast is placed on a rack so that it doesn't cook in the drippings (oil, bouillon, or marinades are used for basting instead of drippings). However, drippings should not be discarded. They should be saved and used for gravies or soups once the fat has been removed. Once they are chilled, it is easy to remove the layer of fat with a spoon. Steaks, stews, and ground meats have all of the visible fat removed, then they are prepared in a manner which will remove any remaining fat.

Since these are not the most tender cuts of meat, although they are very flavorful, it is a good time to start using tenderizers. There are several types of commercial tenderizers that you should investigate. Once you have decided on the type you prefer, use it on your steaks and roasts according to the directions on the container. Remember, you will need less seasoning on your meats if you use a seasoned tenderizer. Wine, vinegar, tomatoes, and other slightly acid liquids are all natural tenderizers, which add flavor and tenderness to a less tender cut of meat. These natural tenderizers have been used for centuries and form the basis for some of our traditional dishes such as Sauerbraten, swiss steak, and marinated lamb.

The grade of beef you buy is important in the low cholesterol diet because the marbling of fat in the meat is different in the different grades of beef. Beef grades include prime, choice, good, and standard or commercial or utility. Prime and choice grades are not advised because the fat is marbled throughout the meat. This marbling gives a tender meat but it is almost impossible for you to remove the marbled fat from the meat and therefore it is not advisable for you to use it. "Good" grade of beef is the best for you to use. Be sure to check with your butcher to see which grade of meat he is using if it is not clearly marked. If he does not have "Good" grade beef he can probably get some for you or perhaps you will have to shop around until you find a meat market or store where it is available. Good grade is still of excellent quality but it has less marbling and a thinner fat covering. Standard and commercial or utility beef is generally used for soups, stews, and recipes that specify a long cooking time.

The round purple U.S. Inspected and Passed stamp on meat gives you grade protection and guarantees that the animal was judged wholesome by a federal inspector and that the plant where it was processed passed sanitary regulations. The dye is not harmful and you may cut it off or not as you wish.

All roasting temperatures in this book should be followed, but the timing is approximate. A great deal depends upon the thickness of the meat, the temperature at which it is put into the oven (room temperature or directly from the refrigerator), and the quality of the meat. If frozen meat is used the cooking time should be increased about 50 percent. A roast meat thermometer should be used whenever possible. The thermometer should be inserted near the thickest part of the meat and care should be taken that the thermometer does not touch any gristle or bone. Also, the thermometer should never touch fat but you will have taken care of that already.

BEEF

It is best to use flank steak, sirloin tip, round of beef, or rump roast for stews because they are lower in fat than other cuts of beef. However, if you must use stew meat, remove all visible fat with a sharp knife and then remove all of the fat which cooks out of the meat. You can do this by braising the meat in liquid until it is barely tender, then cooling the meat in the liquid until it is cold and the fat has risen to the top. The fat is removed and the rest of the recipe is finished. You will probably be amazed at the amount of fat which you can skim off the meat after it has been refrigerated. As it requires quite a while to cool, it is sometimes best to do a quantity in advance and freeze it for your use whenever you decide you want to serve stew or some other dish which requires braising stew meat.

GROUND MEAT

When you use a recipe that includes ground beef, it is very important that you have either very lean ground meat or that you make every effort to remove the fat from the meat. Remember that hamburger is about 25 percent fat and lean ground beef isn't very much leaner. The meats that you should use for ground meat are the same lean meats that you use for other recipes: round, rump, sirloin tip, flank steak, and, if you want to be very extravagant, you can use tenderloin. All of these are low in fat and will be even lower after all the visible fat is removed. If you have a butcher who will remove every bit of visible fat and then grind the meat for you, you are in luck — this is the perfect solution. Very few of us are that lucky but there are other methods for insuring the supply of low fat ground meats. Methods available to the average person include:

1. Buy a large quantity of meat at a frozen food locker. Have all

of the visible fat trimmed off the meat and then have it ground and packaged.

2. Cultivate that wonderful butcher who will trim all of the fat off a piece of meat before grinding it for you.
3. Buy a heavy duty electric grinder and grind the meat yourself after you have trimmed off all of the visible fat. (This is the last resort for most people, it is time consuming and can be messy.)
4. Buy lean ground meat at the supermart and then cook the fat out of it before you finish the recipe. (Brown the meat well, put it in a colander, and pour very hot water over it. Then return the meat to the pan and follow directions for the rest of the recipe.) Some recipes can be adapted to this method but others cannot. It is more practical for dishes such as chili or spaghetti sauce than for meat loaf.

It is a good idea to have a collection of recipes for different kinds of meat loaves to use as entrees and for sandwiches, since you will be unable to use the high fat cold meats that you find in the supermarts. Meat loaves can be made from a variety of recipes. Almost everyone has his favorite, which can be adapted for use in a low cholesterol kitchen. The important things to remember are to use low fat ground meat, egg whites instead of whole eggs, and instant or skim milk instead of whole milk. It is important to use only ground round of beef, which has had the fat removed before it is ground. The bread crumbs, rolled oats, or other fillers in the meat loaf will absorb fat; therefore, the fat doesn't cook out as well as it would in a roast. Always use a shallow pan for meat loaf, not a loaf pan, since you want any fat to drain into the bottom of the pan.

Many people dearly love sausage, but most of the commercially available sausages have a very high percentage of saturated fat and should not be used in a low cholesterol diet. However, if you want to take the time and trouble, you can prepare a sausage that would be allowed even to those who must limit their cholesterol intake. The trick is to replace the saturated fat with oil. The seasonings can be varied, depending upon your family's taste. The Beef Sausage recipe in this chapter is included only as a guide. It should be used as a basic recipe to develop the type most acceptable to your husband. Do not delete the crumbs unless you replace them with potatoes, oatmeal, or some other type of filler because without the filler the oil will cook out very quickly, leaving a dry and unappetizing sausage.

If there is a professional sausage maker in your neighborhood, you can mix the sausage and take it to him to stuff into casings. If you don't have this service available, you can buy some medium size casings, and stuff them yourself, using the sausage stuffing attachment for your grinder or a cookie press. The cookie press is much slower but it will work.

Casings may be bought at many stores. When you are ready to stuff the casings, put one end of the casing over the water faucet, and run lukewarm water through it to clean it out. Press out the water and it is ready to use.

Hamburgers are a great American favorite. Kids love them and most husbands like them too. However, it is not a good idea for your husband to order them in a restaurant or drive-in, because most commercial hamburgers contain fat to make them juicy. Hamburgers are always better if they are made with freshly ground beef. In the low cholesterol diet that beef should be lean beef from which all visible fat has been removed. The resulting hamburger will be rather dry if pure beef is used without any other items. This can be overcome by mixing about 2 tablespoons of vegetable oil into each pound of ground beef or by putting a pat of margarine in the center of each burger. Burgers may be prepared in quantity and frozen for future. They may be cooked from the frozen state if your family likes them rare but it is better to thaw thick ones if your family likes them well done.

Burgers may be cooked according to the method most popular with your family.

Grilled: Heat a grill until it is sizzling hot, rub lightly with oil or sprinkle with salt. Brown the burgers on both sides, reduce the heat, and cook them over medium heat about 4 to 8 minutes on each side for thick burgers and about 2 to 4 minutes on each side for thin burgers.

Skillet cooked: Heat a heavy frying pan until sizzling hot, rub lightly with oil or sprinkle with salt. Brown the burgers on both sides, reduce the heat, and cook them over medium heat about 4 to 8 minutes on each side for thick burgers and 2 to 4 minutes on each side for thin burgers.

Broiled: Arrange patties on cold broiler rack. Broil about 3 inches from the heat, turning once, for about 4 to 6 minutes per side for thick burgers and about 3 to 5 minutes per side for thin burgers.

VEAL

Veal is delicate in flavor when it is cooked properly. Good veal is light pink in color rather than red and has a small amount of very white fat. This small amount of fat means that it is not well suited for broiling but it is excellent for use on a low cholesterol diet. It is best roasted or braised, and should be cooked until it is well done (170°F). The veal leg may be cut into leg roast, heel of the round, round steak, rump roasts, cutlets, and scallops. The veal sirloin may be roasted or cut into sirloin steaks. The roasts may be rolled if desired. All visible fat should be removed.

LAMB

Most people think of lamb as a springtime dish but it is available throughout the year, although supplies may vary in some areas. Properly cooked lamb has a delicious mild flavor and an appetizing aroma. In the past, recipes for lamb usually specified that it be cooked to the well done stage (180°F). Today the accepted procedure is to cook the lamb to the slightly rare or pink stage (165°F). This results in a more juicy, flavorful, and tender product. Cooking with dry heat is generally used for roasts although lamb may be pot roasted if desired. If you find lamb rather dry it may be brushed during roasting with a marinade to add moisture and improve the flavor. Lamb should be served either piping hot or cold. Hot or cold lamb is good but tepid lamb — never.

The recipes in this chapter include some for the leg of lamb, which is the leanest part of the animal. The leg may be cooked whole or it may be split into a half leg roast and a sirloin roast. The sirloin may also be cut into sirloin chops. Ground lamb may be used if you ask your butcher to remove all visible fat from the meat and then grind it for you. If this is not available to you, ground lamb may be purchased and then the fat cooked out of it before it is combined with other ingredients as you do with lean hamburger. Traditionally, ground lamb is quite lean and lamb patties may be broiled as purchased as long as they are not wrapped in bacon. Roasts may be cooked with the bone in or they may be boned, all visible fat removed, rolled and tied. If you buy the whole leg or the sirloin, you will find that it is covered with a whitish brittle fat called the fell. This should be removed before cooking as it tends to make the flavor of the meat strong, as well as adding additional fat to the meat.

PORK

Modern swine breeders and Agricultural Experiment Stations have developed a modern pig that is much more streamlined than its ancestors. However, we still need to buy the leaner cuts and trim them well. Leaner cuts are the tenderloin, fresh ham, sirloin roast, and the center loin, which may be used as roast or for chops. These cuts may be used occasionally if all visible fat is removed and they are prepared so that as much of the remaining fat as possible is removed in cooking.

The tenderloin may be roasted whole or cut across the grain into slices. These slices are very tender and flavorful. They may be grilled or broiled; and since they are cut quite thin, they cook quickly. The fresh ham, center cut loin, and sirloin are usually used as roasts. If you want them boned, ask your butcher to remove all of the visible fat from them, then bone and roll them for you. If this service is unavailable to you, buy the leanest roasts possible, then remove all visible fat with a sharp knife before cooking them. You will probably end up with a rolled roast since the removal of that much fat will leave you with a roast that needs to be rolled and tied in order to form an even shape for roasting.

Pork chops should be center cut and should have all visible fat removed with a sharp knife. They should be broiled or grilled so that as much fat as possible can be removed in cooking. They should not be baked with dressing or a gravy, because when this method of cooking is used the fat remains in the finished gravy or dressing and cannot be as easily discarded. If you are accustomed to preparing pork chops by grilling them until brown then finishing them in the oven, this method may still be used if they are placed on a rack in a Dutch oven or roaster, so that all of the fat drips down into the bottom of the pan.

It is not generally customary in this country to use pork in stews. However, this is a practice in some countries, and you will find recipes in Chapter XII that feature the use of pork.

CANADIAN BACON

Canadian style bacon may be used in the low cholesterol diet. It is much more lean than the regular bacon and has a very good flavor. All visible fat should be removed with a sharp knife and then it may be prepared in any of the ways listed in this chapter. Lean Canadian bacon may also substitute for ham in such dishes as scalloped ham and potatoes or ham and macaroni.

HAM

The use of ham in the low cholesterol diet is rather controversial. If the ham is very lean, it may be used. However, most hams are too fat to be used. The imported Polish and Danish hams are generally the most lean. Some of the American packers are also offering some very lean precooked hams that could be used.

The precooked hams may be glazed and baked for festive occasions. Ask your butcher to remove any visible fat and then slice and tie the ham for you. This makes it much easier to handle the ham after it is baked and the string can be removed just before you serve it. Fully cooked hams should be roasted according to directions on the can or package to an interior temperature of 130°F. This will take about 15 to 20 minutes per pound in a preheated slow oven (325°F).

There are many glazes available for use on baked hams. You can buy them or make your own. Any glaze is satisfactory as long as it contains no saturated fat. One of my favorite glazes is the one my friend Mary Boineau uses on both ham and chicken.

The center cut of smoked ham is generally acceptable if all of the visible fat is removed with a sharp knife. It may be cooked as follows:

Broiled: With a sharp knife, remove all visible fat from a center cut of ham, which has been cut about 1-inch thick. Broil the ham about 2 inches from heat, turning once while broiling. The total cooking time for fully cooked hams will be about 15 minutes and for uncooked ham about 25 minutes.

Pan-broiled: With a sharp knife, remove all visible fat from a center cut of ham which has been cut about ¼- to ½-inch thick. Rub a frying pan lightly with vegetable oil. Cook over low heat for about 3 to 4 minutes per side for fully cooked ham and about 6 to 8 minutes per side for uncooked ham. Turn the ham at least once during cooking.

GRAVY

Your husband likes gravy — I'm sure of that — and would like to continue to enjoy a good gravy with roasts and other meats. Gravy is permissible as long as there is little or no saturated fat in it. The best way to assure yourself that there is no fat in the gravy is to remove all fat possible from the drippings. This can be done by chilling the drippings then just removing the fat, which forms a hard layer on top. If the drippings seem a little scant, you can add some hot water to the pan and then stir and scrape the pan until you have loosened all of those delicious little brown particles that add flavor to gravies. You can use one of the following methods to provide a gravy free of saturated fats and any one of them will provide a tasty gravy:

1. Drippings may be kept on hand in the refrigerator for use in gravy. They will keep well with the layer of fat on top of them for several days. If you must keep them longer, it is advisable to freeze them until needed.
2. Drippings may be removed from the bottom of the Dutch oven or roaster with a baster, put into an ice cube tray and chilled in the freezer for a short time. The fat will rise to the top and can be removed. Then you can use the fat free drippings for gravy.
3. If meat drippings are unavailable, you can make a good gravy using bouillon cubes with a little Kitchen Bouquet for added color, if desired. You can also use bouillon cubes and water to extend your drippings if you do not have enough to make the amount of gravy you need. Remember that most bouillon

cubes contain salt and you will need to adjust the seasoning of your gravies accordingly. Water saved from cooking vegetables may also be used with bouillon cubes for a flavorful gravy.

The recipes in this chapter use various techniques to get rid of as much fat as possible. You will probably have favorite recipes of your own, some of which can be adapted for your low cholesterol kitchen after you have mastered the techniques used here. Remember always that the important thing is to get rid of as much of the saturated fat as possible and to substitute unsaturated fat if fat is necessary to the recipe. Prepare the recipe the first time exactly as it is written; then if you want to add your own touch to it, do so after you have mastered it. Many variations are possible for any given recipe. The technique is the important thing, not the specific seasonings used.

All weights of meat given in these recipes are as purchased, before they are trimmed of all visible fat.

roast sirloin of beef

Serves 6 to 8

4-pound sirloin of beef
  Tenderizer (optional)

Kitchen Bouquet (optional)

Remove all visible fat from beef with a sharp knife. Apply tenderizer according to directions on package. Place roast on rack in 4-quart Dutch oven. Roast may be brushed with kitchen bouquet if a rich brown crust is desired. Cover and cook in a preheated slow oven (325°F) for 1½ hours. Remove cover, insert meat thermometer and continue roasting until desired temperature is reached. Total cooking time should be approximately: 2½ hours for 140°F (rare); 3 hours for 160°F (medium); 3½ hours for 170°F (well done).

Do not baste or turn roast during cooking time. Roast should set about 20 minutes before it is carved.

roast rump of beef

Serves 6 to 8

4-pound rump roast of beef Kitchen Bouquet (optional)
  Tenderizer (optional)

Remove all visible fat from beef with a sharp knife. (You will probably have to untie the strings before you remove the fat from a rolled rump roast, then retie the strings to force the meat back into a roll.) Apply tenderizer according to package directions. The roast may be brushed with kitchen bouquet if desired, or it may be basted during cooking with drippings saved from another roast, with the fat removed and then heated. Since the natural fat has been removed, it is necessary to baste the roast or to brush it with kitchen bouquet or a marinade. Place roast on a rack in a 4-quart Dutch oven and insert meat thermometer. Roast in a preheated slow oven (325°F) until desired temperature is reached, approximately: 2½ hours for 140°F (rare); 3 hours for 160°F (medium); 3½ hours for 170°F (well done).

Roast should set about 20 minutes before carving.

(This method for cooking roast rump of beef and the method for cooking roast sirloin of beef are interchangeable. Either cut of meat may be roasted by either method.)

roast beef tenderloin

Serves 8 to 12

4- to 6-pound beef tenderloin Vegetable oil or margarine

Remove all visible fat, sinews, and connective tissue from tenderloin with a sharp knife. Place on rack in open pan with tail end tucked under rest of roast. Insert meat thermometer in thickest part of the tenderloin. Brush with oil or margarine before and during cooking. Roast in preheated very hot oven (450°F) until thermometer registers rare (140°F). Tenderloin is generally served rare. If you want to serve the tenderloin medium well done, increase cooking time until thermometer registers (160°F).

beef tenderloin steaks

When beef tenderloin is used for steak, it is generally divided into 3 parts: filet mignon, chateaubriand, and tournedos. The chateaubriand is the center of the filet and is generally cooked whole, either broiled or roasted, then sliced at the table. The upper end of the tenderloin is cut into filet mignon steaks, the tail is cut into tournedos, and the very tip is used for braised tenderloin tips to be served with noodles or rice. All visible fat, sinews, and connective tissue is removed with a sharp knife before the steaks are cut. Since the steaks are so lean, they need to be sautéed in vegetable oil or margarine, or brushed with the oil or margarine if they are broiled. Sauté them quickly, about 3 to 4 minutes per side for 1-inch steaks and 4 to 5 minutes per side for 1½-inch steaks. To broil, place in a preheated broiler and broil about 2 to 3 minutes per side for 1-inch steaks or 4 to 5 minutes per side for 1½-inch steaks and 5 to 6 minutes per side for 2-inch steaks.

Cathy's pot roast

Serves 8 to 10

4- to 5-pound rump roast
  of beef
3 ounces stuffed olives

2 ounces capers
2 cloves garlic
½ cup hot water

Remove all visible fat from beef with a sharp knife. (You will probably have to untie the strings before you can remove the fat from a rolled rump roast. The roast should be rolled and retied after the fat is removed.) Cut little crescent shaped pockets in the roast about ½ inch across and about ¾ inch deep. Stuff each pocket with olives, capers, and a thin sliver of garlic or you can put the stuffing on the meat before you roll it and tie it again. Press the meat back into place over the stuffing. Place roast on rack in a Dutch oven and pour hot water in the bottom. Cover and bake in a preheated slow oven (325°F) 2½ to 3 hours or until roast is well browned and tender. Remove roast and let it set 20 minutes before serving.

onion pot roast

Serves 4 to 6

2½-pound round of beef cut   1 package onion soup mix
  2 inches thick

Remove all visible fat from round of beef with a sharp knife. Put beef on heavy duty aluminum foil. Spread onion soup mix over beef, cover with foil and close tightly so that no steam will escape. Put package of meat on cookie sheet and bake in a preheated moderate oven (350°F) 2½ to 3 hours or until tender.

pot roast with vegetables

Serves 4 to 6

2½- pound round of beef   6 medium onions, peeled
     cut 2-inches thick   and left whole
  2 teaspoons salt   6 medium potatoes, pared
  ¼ teaspoon pepper   and cut into halves
  ½ teaspoon monosodium   6 medium carrots, peeled
     glutamate (MSG)   and cut into halves
     (optional)   3 large fresh green peppers,
  1 teaspoon ground oregano   cleaned and cut into
     (optional)   wedges (optional)
  ½ cup hot water

Remove all visible fat from beef with a sharp knife. Put beef into Dutch oven, cover with salt, pepper, monosodium glutamate, oregano, and water. Cover tightly and bake in a preheated moderate oven (350°F) 1½ hours. Add onions, potatoes, carrots, and green peppers. Cover and cook for another hour or until meat and vegetables are tender. Serve hot.

spicy pot roast

Serves 8 to 10

4-pound round of beef
　　cut 2-inches thick
3 tablespoons vegetable oil
2 teaspoons salt
¼ teaspoon pepper
½ cup water
1 cup tomato sauce
½ cup thinly sliced onions

2 minced cloves of garlic
2 tablespoons brown sugar
½ teaspoon dry mustard
½ cup lemon juice
½ cup catsup
1 tablespoon Worcester-
　　shire sauce

Remove all visible fat from beef with a sharp knife. Brown beef on both sides in hot oil in a Dutch oven. Add salt, pepper, water, tomato sauce, onions, and garlic. Cover tightly and simmer 1½ hours. Combine brown sugar, mustard, lemon juice, catsup, and Worcestershire sauce and pour over meat. Cover and continue to simmer about 1 hour or until meat is tender. Serve hot with sauce.

roast beef hash

Serves 4 to 6

2 cups ground cold roast
　　beef
2 cups diced cooked
　　potatoes
½ cup finely chopped
　　onions
¼ cup finely chopped fresh
　　green peppers

2 tablespoons Worcester-
　　shire sauce
2 teaspoons salt
¼ teaspoon pepper
1 cup hot meat stock or
　　drippings
4 tablespoons (½ stick)
　　margarine

Combine roast beef, potatoes, onions, green peppers, Worcestershire sauce, salt, pepper, and meat stock. Use margarine to coat the inside of a 1½ quart casserole. Put hash into casserole and bake in a preheated moderate oven (350°F) 30 to 45 minutes or until hash is well browned and crusty.

The French and the Italians serve the broth from this meat and vegetable dish as a first course. The vegetables give the soup a wonderful flavor and it is a good light beginning for a moderately heavy meal.

boiled beef with vegetables

Serves 4 to 6

2½-pound round of beef cut 2-inches thick
2 or more quarts boiling water
1 tablespoon salt
1 tablespoon dried parsley
1 tablespoon leaf oregano
1 teaspoon monosodium glutamate (MSG)
½ teaspoon coarse ground black pepper
6 beef bouillon cubes

6 medium onions, peeled and left whole
6 medium potatoes, pared and cut into halves
6 medium carrots, peeled and cut into halves
3 large fresh green peppers, cleaned and cut into quarters
1 medium size cabbage, cleaned and cut into 6 wedges

Remove all visible fat from beef with a sharp knife. Put beef into heavy 6-quart pan and cover with boiling water. Add salt, parsley, oregano, monosodium glutamate, black pepper and bouillon cubes. Bring to a simmer and simmer about 2½ to 3 hours or until tender. If necessary, add boiling water to cover, while meat is simmering. *Do not boil.* Remove meat when it is tender and cover with aluminium foil to keep it warm until it is sliced just before serving time. The vegetables must be added at varying times so that they will all be cooked at the same time. The onions are added first, the broth is brought to a boil and they are cooked 5 minutes. The potatoes and carrots are then added, the broth is brought back to a boil and everything is cooked another 10 minutes. The cabbage and green peppers are then added, the broth is brought back to a boil once again and all of the vegetables are cooked another 10 minutes or until tender. When all vegetables are cooked, remove from the broth and serve.

shaker flank steak

Serves 6 to 8

3- pound beef flank steak
2 tablespoons all purpose
   flour
2 tablespoons margarine
1 teaspoon salt
¼ teaspoon pepper
½ cup chopped celery

½ cup finely chopped carrots
¼ cup finely chopped fresh
   green peppers
¼ cup finely chopped onions
3 tablespoons lemon juice
½ cup catsup
½ cup water

Remove the membrane and all visible fat from beef with a sharp knife. Score the steak about ⅛ -inch deep at about 1-inch intervals in a diamond pattern. Dust steak with flour and sauté in margarine in heavy kettle until well browned on both sides. Add salt, pepper, celery, carrots, green peppers, onions, lemon juice, catsup, and water. Cover tightly and simmer 1 to 1½ hours or until meat is tender. The meat will have a rich sauce formed from the vegetables.

London broil

Serves 4 to 6

1 beef flank steak, about
   2 pounds
1 cup Italian style vinegar
   and oil dressing

1 teaspoon salt
½ teaspoon pepper
2 tablespoons soft
   margarine

Remove membrane and all visible fat from beef with a sharp knife. Score the steak about ⅛ -inch deep at about 1-inch intervals in a diamond pattern. Cover steak with salad dressing and let it marinate several hours in the refrigerator.

Drain meat well and broil about 2 inches from the flame for 5 minutes on each side. Flank steak should never be overcooked. Season with salt and pepper when you turn the meat and brush with soft margarine. Season second side and brush with margarine again after steak is cooked. Slice steak on the diagonal with a very sharp knife and serve in thin slices. If you desire, the steak may be cooked over charcoal in lieu of broiling.

charcoal broiled round steak

Serves 4 to 6

2½ - pound beef round steak,
    cut 1½ inches thick
    tenderizer

½ cup vegetable oil
½ cup lemon juice

Remove all visible fat from beef with a sharp knife. Sprinkle tenderizer on meat according to directions on package. Grill over hot coals, turning often. Baste with a mixture of oil and lemon juice. Test for doneness after 30 minutes. Let stand about 5 minutes and then slice diagonally to serve.

broiled round steak

Serves 4 to 6

2½ - pound beef round steak,
    cut 1½ inches thick
    tenderizer

½ cup vegetable oil
½ cup orange juice
½ cup sherry

Remove all visible fat from beef with a sharp knife. Sprinkle tenderizer on all surfaces of meat according to directions on tenderizer package. Broil about 10 to 15 minutes on one side until brown, turn and broil on alternate side until brown. Combine oil, orange juice, and sherry and use to baste the steak while it is broiling. Let stand about 5 minutes and then slice on the diagonal to serve.

Swiss steak

Serves 4 to 6

2- pound beef round steak,
   cut ½ inch thick
2 tablespoons all purpose
   flour
2 teaspoons salt
⅛ teaspoon pepper
½ teaspoon monosodium
   glutamate (MSG)
   (optional)

3 tablespoons vegetable oil
2 cups canned tomatoes
   with juice
1 teaspoon Worcestershire
   sauce
½ cup chopped onions
½ cup chopped fresh green
   peppers

Remove all visible fat from beef with a sharp knife and cut into serving size portions. Combine flour, salt, pepper, and monosodium glutamate; then pound it into round steak with the back of a cleaver or the side of a saucer. Heat oil in Dutch oven and brown meat in oil on both sides. Add tomatoes, Worcestershire sauce, onions, and green peppers to meat. Cover and simmer slowly or bake in a pre-heated moderate oven (350°F) 1½ to 2 hours or until meat is tender. Add a little hot water while cooking if it looks dry. Serve hot with rice, noodles or potatoes.

frozen beef cubes

Yields 2 to 2¼ quarts

6 pounds beef stew meat
¼ cup vegetable oil
1 tablespoon salt
1 teaspoon pepper

1 teaspoon monosodium
   glutamate (MSG)
   (optional)
1 quart hot water

Remove all visible fat from beef with a sharp knife. Brown beef in hot oil in Dutch oven or heavy pot. Add salt, pepper, monosodium glutamate and hot water. Cover tightly and simmer 1 to 2 hours or until barely tender. Cool, remove fat and freeze. Allow about ½ cup per person.

The above prepared frozen beef cubes could be used in making beef stew. In the following recipe, substitute 3 cups of the beef cubes and 2 cups of broth (either from the frozen beef cubes or prepared from beef bouillon cubes) for the beef, flour, 1 teaspoon salt, pepper, oil, and hot water. Bring the beef cubes and broth to a boil and then proceed to add the vegetables and dumplings as directed.

This recipe can be varied according to the type and size cut of the vegetables used. A total of 7½ cups of vegetables is just about right but the kind depends on your family's preference. Tomato juice may also be used for part of the liquid if you like a tomato flavor in your stew. The gravy may be thickened with about 3 to 4 tablespoons of flour stirred into ½ cup of cold water just before serving if you like a thicker gravy.

old fashioned beef stew

Serves 6

3- pound round of beef, cut into 2-inch cubes
½ cup all purpose flour
1 teaspoon salt
½ teaspoon pepper
3 tablespoons vegetable oil
1 quart hot water
2 cups diced potatoes
2 cups diced carrots
2 small whole onions
1 cup diced celery
½ cup diced fresh green peppers
2 beef bouillon cubes
2 teaspoons salt
dumplings
(recipe follows)

Remove all visible fat from beef with a sharp knife. Combine flour, 1 teaspoon salt, and pepper. Dredge meat in flour mixture and brown in hot oil in Dutch oven or heavy pan. Add hot water, cover, and simmer 2 hours, adding more hot water if necessary. Add potatoes, carrots, onions, celery, green peppers, bouillon cubes, and 2 teaspoons salt. Cook uncovered 10 minutes, add dumplings, cook another 10 minutes uncovered; cover pan tightly and cook another 10 minutes. Serve hot.

dumplings

Serves 6

2 cups all purpose flour
1 tablespoon baking
   powder
1 teaspoon salt

⅓ cup instant dry milk
¼ cup vegetable oil
¾ cup water

Sift flour, baking powder, salt, and instant dry milk together into a mixing bowl. Stir oil into the water and add it all at once to the flour mixture. Mix lightly to form a soft dough. Drop by table-spoonsful on top of stew. Simmer 10 minutes uncovered, cover tightly and simmer 10 more minutes. (Don't remove that cover; it really will ruin the dumplings.)

oven stew

Serves 6

2- pound round of beef, cut
   into 2-inch cubes
 2 cups cubed carrots
½ cup sliced onions
½ pound sliced fresh
   mushrooms
 1 cup sliced celery
½ cup water

½ cup tomato puree
¼ cup chili sauce
 1 teaspoon Italian
   seasoning
 2 teaspoons salt
⅛ teaspoon pepper
½ cup red table wine

Remove all visible fat from beef with a sharp knife. Combine beef with carrots, onions, mushrooms, celery, water, tomato puree, chili sauce, Italian seasoning, salt, pepper, and wine in a 3-quart casserole. Cover casserole and bake in a preheated slow oven (325°F) for 2 hours. Remove cover, stir stew, and continue to cook uncovered 1 hour or until meat is tender.

braised beef tips

Serves 4 to 6

2 pounds beef sirloin or
   tenderloin tips
¼ cup all purpose flour
1 teaspoon salt
⅛ teaspoon pepper
1 tablespoon paprika
3 tablespoons vegetable oil
½ cup chopped fresh green
   peppers

½ cup chopped onions
4 cups hot water
6 beef bouillon cubes
½ teaspoon monosodium
   glutamate (MSG)
   (optional)
¼ cup all purpose flour
½ cup cold water

Remove all visible fat from beef with a sharp knife and cut into 1-inch pieces. Combine ¼ cup flour, salt, pepper, and paprika. Dredge the meat in the flour mixture and brown in hot oil in heavy saucepan. Add green peppers, onions, hot water, bouillon cubes, and monosodium glutamate; cover and simmer about 1 to 1¼ hour or until meat is tender. Add ¼ cup flour to cold water and stir to form a smooth paste. Stir paste into meat mixture and cook and stir until gravy is thickened. Serve over hot noodles or rice.

This is a traditional Iowa recipe. I have never seen it prepared by anyone who did not have an Iowa background. It sounds unusual but it is delicious and that gravy is wonderful on mashed potatoes. It is possible to use it on a low cholesterol diet because the fat in the gravy is not from the round steak, which is very low in fat, but from the oil in which you cooked the meat.

Iowa beefsteak

Serves 4 to 6

1½ - pound beef round steak,
     cut ½-inch thick
¼ cup all purpose flour
1 teaspoon salt

¼ teaspoon pepper
3 tablespoons vegetable oil
½ cup hot water
¼ cup all purpose flour

½ teaspoon monosodium
     glutamate (MSG)
     (optional)

2 cups cold water or
     reconstituted instant
     dry milk

Remove all visible fat from beef with a sharp knife and cut into serving size portions. Combine ¼ cup flour, monosodium glutamate, salt, and pepper. Pound as much of the flour mixture as possible into the steak with the back of a cleaver or the side of a saucer. Heat oil in heavy frying pan and brown the steak well in the hot oil. Add the hot water, cover tightly and simmer for 15 to 20 minutes or until steak is tender. Remove steak to a heated platter and cover with foil to keep it warm. Put the second ¼ cup flour in the frying pan and stir constantly until it is browned. Add the cold water all at once and cook over low heat stirring constantly until all of the lumps are dissolved and the gravy is bubbling. Add salt and pepper to the gravy if necessary and serve hot.

This is a good dish to prepare ahead of time and freeze or refrigerate until you need it.

barbecued steak

Serves 4 to 6

2- pound beef round steak,
     cut 1½ inches thick
1 teaspoon salt
¼ teaspoon pepper
2 tablespoons vegetable oil
½ cup chopped onions
½ cup chopped fresh green
     peppers

2 tablespoons brown sugar
2 tablespoons salad mustard
2 tablespoons Worcester-
     shire sauce
1 tablespoon lemon juice
1 teaspoon ground oregano
2 cups canned tomatoes
     with juice

Remove all visible fat from the round steak with a sharp knife and cut it into serving size pieces. Pound salt and pepper into the round steak. Heat the oil in a heavy frying pan and brown the steak well in the hot oil. Put the meat in a casserole with onions and green peppers. Combine brown sugar, mustard, Worcestershire sauce, lemon juice, oregano, and canned tomatoes. Pour this mixture over the meat and vegetables. Cover the casserole and bake it in a preheated moderate oven (350°F) for 2 to 2½ hours or until tender. Serve with rice or noodles or on hard crusty bread.

My mother often served this for Sunday dinner in Iowa. She prepared it in a heavy iron skillet and served it with lots of hot mashed potatoes and cole slaw. It was one of the first meat dishes that I learned to prepare.

farmer's steak

Serves 4 to 6

2- pound beef round steak, cut 2-inches thick	¼ teaspoon pepper
	3 tablespoons vegetable oil
½ cup all purpose flour	½ cup chopped onions
1 tablespoon salt	1 cup or more water

Remove all visible fat from beef but do not cut into portions until ready to serve. Combine flour, salt, and pepper, and pound as much as possible into the round steak. Heat oil in heavy frying pan and brown the meat on both sides. Add onions and 1 cup water. Cover and simmer gently about 1½ hours or until meat is tender. Add more water if necessary.

pepper steak

Serves 4 to 6

2- pound beef round steak	3 tablespoons vegetable oil
2 tablespoons all purpose flour	1 teaspoon Worcestershire sauce
2 teaspoons salt	2 cups hot water
⅛ teaspoon pepper	4 beef bouillon cubes
½ teaspoon monosodium glutamate (MSG) (optional)	4 large fresh green peppers, cut into ¾-inch julienne strips

Remove all visible fat from the beef with a sharp knife, and cut into serving size pieces. Combine flour, salt, pepper, and mono-sodium glutamate, and pound into the round steak. Heat oil in a Dutch oven and brown meat well. Combine Worcestershire sauce, water, and bouillon cubes, and add them to the meat. Simmer the meat slowly on top of a range or in a preheated moderate oven (350°F) for 2 to 2½ hours or until meat is almost tender. Add green peppers to meat and simmer ½ hour longer or until meat is tender. Serve with rice, noodles, or potatoes.

stuffed round steak

Serves 4 to 6

2½ - pound beef round steak, cut ½-inch thick	¼ cup finely chopped onions
tenderizer	1 teaspoon salt
4 cups dry bread cubes	⅛ teaspoon pepper
¼ cup hot beef bouillon	¼ teaspoon ground thyme
¼ pound (1 stick) melted margarine	1 teaspoon ground sage
	¼ cup raisins

Remove all visible fat from the beef with a sharp knife. Apply the tenderizer according to package directions. Meat will be in pieces and must be reformed into an oblong. This is done by placing it on strings that have been evenly spaced on a chopping board in preparation for tying the round steak into a roll around the dressing.

Combine bread cubes, bouillon, margarine, onions, salt, pepper, thyme, sage, and raisins, and mix lightly to form dressing. Place the dressing on the round steak. Tie the strings around the meat and dressing to form a long roll. Put this roll on rack in 4-quart Dutch oven. Cover and cook it in a moderate oven (350°F) for 1 hour. Uncover and continue to cook for 45 minutes longer or until meat is tender and browned.

chili con carne

Serves 6 to 8

2 pounds lean ground beef
4 cups tomatoes and juice
½ cup tomato paste
1 cup diced fresh green
   peppers
1 cup diced onions

2 no. 2 cans drained
   kidney beans
1 tablespoon chili powder
1 teaspoon garlic salt
1 tablespoon salt
½ teaspoon pepper

Brown the meat in a heavy saucepan. Put the browned meat in a colander and run 2 quarts of very hot water over the meat to wash any fat away. Return the meat to the saucepan. Add tomatoes, tomato paste, green peppers, onions, kidney beans, chili powder, garlic salt, salt, and pepper. Simmer for 1½ to 2 hours.

baked beef and macaroni

Serves 4 to 6

1 cup sliced onions
1 cup julienne fresh green
   peppers
2 tablespoons vegetable oil
1 pound ground beef
   (round steak)
1 cup tomato sauce
3 beef bouillon cubes
2 cups hot water
2 cups canned tomatoes
   and juice

1 tablespoon Worcester-
   shire sauce
2 teaspoons salt
¼ teaspoon pepper
½ teaspoon ground oregano
1 teaspoon Italian
   seasoning
1½ cups uncooked elbow
   macaroni

Sauté onions and green peppers in oil until they are golden. Add the ground beef and cook and stir until meat is well browned. Add tomato sauce, bouillon cubes, hot water, tomatoes, Worcestershire sauce, salt, pepper, oregano, and Italian seasoning to the meat mixture; cover and simmer over low heat for about 20 minutes. Combine the meat mixture with uncooked macaroni and pour into a 3-quart casserole. Cover the casserole and bake in a moderate oven (350°F) for 30 minutes. Remove the cover and stir the contents of the casserole. Continue to bake uncovered for another 15 minutes or until macaroni is tender.

firm meat loaf

Serves 4

1 pound ground round of beef	¼ teaspoon ground allspice
2 tablespoons soy sauce	½ cup rolled oats
½ teaspoon salt	⅓ cup instant dry milk
⅛ teaspoon pepper	½ cup water
1 egg white	½ cup finely chopped onions

Combine the ground beef, soy sauce, salt, pepper, egg white, allspice, rolled oats, instant dry milk, water, and chopped onions. Mix thoroughly. Form into a loaf and place it in shallow pan. Bake the loaf in a preheated moderate oven (350°F) for 1 hour or until loaf is browned.

spicy meat loaf

Serves 6 to 8

2 pounds ground round of beef	2 egg whites
1 tablespoon Worcestershire sauce	1 cup catsup
	3 cups day old bread cubes
1 teaspoon salt	½ cup finely chopped onions
¼ teaspoon pepper	

Combine the ground beef, Worcestershire sauce, salt, pepper, egg whites, catsup, bread cubes, and onions. Mix thoroughly. Form into a loaf and place it in a shallow pan. Bake the loaf in a preheated moderate oven (350°F) for 1½ hours or until loaf is lightly browned.

onion soup meat loaf

Serves 6 to 8

2 pounds ground round of beef
½ package dehydrated onion soup
2 egg whites

2 cups cracker crumbs
1 cup hot water
½ teaspoon monosodium glutamate (MSG) (optional)

Combine the ground beef, dehydrated onion soup, egg whites, cracker crumbs, water, and monosodium glumatate. Mix thoroughly. Form into a loaf and place it in a shallow pan. Bake the loaf in a preheated moderate oven (350°F) for 1¼ hours or until browned.

California meat loaf

Serves 4

1 pound ground round of beef
1 cup corn flakes
2 egg whites
1 teaspoon salt
⅛ teaspoon pepper

⅓ cup instant dry milk
½ cup water
¼ cup catsup
1 tablespoon Worcestershire sauce
1 cup raisins

Combine the ground round, corn flakes, egg whites, salt, pepper, instant dry milk, water, catsup, Worcestershire sauce, and raisins. Mix thoroughly. Form into a loaf and place it in a shallow pan. Bake the loaf in a preheated moderate oven (350°F) for 1 hour or until loaf is browned.

meat loaf with herbs

Serves 6

1½ pounds ground round of
     beef
1 cup dry bread crumbs
2 egg whites
1 cup tomato sauce
½ cup finely chopped
   onions

½ cup finely chopped fresh
   green peppers
1½ teaspoon salt
⅛ teaspoon ground thyme
½ teaspoon ground oregano
½ teaspoon crushed Italian
   seasoning

Combine the ground beef, bread crumbs, egg whites, tomato sauce, onions, green peppers, salt, thyme, oregano, and Italian seasoning. Mix thoroughly. Form into a loaf and place it in a shallow pan. Bake the loaf in a preheated moderate oven (350°F) for 1½ hours or until lightly browned.

beef sausage

Yields about 8 pounds of sausage

6 pounds round of beef
1 pound pork tenderloin
1 cup vegetable oil
1 cup red wine or water
3 tablespoons salt

2 teaspoons pepper
4 minced cloves of garlic
3 tablespoons paprika
2 teaspoons monosodium
   glutamate (MSG)
3 cups dry bread crumbs

Remove all visible fat from the meat with a sharp knife. Cut the meat into about 1-inch cubes and grind the pork and beef together using a coarse blade.

Combine oil, wine or water, salt, pepper, garlic, paprika, and monosodium glutamate. Mix well and pour over meat and bread crumbs. Blend using your hands or a mixer. Pack the meat mixture into a bowl, cover, and refrigerate overnight to blend the ingredients.

The next day fry a little of the sausage to test its flavor before stuffing it into the casings. Correct the seasoning.

Mix the meat well again and stuff it into the casings. This takes time, patience, and a little practice, but it is well worth it. In order to stuff the casings, remove the grinder blade from your mixer and attach the sausage stuffing attachment. Push a length of the casings up over the stuffer and force the meat mixture into the casings. Tie each length of casings at each end, twist it into about 6-inch sausages. Tie the sausages at each end and allow them to marinate a day or so before you cook them.

These sausages are better baked or fried than boiled. They may be smoked if desired. It is important that all equipment be sterilized before it is used in order to prevent contaminating the meat mixture.

pure beef burgers

Serves 4

1 pound ground round of
   beef
1 teaspoon salt

¼ teaspoon pepper
4 margarine patties
   (optional)

Add salt and pepper to ground round of beef. Divide into 4 equal portions. Shape each portion lightly into a burger around a margarine patty. Cook as directed earlier in the chapter. Serve hot.

hamburger patties

Serves 4

1 pound ground round of
   beef
1 teaspoon salt
¼ teaspoon pepper
¼ cup dry bread crumbs

2 tablespoons finely
   chopped onions
¼ teaspoon monosodium
   glutamate (MSG)
   (optional)
2 tablespoons vegetable oil
   (optional)

Combine ground round of beef, salt, pepper, bread crumbs, onions, monosodium glutamate, and oil. Mix lightly. Divide into 4 or 8 equal portions. Shape each portion into 4 thick or 8 thin burgers and cook as directed earlier in the chapter. Serve hot.

sloppy joes

Serves 4 to 6

½ cup chopped onions
½ cup chopped fresh green peppers
1 tablespoon vegetable oil
1 pound ground round of beef
2 tablespoons flour

2 teaspoons prepared mustard
1 cup catsup
1 teaspoon salt
¼ teaspoon pepper
¼ to ½ cup hot water

Sauté the onions and green peppers in oil until the onions are golden. Add the ground round of beef and cook it until the meat is browned. Sprinkle flour over the meat and continue to cook and stir for 1 minute. Add mustard, catsup, salt, pepper, and ¼ cup hot water. Simmer for 10 minutes. Add remaining hot water if mixture becomes too thick. Serve hot on toasted buns.

hobo burgers

Serves 4

4 12-inch squares of heavy aluminum foil
1 pound ground round of beef
4 margarine patties
4 thick onion slices
½ cup frozen peas

4 thick tomato slices
1 julienne slices fresh green peppers
1 medium size white potato, quartered
2 teaspoons salt
¼ teaspoon pepper

Place aluminum foil squares on a working surface. Form the ground round of beef into 4 burgers with a patty of margarine in the center of each. Put 1 burger patty, 1 onion slice, 2 tablespoons frozen peas, 1 tomato slice, 1 green pepper slice, and 1 quarter of potato on each aluminum square. Season them with salt and pepper. Seal the foil tightly and bake in preheated hot oven (425°F) for about 45 minutes or until vegetables and meat are done. Serve hot.

frizzled dried beef

Serves 4

2 tablespoons (¼ stick) margarine
4 ounces shredded dried beef

3 tablespoons all purpose flour
2 cups reconstituted instant dry milk
¼ teaspoon pepper

Heat the margarine in a saucepan. Add the dried beef, cook and stir over moderate heat until edges of the beef begin to frizzle. Add flour and continue to cook and stir for 3 or 4 minutes, until flour is light brown. Add milk and cook, stirring constantly, until the mixture bubbles and is thick and smooth. Season with pepper and serve over toast, hot biscuits, or mashed potatoes.

roast veal

Insert a meat thermometer in thickest part of the roast. Be sure that the thermometer is touching neither sinew nor bone. Place the roast on rack in open pan or roaster. Do not cover. Do not add water. Roast in preheated slow oven (325°F) for about 25 to 35 minutes per pound or until the thermometer registers 180°F. The roast may be brushed several times during roasting with margarine or oil mixed with herbs or other seasonings. The roast will be easier to carve if allowed to stand for 20 minutes after it is removed from the oven.

pot roast of veal

Serves 6 to 8

4- pound veal roast
¼ cup all purpose flour
2 teaspoons salt
¼ teaspoon pepper
¼ teaspoon ground thyme
1 teaspoon monosodium
   glutamate (MSG)
   (optional)
3 tablespoons vegetable oil

1 cup hot water
2 cups potatoes, cut in
   2-inch cubes
2 cups carrots, cut in
   2-inch cubes
1 cup sliced onions
1 teaspoon salt
¼ cup cold water

Remove all visible fat from the veal with a sharp knife. Combine flour, 2 teaspoons salt, pepper, thyme, and monosodium glutamate. Roll the meat in the flour mixture and brown it on all sides in hot oil. Place roast on rack in 4-quart Dutch oven or roaster. Pour water in the bottom of the Dutch oven. Cover and roast in a preheated moderate oven (350°F) for 1½ hours. Place potatoes, carrots, and onions around the meat. Sprinkle the vegetables with 1 teaspoon salt, cover and return to oven. Roast for another hour or until the vegetables and meat are tender. Remove the meat and vegetables to hot platter. Stir any remaining flour mixture into ¼ cup cold water to form a smooth paste. Add flour paste to meat drippings to form a gravy, stirring constantly and cooking until smooth.

braised veal chops

Serves 6

6 veal loin chops
1½ teaspoons salt
¼ teaspoon pepper
¼ cup vegetable oil
½ cup chopped onions
½ cup chopped fresh green
   peppers

1 cup tomatoes and juice
¼ cup dry sherry
1 6-ounce can sliced
   mushrooms, drained
2 tablespoons chopped
   parsley

Remove all visible fat from the veal with a sharp knife. Sprinkle the chops with salt and pepper. Brown the chops in hot oil. Put the chops in a 2½-quart casserole. Brown the onions and green peppers in oil. Pour the onions and peppers, with their oil, over the chops. Add tomatoes, sherry, mushrooms, and parsley to the meat. Cover and cook in a preheated moderate oven (350°F) for 1 hour or until meat is tender. Serve sauce over chops.

veal with wine sauce

Serves 4 to 6

2 pounds very thin veal cutlets
2 slightly beaten egg whites
¾ cup dry bread crumbs
6 tablespoons (¾ stick) margarine

½ teaspoon dry mustard
1 teaspoon salt
¼ teaspoon pepper
1 tablespoon Worcestershire sauce
½ cup white table wine

Remove all visible fat from the veal with a sharp knife. Dip the cutlets in beaten egg white and then in bread crumbs. Let them stand 10 minutes to dry the coating. Heat the margarine in heavy frying pan and brown the cutlets. Remove the cutlets and keep them warm. Put mustard, salt, pepper, Worcestershire sauce, and wine in the frying pan. Stir to loosen the brown bits in the frying pan. Bring sauce to a boil and serve it hot over veal cutlets.

braised veal steaks

Serves 4 to 6

2- pound veal steak
¼ cup all purpose flour
1 teaspoon salt
¼ teaspoon pepper

¼ teaspoon thyme
¼ cup (½ stick) margarine
½ cup reconstituted instant dry milk

Remove all visible fat from the veal with a sharp knife. Combine flour, salt, pepper, and thyme. Dredge the veal in the flour mixture. Heat the margarine in a heavy frying pan and fry the steak on both sides until browned. Pour milk over the steak, cover tightly, and simmer over low heat for about 1 hour or until the steak is tender.

veal with carrots

Serves 4 to 6

2 pounds veal round steak	¼ cup vegetable oil
¼ cup flour	1 teaspoon garlic salt
1 teaspoon salt	6 medium carrots, pared
¼ teaspoon pepper	and halved
¼ teaspoon marjoram	½ cup white table wine

Remove all visible fat from the veal with sharp knife. Cut the veal into 2-inch pieces. Combine flour, salt, pepper, and marjoram. Dredge the veal in the flour mixture. Brown the veal in hot oil in frying pan. Add garlic salt, carrots, and wine and cover tightly. Simmer over low heat for 30 minutes or until veal and carrots are tender.

veal stew

Serves 6 to 8

2 pounds round of veal,	1 cup hot water
cut into 1½-inch cubes	2 beef bouillon cubes
2 cups thinly sliced onions	1 cup thinly sliced fresh
¼ cup vegetable oil	green peppers
1 tablespoon paprika	2 cups canned tomatoes
2 teaspoons salt	and juice
¼ teaspoon pepper	1 cup sliced fresh
	mushrooms

Remove all visible fat from the veal with a sharp knife. Fry onions in hot oil in Dutch oven until golden. Stir paprika, salt, and pepper into onions. When thoroughly blended add the veal, stir and cook until the veal is lightly browned. Add the hot water and bouillon cubes, cover, and simmer over low heat for about 30 minutes or until meat is barely tender. Add the green peppers, tomatoes and mushrooms. Cover tightly and continue to cook for an additional 30 minutes or until the meat and vegetables are tender.

veal and ham loaf

Serves 6 to 8

1½ pounds ground round of veal
½ pound ground center cut uncooked ham
½ teaspoon garlic salt
½ cup finely chopped onions

2 cups cracker crumbs
2 teaspoons salt
½ teaspoon pepper
2 slightly beaten egg whites
⅓ cup instant dry milk
¾ cup water

Combine the veal, ham, garlic salt, onions, cracker crumbs, salt, pepper, egg whites, instant dry milk, and water. Mix thoroughly. Form into a loaf and place it in a shallow pan. Bake the loaf in a preheated moderate oven (375°F) for 1¼ hours.

veal burgers

Serves 4

1 pound ground round of veal
1 teaspoon salt

¼ teaspoon pepper
4 margarine patties

Add salt and pepper to the ground veal. Divide the meat into 4 equal portions. Shape each portion lightly into a burger around a margarine patty. Grill the burgers on a lightly greased grill for about 8 minutes on each side or until well browned. (2 tablespoons vegetable oil can be mixed with the ground veal instead of using the margarine patties if you prefer.)

roast lamb

Insert a meat thermometer into the thickest part of the roast. Be sure that the thermometer is touching neither sinew nor bone. Place the roast on a rack in an open pan or roaster. Do not cover. Do not add water. Roast the lamb in a preheated slow oven (325 °F) for 25 to 35 minutes per pound until thermometer reads 165°F for rare or 180°F for well done. The roast may be brushed several times during roasting with a marinade or rubbed with seasoning before roasting. The roast will be easier to carve if it is allowed to stand for 20 minutes after it is removed from the oven.

Variations
Swedish Style Roast Lamb: Roast as directed above using 1 cup hot black coffee combined with 1 tablespoon sugar and 2 tablespoons instant milk as a marinade.
Barbecued Roast Lamb: Roast as directed above using your favorite barbecue sauce as a marinade.
Savory Roast Lamb: Roast as directed above using a marinade made by combining 1 teaspoon garlic salt, ½ teaspoon salt, ½ teaspoon ground oregano, 1 teaspoon paprika, ½ teaspoon pepper, ¼ cup vinegar, and ¼ cup vegetable oil.

Lamb is generally served with mint or tart red jelly or with mint sauce. There are many good recipes for mint sauce but this is my favorite:

mint sauce

Yields 2 cups of sauce

1 tablespoon sugar
1 cup boiling water

1 cup vinegar
3 tablespoons freshly
      chopped mint

Pour boiling water over sugar and stir to dissolve. When sugar mixture is cool, add vinegar and mint. Let the sauce stand at least 24 hours before it is served. Serve at room temperature.

barbecued leg of lamb

Serves 6 to 8

1 leg of lamb (about 5 pounds)
2 cups Italian or French vinegar and oil dressing

2 teaspoons monosodium glutamate (MSG) (optional)

Have your butcher bone the leg of lamb and then remove all visible fat. Do not have him roll and tie the roast. You want a butterfly roast which will lie flat on the barbecue. Place boned leg of lamb in a shallow bowl. Combine the salad dressing with the monosodium glutamate, and pour it over the lamb. Marinate the lamb for at least 3 hours and up to 2 days in the refrigerator. Turn the roast occasionally.

Broil the lamb on a preheated low heat broiler. Turn the meat frequently and baste with marinade during broiling. It will take about 40 minutes to cook the meat so that it is well done on the edges and rare in the center. It may be broiled longer if desired. This method of broiling will give you both rare and well done meat to suit all your guests or family.

barbecued lamb roll

Serves 6 to 8

1 leg of lamb (about 5 pounds)
3 cloves of garlic
¼ cup vegetable oil

1 teaspoon lemon pepper marinade
2 teaspoons salt

Remove all visible fat from the lamb with a sharp knife, roll and tie for cooking on the spit of a rotisserie. Cut slits in the flesh of the meat and insert slivers of garlic. Put the meat on the spit and cook according to the directions that came with your rotisserie. Cook until crusty and brown. Brush the lamb while it is cooking with a mixture of the oil, pepper marinade, and salt. (Lemon pepper marinade is black pepper with lemon flakes in it. If it is not available to you, use black pepper.)

broiled lamb chops

lamb sirloin chops, cut ½ to
  ¾ inch thick
salt

pepper
Italian or French vinegar and
  oil dressing (optional)

Remove all visible fat from the chops with a sharp knife. Broil 3 to 4 inches from the heat for 8 to 10 minutes. Turn the chops and broil for 5 to 8 minutes until done. The chops should be seasoned after they are turned. If the chops are dry they may be brushed a couple of times on each side with Italian or French vinegar and oil dressing. Serve hot.

grilled lamb chops

lamb sirloin chops, cut ½ to
  ¾ inch thick

salt
pepper

Remove all visible fat from the chops with a sharp knife. Place the chops on a lightly oiled preheated griddle. Grill the chops for 5 to 7 minutes. Turn them and continue grilling for about 7 minutes or until done. Season the chops with salt and pepper. Serve hot. The chops may be brushed with marinade after they are turned. A vinegar and oil base dressing may be used or one of the marinades used with roast lamb.

lamb stew

Serves 6 to 8

2 pounds sirloin of lamb,
    cut into 2-inch cubes
3 tablespoons vegetable oil
¼ cup minced onion
¼ teaspoon dehydrated
    garlic
¼ cup all purpose flour
1 teaspoon salt
⅛ teaspoon pepper
3 cups boiling water

2 cups cubed carrots
1 cup sliced onions
2 cups cubed potatoes
2 teaspoons Worcestershire
    sauce
2 tablespoons chopped
    parsley

Remove all visible fat from the lamb with a sharp knife. Sauté onion in oil in a Dutch oven until golden. Remove the onion from the oil. Combine flour, salt, and pepper. Dredge the lamb in flour mixture and brown it well in hot oil. Add onions, garlic, and water to the lamb, cover, and simmer for 1½ hours or until the lamb is tender. Chill the lamb in the broth until cold. Skim any fat from the surface of the broth. Return the lamb to the heat, bring it to a boil and add carrots, sliced onions, potatoes, and Worcestershire sauce. Simmer for about 30 minutes or until vegetables are done. Sprinkle the stew with parsley and serve hot.

Variation

Irish Lamb Stew: Omit browning the lamb. Use the flour mixture combined with ½ cup cold water to thicken the stew after the vegetables are done.

lamb patties

Serves 4

1 pound ground sirloin or
    leg of lamb
1 teaspoon salt

⅛ teaspoon pepper
½ teaspoon monosodium
    glutamate (MSG)
    (optional)

Combine the ground lamb, salt, pepper, and monosodium glutamate. Mix lightly. Divide the lamb into 4 to 8 equal portions. Shape each portion into 4 thick or 8 thin patties. Arrange the patties on a cold broiler rack. Broil the patties about 3 inches from the heat. The patties should be cooked about 4 to 6 minutes per side for thick patties and about 3 to 5 minutes per side for thin patties. They may also be skillet cooked or grilled.

roast pork

Insert a meat thermometer in the thickest part of the roast. Be sure that the thermometer is touching neither sinew nor bone. Place the roast on rack in open pan or roaster. Do not cover. Do not add water. Roast the pork in a preheated slow oven (350°F) for about 35 to 40 minutes per pound or until thermometer registers 185°F. Be sure to calculate the cooking time on weight of the roast after all visible fat is removed. The roast may be brushed several times during roasting with a marinade or rubbed with seasoning before roasting. Roast will be easier to carve if it is allowed to stand 20 minutes after it is removed from the oven.

Variations

Orange Glazed Roast Pork: Roast the pork as directed above, using a marinade made by combining ¼ cup vegetable oil, ¼ cup lemon juice, ¼ cup sherry, ¼ cup orange marmalade, ⅛ teaspoon ground thyme, ¼ teaspoon ground oregano, 2 teaspoons salt, ¼ teaspoon pepper, ½ teaspoon monosodium glutamate, and ½ teaspoon Italian seasoning.

Barbecued Roast Pork: Roast the pork as directed above using your favorite barbecue sauce as a marinade.

Canadian bacon

Broiled: Cut bacon into ¼-inch thick slices. Broil the bacon 3 inches from the heat for about 3 minutes on each side.

Pan broiled: Preheat a frying pan. Cut the bacon into ¼-inch thick slices. Brown the bacon on both sides, reduce the heat and finish cooking.

Baked: Remove all visible fat from about a 2 to 2¼-pound piece of bacon. Put the bacon in a shallow baking pan and cook it uncovered in a slow oven (325°F) for 1 hour. The bacon may be basted every 15 minutes with a mixture of ½ cup brown sugar, ½ cup pineapple juice, and ¼ teaspoon dry mustard.

Mary's fruit and honey glaze

Yields 2½ cups

1 cup canned apricot halves with juice
1 cup canned pineapple tidbits with juice
1 tablespoon soy sauce
¼ cup honey
2 tablespoons brown sugar
1 teaspoon pickling spice

Combine apricots, pineapple, soy sauce, honey, brown sugar, and pickling spice in blender to form a puree. Brush ham with the puree several times during baking.

lima beans and ham

Serves 4

1 pound large dried lima beans
water to cover beans
1 pound center cut uncooked ham
½ cup thinly sliced onions
1 finely chopped garlic clove
½ cup red table wine
1 teaspoon Worcestershire sauce
¼ teaspoon pepper
¼ teaspoon ground thyme

Cover the lima beans with water and soak overnight. Simmer the beans gently in the same water until tender. Remove all visible fat from the ham and cut into 1-inch cubes. Brown the ham in a lightly greased frying pan. Combine beans, ham, onions, garlic, wine, Worcestershire sauce, pepper, and thyme. Mix lightly and pour into a 2½- or 3-quart casserole. Cover and bake in preheated moderate oven (350°F) for 2 hours.

fruited ham slice

Serves 4

1 pound center cut uncooked ham slice	¼ cup brown sugar
2 cups hot crushed pineapple with juice	½ teaspoon ground cinnamon
	2 tablespoons margarine

Remove all visible fat from the ham and brown it in a lightly greased frying pan. Put the ham in the bottom of a shallow 1½-quart casserole. Spread the pineapple on the ham. Sprinkle with brown sugar and ground cinnamon. Dot it with small amounts of margarine. Cover and bake in a preheated slow oven (325°F) for 30 minutes. Uncover and bake for another 15 minutes or until the fruit is lightly browned.

scalloped ham and potatoes

Serves 4

1 pound center cut uncooked ham slice	1 teaspoon monosodium glutamate (MSG) (optional)
4 cups thinly sliced raw potatoes	¼ teaspoon pepper
½ cup instant dry milk	1½ cups warm water
¼ cup all purpose flour	

Remove all visible fat from the ham and cut it into 1-inch cubes. Combine the ham and potatoes. Combine instant milk, flour, monosodium glutamate, and pepper. Put the ham and potato mixture into a greased 1½-quart casserole, sprinkling the flour mixture into the ham and potatoes as you put them into the casserole. Pour warm water over the potatoes and ham and bake in a preheated moderate oven (350°F) for about 1¼ hours or until the potatoes are tender and the casserole is browned. Do not cover the casserole during baking period.

brown gravy

Yields 2 cups

2 cups cold stock or drippings
¼ cup all purpose flour

Salt and pepper to taste
½ teaspoon Kitchen Bouquet (optional)

Add flour to the cold stock and stir or beat it until smooth. Pour it into a saucepan and heat, stirring constantly. Cook and stir the gravy for about 5 minutes or until it is smooth and the flour is cooked. Correct the seasoning, add kitchen bouquet if desired, and serve hot.

cream gravy

Yields 2 cups

2 cups cold stock
¼ cup all purpose flour

½ cup instant dry milk
Salt and pepper to taste

Add flour and instant milk to the cold stock and stir or beat it until smooth. Pour the gravy into a saucepan and heat it, stirring constantly. Cook and stir the gravy for about 5 minutes or until it is smooth and the flour is cooked. Correct the seasoning and serve hot.

mushroom gravy

Yields 2¼ cups

½ cup sliced, drained
   canned mushrooms
1 tablespoon vegetable oil

2 cups cold stock and
   juice from mushrooms
¼ cup all purpose flour
   Salt and pepper to taste

Brown the mushrooms in hot oil. Add flour to the cold stock and
stir or beat it until smooth. Pour the gravy into a pan with the
mushrooms and heat, stirring constantly. Cook and stir the gravy
for about 5 minutes or until it is smooth and the flour is cooked.
Correct seasonings and serve hot.

pan gravy

Yields 2 cups

¼ cup vegetable oil or
   margarine (½ stick)
¼ cup flour
2 cups cold water, meat
   stock or bouillon

½ teaspoon Kitchen Bouquet
   (optional)
   Salt and pepper to taste

Brown flour with oil or margarine in a saucepan, stirring constantly,
until it is bubbling and browned. Remove it from the heat and add
the cold liquid and kitchen bouquet. Return the gravy to the heat
and, stirring constantly, cook for about 1 or 2 minutes or until
smooth. Correct the seasoning and serve hot.

onion gravy

Yields 2¼ cups

1 cup chopped onions
2 tablespoons vegetable oil
2 cups cold stock or
   bouillon

¼ cup all purpose flour
   Salt and pepper to taste

Brown onions in hot oil until golden. Add flour to the cold liquid and stir or beat it until smooth. Pour the gravy into a pan with the onions and heat, stirring constantly. Cook and stir the gravy for about 5 minutes or until it is smooth and the flour is cooked. Correct the seasoning and serve hot. (If a brown gravy is preferred, add the flour to the onions and continue to stir and cook the flour with onions until browned. Add the stock and continue as directed.)

tomato gravy

Yields 2 cups

¼ cup finely chopped onions
¼ cup finely chopped fresh
   green peppers
3 tablespoons margarine
3 tablespoons flour
1 cup water

¼ cup tomato puree
1 teaspoon sugar
1 teaspoon salt
¼ teaspoon dehydrated
   garlic
⅛ teaspoon black pepper

Sauté onions and green peppers in margarine. Add flour and cook and stir the mixture until bubbling. Add water, tomato puree, sugar, salt, garlic, and pepper. Stir and cook the gravy for about 5 minutes or until it is smooth and the flour is cooked. Serve hot.

fish

If you are used to serving fish to your family, you don't need this chapter; all you need is to remember not to use saturated fats when you are preparing fish and to use shrimp sparingly. However, if you have as little experience preparing fish as I had when the doctor said that my husband should have several servings of fish each week, then this chapter is for you. I can only remember having fresh fish once before I left our little Iowa town for college. A friend of my father's had sent us a whole fresh salmon that he had caught on a fishing trip. My mother fried it because that was the only way she knew to prepare fish. It was delicious and we all loved it but there was no repeat performance since my father was not a fisherman and there was no other source of fresh fish in our area. Of course, that was years ago. Today people in Iowa have frozen fish available to them in the stores, just as everyone else does, so that there is no need now to go without the fresh or frozen fish your family likes and needs.

One of the first things to keep in mind is that we are talking about serving fish. Shrimp should be used sparingly. Most doctors say not more than one 4-ounce serving per week. Shrimp is low in fat but it does contain cholesterol. It has less cholesterol than meat but more than other fish or seafood. Since over 240 species of fish and shellfish are sold in the United States, there is certainly enough variety amongst which to choose that you need never complain about lack of variety in the kinds of fish that you serve.

Fish plays an important part in the low cholesterol diet because it is low in calories, contains only small amounts of cholesterol and the fat is less saturated than that in meat — in many cases the fat is even unsaturated.

Fish and your husband's diet are similar to a bridegroom and his in-laws. He might as well learn to know and like them, because they are going to be an important part of his life from now on. Because most doctors advise you to restrict the number of servings of meat per week, fish is more important in your menu planning than it ever was before. Even though Catholics are no longer required to eat fish on Friday, more fish is being bought in the United States. Evidently fish is becoming more popular. People are realizing just how good it is and how good it is for them.

Fresh fish is best at the peak of its season, just as you'd expect of fresh fruits and vegetables. And, like fresh fruits and vegetables, fish are least expensive just when they are at their peak. The peak of the season can be the time that your husband takes off on a fishing trip, or when the commercial fishing fleets have their greatest hauls. Whatever fish is in season is the kind to feature in your menu planning. Since your husband probably doesn't go fishing that often, it pays to cultivate your fish dealer as you do your meat dealer. He can advise you of the best buys in fish at any given time. Of course, if your only source of fish is the supermart, you will have to acquaint yourself with the various species of fish and learn how to prepare them so that your husband will enjoy them, instead of mourning the steaks and prime ribs now missing from his diet. Take the positive approach. Serve such delicious, mouth-watering fish that he will seldom miss the meals he used to enjoy.

Fresh fish should have a mild odor, bright clear eyes, red gills that are free from slime, iridescent skin, and firm flesh. Of course, fish cut in fillets or steaks don't show the condition of their eyes or gills, but you can still look for the mild odor and firm flesh; also, be sure there is no trace of browning or drying. Fresh fish should be put in the refrigerator in its original wrapper as soon as possible after you buy it. A storage temperature of 35-40°F is needed to keep it fresh, and it should not be held in the refrigerator longer than a day or so before you cook it.

Frozen fish is available throughout the year. The fish should be frozen solid and have little or no odor. It should be wrapped in a moisture- and vapro-proof material and there should not be much space between the fish and the wrapping, although sometimes the fish is coated with a thin glaze of ice to keep it from drying out. Any discoloration in the frozen fish indicates poor quality and you shouldn't buy it. Frozen fish should be stored at 0°F or lower, to keep its quality. If the temperature is higher than zero chemical changes will cause the fish to lose color, flavor, texture, and nutritive value. Frozen fish should not be stored over six months if you want to serve it at its peak flavor.

Canned fish comes in a variety of species, too. Salmon, tuna, mackerel, and sardines are the most popular kinds although we also like bonita. Canned fish should be stored in a cool dry place for not over a year.

Cooked fish may be stored in either the freezer or the refrigerator. Be sure to put it in a covered, air-tight container. If you are going to freeze it, wrap it in a moisutre- and vapor-proof material, and it is best not to keep it frozen over three months.

When you get ready to thaw frozen fish, keep the following guidelines in mind:

1. Schedule your thawing so that you will use the fish as soon as possible after it is thawed. Do not hold thawed fish more than a day before cooking it.
2. Put individual packages of fish in the refrigerator to thaw. Allow 24 hours for thawing 1-pound packages. If you must thaw it more quickly, put the package under cold running water and allow one to two hours to thaw a 1-pound package.
3. Do not thaw fish at room temperature or in warm water.
4. Do not refreeze fish after it has been thawed.
5. Frozen fillets or steaks may be cooked without thawing, if additional cooking time is allowed. Fillets or steaks to be breaded or whole fish to be stuffed should be thawed before you use them.

The thing to learn thoroughly before you buy fish at the super-mart is "The Market Forms of Fish." The different market forms of fish are:

Whole Fish are sold just as they come from the water. Before you cook them they must be scaled, eviscerated, and usually the heads, tails and fins are removed; however, some small fish, such as smelts, are cooked with only the entrails removed. This is how your husband or other fishermen usually bring fish home. Believe me, unless you have a man around to clean them or you are the hardy type and used to doing this sort of thing, it is a good idea to avoid fish in this form. You will need about 11 ounces per serving of this type of fish.

Dressed Fish are sold scaled, eviscerated, and sometimes the head, tail and fins are removed. The smaller size fish prepared this way are called pan-dressed. This kind of fish is all ready to cook and it is the simplest way to buy it if you are buying a whole fish. You will need about 8 ounces per serving of this kind of fish.

Steaks are cross-section slices from a large dressed fish cut ⅝- to 1-inch thick. A cross section of the backbone is usually the only bone in a steak. You will need about 5 ounces per serving of this type of fish.

Chunks are cross sections of a large dressed fish, cut in thicker pieces than steaks. A cross section of the backbone is usually the only bone in a chunk. You will need about 5 ounces per serving of this kind of fish.

Fillets are the sides of the fish cut lengthwise away from the backbone. They are practically skinless and may or may not be skinned. Butterfly fillets are both sides of the fish cut lengthwise away from the backbone and held together by the uncut flesh and skin of the belly. These fillets are practically boneless. You will need about 5 ounces per serving of fillets.

Fish is so good that it is hard to believe how easy it is to prepare. It is cooked at a low or moderate heat because if cooked at too high a temperature or for too long a time it will get dry and tough. About the only exception to this is oven-frying, by which you cook the fish at a high temperature to simulate frying, but then it is encased in a batter, which coats the fish to protect it from the high heat.

It is easy to tell when fish is cooked. Raw fish has a watery, translucent look. After it has been cooked, fish becomes opaque and milky white, the flesh separates easily into layers or flakes. If there are any bones in the fish, the flesh will fall away from the bones easily. Most cooked fish tends to break easily so it should be handled with care.

When you are first learning to prepare fish it is helpful to remember the basic methods: baking, broiling, frying, poaching, and steaming. (A table at the end of this chapter lists some common species of fish and some ways in which they are best prepared.)

BAKING FISH
Baking is a form of dry heat cooking and is one of the easiest

ways to cook fish. However, care should be taken to bake fish at a moderate temperature. Fish should be cooked in a preheated 350°F oven for a relatively short period of time. This keeps the fish moist and flavorful. Fish that are not baked with a topping or sauce should be basted with oil or a marinade to keep the surface moist. Frozen fish can be baked without defrosting if you allow for extra baking time, and if the recipe does not call for stuffing the fish or dipping it in milk or egg white and milk and rolling in bread crumbs.

BROILING FISH

Broiling is also a form of dry heat cooking, but the heat is more direct and more intense than in baking. It is better to use fillets, steaks, or pan dressed fish cut about 1-inch thick for broiling because the intense heat tends to dry out thinner fish. Fish should be thawed before it is broiled and should be brushed with an oil, marinade, or basting sauce before it is put under the broiler and again while it is being broiled. The directions for your own particular broiler should be followed. However, it is a general rule to broil the fish about 3 to 4 inches from the source of heat and put thicker cuts further from the heat than thinner ones. The length of time it takes to broil fish will depend upon the thickness of the fish and its distance from the source of heat. Cooking time will range from 10 to 15 minutes to reach the flaking stage. Generally, fish do not need to be turned while they are broiling, because the heat of the pan will cook the underside of the fish as well. Turn thicker pieces, such as pan dressed fish, when half of the broiling time is up; baste again with oil or sauce. Always serve broiled fish very hot.

CHARCOAL BROILING FISH

Charcoal broiling is becoming a very popular outdoor sport. It is a wonderful way to keep the heat out of the house in the summer and your husband busy cooking for company while you prepare the rest of the dinner. Fish are a natural for this sort of cooking because they cook so quickly. Pan dressed fish, fillets, and steaks are all suitable for charcoal broiling. The fish should be thawed before it is broiled and, because it flakes easily, it is wise to use a well greased, long handled, hinged wire grill. Thicker cuts of fish are preferable as they tend to dry out less than the thin ones, but they still should be basted generously before and during cooking. Fish are generally cooked about 4 inches from moderately hot coals for 15 to 20 minutes, depending upon the thickness of the fish. French or Italian style salad dressings make a good brushing sauce for fish because their oil and spices keep the fish moist and flavorful. However, it is best not to use a sauce with a high sugar content since it burns too easily and may spoil your fish.

FRYING FISH

Frying means cooking in fat, and for our purpose it means cooking in oil. Fortunately, oil is very good for frying because it does not smoke as easily as some of the animal fats. It can be heated to the correct frying temperature, and it will not usually add any odor to the fish because it doesn't decompose and smoke as easily as some saturated fats. The temperature of the oil is very important: if it is too cold you will get a pale, greasy, fat soaked product; if it is too hot the fish will burn on the outside before cooking thoroughly inside. Before frying, frozen fish must be thawed, separated, and cut into pieces of serving size. Some breaded fish are frozen in separated pieces and are fried without thawing according to the directions on the package. Fish should be drained (right after it is fried) to remove excess oil and should be served hot. It is not advisable to buy the breaded fish portions unless you read the list of ingredients. Make sure that no forbidden ingredients are used.

Fish should not be dipped in whole egg. Egg white mixed with milk makes a very satisfactory dip for fish and many other items. You can also dip fish in oil or in reconstituted instant dry milk, then in bread or cornflake crumbs — not in cracker crumbs because crackers contain saturated fat.

Deep fat frying means cooking in a deep layer of hot fat; for us this means a deep layer of hot oil. It is a quick method of cooking — a tasty and appetizing way to cook tender fish.

For deep fat frying you need an electric fryer or a heavy, deep saucepan with a fry basket to fit it and a deep fat frying thermometer. You should use enough oil to float the fish but not enough to fill the pan more than half full. You have to allow room for the fish and for the oil to bubble while the fish is cooking. The fish may be dipped in a liquid and coated with a breading or dipped in a batter. This coating will keep the fish moist during frying and will also give a delicious crispness to the finished product. Place only one layer of fish at a time in the basket and allow enough room so that the pieces do not touch each other. Lower the basket slowly into the hot oil, when it has reached the right temperature, to prevent excessive bubbling. If the oil is at the right temperature, a crust will form almost immediately, holding the juices in and the oil out of the crust. Fish should be fried until it is golden brown, which is usually about 3 to 5 minutes.

The directions for frying fish should not be confined to the species of fish listed in these recipes. The methods can be applied to a great variety of fish. They are meant to be basic directions for any type of fish as well. One of the best ways to serve halibut is to cut the steaks into 1-inch cubes, dip it in your favorite coating mixture, then either pan fry or deep fat fry the cubes. It isn't scallops, but it is awfully good.

OVEN-FRYING FISH

Oven-frying is not really frying because you don't use that much oil. It is a method of cooking fish in a very hot oven, which simulates frying. Fish is cut into serving size portions, dipped in salted, reconstituted instant dry milk, and coated with fine, dry crumbs. The fish is then placed in a shallow, well greased pan. A little oil is poured over the fish and it is baked at 500°F. The fish does not need to be turned or basted and the cooking time is short. The crumb coating and the high temperature prevent the juices from escaping and form an attractive brown crust. All in all, it is the answer to the question: What to have when you want to serve something quick and simple? Be sure to have your oven preheated and hot; it just doesn't work in a cool oven.

POACHING FISH

Poaching means cooking in a simmering liquid. The fish is placed in a single layer in a shallow, wide pan (such as a large frying pan) and barely covered with liquid. The liquid can be a stock, lightly salted water, white wine and water, or water with various herbs in it. It is important not to overcook the fish and it is important that the liquid should just simmer, not boil. The fish should cook in the simmering liquid, in a covered pan, about 10 to 15 minutes, or until the fish flakes easily when tested with a fork. It can then be served with a sauce or used in a salad or some other fish dish, such as a casserole. A whole poached salmon lends a most glamorous note to a buffet.

STEAMING FISH

Steamed fish is cooked by the steam from hot water. It is an excellent means of cooking fish to retain their natural juices and flavors. A steamer is ideal but any deep pan with a tight cover may be used if a rack will fit it. The rack is to keep the fish out of the water. The water used may be plain, seasoned with herbs, or combined with wine. The fish are placed on a rack over rapidly boiling water. The pan is covered and the fish are allowed to steam for 10 to 15 minutes, or until they flake easily when tested with a fork. Steamed fish are served with a sauce or used in the same way as poached fish.

FISH COOKED IN FOIL

Individual portions of fish may be baked in the oven or prepared outside on the grill in the same way as Hobo Hamburgers. In other words, you can put a single portion of fish, along with some sauce and thinly sliced vegetables, in a foil packet. It will cook beautifully without dirtying any pans and will be very tasty as well. This method takes longer on the grill than it does in an oven, but either method is satisfactory.

FISH STEWS

We could not discuss the methods of cooking fish without mentioning the wonderful fish stews found in so many different countries. Of course, fish stews made with seafood can not be used very often but some wonderful stews are made with the fish that is available and allowed. Do what the natives in other countries do, make your stew with the fish available where you live. The recipe for Fisherman Stew is a good example and might encourage you to develop your own family favorite.

FISH IN CANS

In this chapter, we discuss fish fillets and steaks more than we do different species of fish. This is because fish names will vary from one section of the country to another. The same fish will be called

different names in different places. Most fish recipes are interchangeable as far as the basic recipes are concerned. They can be
used for whatever type of fish you prefer and whatever is available
in your section of the country.

Of course, canned salmon and tuna are called by the same name
throughout the country. They are available everywhere and everywhere they are good and not too expensive. One nice thing about
fish — it is kind to your budget. A housewife always appreciates
that and so does her husband, for that matter. It is much less
expensive to have a fish fry outside in your yard than to serve a
standing rib roast to the same group of friends — and much
better for your husband's health as well.

I grew up in an area and at a time in which fresh fish was not
available. We concentrated on canned tuna and salmon, with an
occasional can of sardines. My father's favorite was tunafish,
noodles, and mushrooms, which we used to have occasionally. You
can still serve it if you make your own noodles with egg whites or
you can use the recipe for Tuna, Macaroni, and Mushrooms. All
the ingredients for it are available at the supermart.

There are times when a hot sandwich seems like just the thing
for lunch or after a golf game. Since most luncheon meats are out
and the amount of cold roast to be used may be limited, it is a
good idea to have sandwich recipes that utilize fish. Fish salad
sandwiches are always good, but there are times when a hot
sandwich seems more suitable. This is the time to serve Texas
Tuna or Salmon Burgers.

Both tuna and salmon loaves are good hot and make excellent
sandwiches. They should not be packed in a lunch, however,
unless the lunch can be kept refrigerated. But if a refrigerator is
available, they may be wrapped in aluminum foil and kept chilled
until lunch time. (The aluminum foil is to keep the salmon odor
away from the rest of the food in the refrigerator as well as to
protect the sandwich.)

SAUCES TO SERVE WITH FISH

Lemon juice is always good with fish and so is vinegar. I had
never tried vinegar until I was in Britain and was served it with
fish and chips. It is delicious. I was so surprised to find how much
it added to the taste of the fish and chips. Now we use vinegar

with our fish and we even use different kinds of vinegar. I discovered that if I steeped herbs in vinegar I could get a flavorful vinegar that is excellent with fish. Use 1 tablespoon of herbs to 1 cup of vinegar, cover the herbs with the vinegar, and let it steep for a few days before removing the herbs. I think that our favorite is dill vinegar, but you can try different herbs to see which you prefer. I even use the juice from sweet pickles with herbs for fish. Many other sauces are excellent with fish. You can, of course, use any of them that contain no saturated fats. Toward the end of this chapter are some that you might enjoy.

baked stuffed fish

Serves 6

3- pound dressed fresh or frozen fish	1 slightly beaten egg white
1 teaspoon salt	½ teaspoon ground sage
⅛ teaspoon pepper	½ teaspoon salt
½ cup chopped celery	¼ teaspoon ground thyme
¼ cup chopped onions	⅛ teaspoon pepper
¼ cup vegetable oil	2 tablespoons vegetable oil
1 quart dry bread crumbs	

Thaw the fish, if frozen. Clean, wash, and dry the fish. Sprinkle the inside of the fish with 1 teaspoon salt and ⅛ teaspoon pepper. Place the fish on a well greased bake-and-serve platter.

Sauté the celery and onions in hot oil until the onions are golden. Add bread crumbs, egg white, sage, ½ teaspoon salt, and ⅛ teaspoon pepper to the vegetables and toss together to form a dressing.

Stuff the fish loosely with the dressing. Brush the fish with 2 tablespoons oil. Bake in a preheated moderate oven (350°F) for 45 to 60 minutes or until fish flakes easily when tested with a fork.

rainbow trout with mushroom herb stuffing

Serves 6

6 pan-dressed fresh or
   frozen rainbow trout
1½ teaspoons salt
4 cups soft bread crumbs
½ cup (1 stick) margarine
1 cup sliced fresh or
   canned mushrooms
⅔ cup sliced green onions

½ teaspoon salt
¼ cup chopped parsley
2 tablespoons chopped
   pimientos
1⅓ tablespoons lemon juice
½ teaspoon ground
   marjoram or thyme
2 tablespoons vegetable oil

Thaw the fish if frozen; clean, wash, and dry it. Sprinkle 1½ teaspoons salt evenly over the inside and outside of the fish.

Sauté bread crumbs in margarine until lightly browned, stirring frequently. Add mushrooms and onions and cook until the mushrooms are tender. Add ½ teaspoon salt, parsley, pimientos, lemon juice, and marjoram or thyme; toss lightly. Stuff the fish with the dressing and arrange them in a single layer in a well oiled baking pan. Brush with oil. Bake in a preheated moderate oven (350°F) 25 to 30 minutes or until fish flakes easily when tested with a fork. Serve plain or with your favorite fish sauce.

broiled fillets or steaks

Serves 6

2 pounds fresh or frozen
   steaks or fillets
2 tablespoons vegetable oil
2 tablespoons lemon juice

1 teaspoon salt
½ teaspoon paprika
⅛ teaspoon pepper

Thaw the fish, if frozen. Cut fish into six portions and place in a single layer, skin side down on a well greased baking pan, about 15 × 10 inches. Combine the remaining ingredients and mix them well to form a basting sauce. Pour sauce over the fish. Broil the fish about 4 inches from the heat for about 10 to 15 minutes or until the fish flakes easily when tested with a fork. Baste the fish once during the broiling.

If your husband likes a spicy fish, this is just the one for him. You can vary it by changing the spices to suit your taste.

spicy red snapper

Serves 6

2 pounds fresh or frozen red snapper fillets	¼ cup vegetable oil
⅓ cup steak sauce	1 tablespoon vinegar
¼ cup catsup	1 teaspoon salt
	½ teaspoon curry powder

Thaw the fish, if frozen. Cut the fillets into serving size pieces. Combine the remaining ingredients and mix them thoroughly. Place the fish, skin side up, on a well greased broiler pan and brush with the sauce. Broil about 3 inches from heat for 4 to 5 minutes. Turn the fish carefully, and brush it with more sauce. Broil 4 to 5 minutes longer, basting occasionally, until fish flakes easily when tested with a fork.

smoky broiled catfish

Serves 6

6 pan dressed, skinned, fresh or frozen catfish	1 clove of garlic, finely chopped
⅓ cup soy sauce	½ teaspoon ground ginger
3 tablespoons vegetable oil	½ teaspoon salt
1 tablespoon liquid smoke	Lemon wedges as desired

Thaw the fish, if frozen. Clean, wash and dry them. Combine soy sauce, oil, liquid smoke, garlic, ginger, and salt and mix thoroughly. Brush the inside of the fish with the sauce. Place the fish on a well greased broiler pan and brush with more sauce. Broil the fish about 3 inches from the heat for 4 to 6 minutes. Turn carefully and brush other side of the fish with sauce. Broil 4 to 6 minutes longer, twice basting with sauce, until fish flakes easily when tested with a fork. Serve with lemon wedges.

barbecued fillets or steaks

Serves 6

2 pounds fresh or frozen steaks or fillets	1 cup tomato sauce
¼ cup chopped onions	2 tablespoons lemon juice
2 tablespoons chopped fresh green peppers	1 tablespoon Worcester- shire sauce
1 clove of garlic, finely chopped	1 tablespoon sugar
2 tablespoons vegetable oil	2 teaspoons salt
	¼ teaspoon pepper

Thaw the fish, if frozen. Saute the onions, green peppers, and garlic in oil until tender. Add all remaining ingredients and simmer them for 5 minutes, stirring occasionally. Cool the sauce. Cut the fish into six portions and place them in a single layer in a shallow baking dish. Pour the sauce over the fish and let them stand for 30 minutes, turning the fish once. Remove the fish from the sauce and reserve the sauce to baste the fish. Place the fish in well greased, hinged wire grills. Cook about 4 inches from moderately hot coals for 5 to 8 minutes. Baste with sauce, turn, and cook 5 to 8 minutes longer or until fish flakes easily when tested with a fork.

deep fat fried fillets or steaks

Serves 6

2 pounds fresh or frozen
  steaks or fillets
¼ cup reconstituted instant
  dry milk
1 egg white

1 teaspoon salt
⅛ teaspoon pepper
1½ cups dry bread crumbs
  Vegetable oil for frying

Thaw the fish, if frozen. Cut the fish into six portions. Combine the milk, egg white, salt and pepper. Dip fish in the milk mixture and roll it in crumbs. Place in a single layer in a fry basket and fry in deep oil at 350°F for 3 to 5 minutes, or until fish are brown and flake easily when tested with a fork. Drain on absorbent paper. Serve hot.

Tennessee fried catfish

Serves 6

6 pan dressed, skinned,
  fresh or frozen catfish
2 teaspoons salt
¼ teaspoon pepper

2 egg whites
¼ cup reconstituted instant
  dry milk
2 cups cornmeal

Thaw the fish, if frozen. Clean, wash, and dry the fish. Sprinkle both sides of the fish with salt and pepper. Combine the egg whites and milk. Dip the fish in the egg white mixture, then roll in cornmeal. Fry the fish in a heavy frying pan containing about ⅛ inch of hot, but not smoking, oil. When the fish is brown on one side, turn it carefully and brown it on the other side. Cooking time should be about 10 minutes, depending on the thickness of the fish. Drain on absorbent paper. Serve hot.

Some people like to dip fish in evaporated skim milk instead of in an egg milk mixture. In either case the fillets should end up with a delicious, crisp coating, which also keeps the fish moist.

pan fried fillet of sole

Serves 4

1 pound fresh or frozen
   fillet of sole
¼ cup evaporated skim milk
½ cup fine dry bread crumbs
½ teaspoon salt

¼ teaspoon paprika
⅛ teaspoon pepper
3 tablespoons vegetable oil
Lemon wedges, as desired

Thaw the fish, if frozen. Dip the fish in evaporated milk and then into a mixture of bread crumbs, salt, paprika, and pepper. Heat the oil in heavy frying pan. Fry the fillets over medium heat for about 3 minutes on each side, or until the fish flakes easily when tested with a fork. Serve hot with lemon wedges.

oven-fried fillets or steaks

Serves 6

2 pounds fresh or frozen
   steaks or fillets
½ cup reconstituted instant
   dry milk

1 teaspoon salt
1½ cups cornflake crumbs or
   toasted dry bread
   crumbs
¼ cup vegetable oil

Thaw fish if frozen. Cut fish into six portions. Combine milk and salt. Dip fish in milk and roll in crumbs. Place fish, single layer, skin side down on a well greased baking pan. Pour oil over fish and bake in a preheated very hot oven (500°F) for 10 to 15 minutes or until fish are brown and flake easily when tested with a fork.

You can vary the amount and type of mustard in this sauce to suit your husband's taste. You can also substitute horseradish for the mustard with good results.

poached fish with mustard sauce

Serves 6

2 pounds fresh or frozen steaks or fillets
2 cups boiling water
¼ cup lemon juice
2 tablespoons onions, finely chopped
1 teaspoon salt
3 peppercorns
1 tablespoon chopped parsley
1 bay leaf
Mustard sauce

Thaw the fish, if frozen. Remove any skin or bones. Cut the fish into serving size portions and place in a well greased 10-inch frying pan. Add water, lemon juice, onions, salt, peppercorns, parsley, and bay leaf to the fish. Cover and simmer 10 to 15 minutes, or until fish flakes easily when tested with a fork. Carefully remove the fish from the liquid to a hot platter. Pour mustard sauce over fish. Serve hot.

mustard sauce

Yields 1 cup

¼ cup (½ stick) margarine
2 tablespoons all purpose flour
½ teaspoon salt
⅛ teaspoon pepper
1½ cups reconstituted instant dry milk
1 tablespoon salad mustard
1 tablespoon chopped parsley

Melt the margarine. Stir in the flour, salt, and pepper. Add the milk gradually and cook until it is thick and smooth, stirring constantly. Add the mustard and parsley and blend well. Serve hot.

whitefish in foil

Serves 6

2 pounds fresh or frozen
   whitefish fillets
1 cup sliced fresh green
   peppers
½ cup thinly sliced onions

¼ cup vegetable oil
2 tablespoons lemon juice
2 teaspoons salt
1 teaspoon paprika
⅛ teaspoon pepper

Thaw the fish, if frozen. Cut the fish into serving size portions. Cut six pieces of heavy duty aluminum foil 12 × 12 inches. Grease the foil lightly. Place a portion of fish skin side down on each portion of foil. Top each portion of fish with ⅙ of the green peppers and onions. Combine oil, lemon juice, salt, paprika, and pepper to form a sauce. Pour the sauce over the fish. Bring the foil up over the fish and close all edges with tight double folds. Make six packages.

Place packages on a grill about 5 inches from moderately hot coals. Cook for 45 to 60 minutes or until fish flakes easily when tested with a fork. Serve hot. Or place the packages in preheated moderate oven (350°F) for about 25 minutes, or until fish flakes easily when tested with a fork.

Serve an individual packet to each person.

fisherman stew

Serves 6

2 pounds fresh or frozen
   salmon, halibut, or
   other firm fish
¼ cup (½ stick) margarine
1½ cups sliced celery
½ cup chopped onions
1 clove of garlic, minced
2 cups canned tomatoes
   and juice

1 cup canned tomato sauce
2 teaspoons salt
½ teaspoon paprika
½ teaspoon chili powder
¼ teaspoon pepper
7 ounces uncooked
   spaghetti
2 cups boiling water

Thaw the fish, if frozen. Cut it into 1-inch chunks. Heat margarine in a heavy saucepan and sauté the celery, onions, and garlic in it until tender. Add the tomatoes, tomato sauce, salt, paprika, chili powder, and pepper. Bring the mixture to a boil. Reduce the heat and simmer, covered, for 20 minutes. Add uncooked spaghetti and boiling water. Cover the pan and simmer for 10 minutes. Add the fish, cover the pan, and cook slowly for another 10 minutes, or until the fish flakes easily when tested with a fork. Serve hot.

tuna, macaroni, and mushrooms

Serves 6

1   12½-ounce can of tuna in vegetable oil
1   cup canned mushrooms
2   tablespoons oil from tuna
¼   cup all purpose flour
¼   cup instant dry milk
½   teaspoon salt
¼   teaspoon white pepper
2   cups mushroom liquid and water
3   cups cooked, drained macaroni
3   tablespoons chopped pimiento
½   cup dry bread crumbs

Drain the tuna and reserve its oil. Drain the mushrooms and reserve the liquid. Put the oil from the tuna in a heavy saucepan. Stir flour, instant dry milk, salt, and pepper into the oil and cook, stirring until well blended. Add the mushroom liquid and water to the flour mixture. Cook, stirring constantly, until a smooth sauce is formed. (You can use a can of mushroom soup made with vegetable oil in place of this sauce if you like.)

Combine the tuna, mushroom sauce, macaroni, and pimiento and pour into a greased 2-quart casserole. Top with crumbs and bake in a preheated moderate oven (350°F) for 1 hour if macaroni is cold or 45 minutes if macaroni is hot when combined with the sauce.

This Jambalaya is also good made with salmon or left over flaked fish instead of the tuna.

tuna jambalaya

Serves 6

2 9¼-ounce cans of tuna in vegetable oil
¼ cup chopped onions
¼ cup chopped fresh green peppers
½ cup diced celery
2 cups canned tomatoes and juice

2 cups canned tomato sauce
1 cup canned mushrooms
1 teaspoon salt
½ teaspoon chili powder
½ teaspoon thyme
¼ teaspoon pepper
2 cups instant rice

Drain the oil from the tuna into saucepan. Saute the onions, green peppers, and celery in this oil until the vegetables are crisp tender. Add tomatoes, tomato sauce, mushrooms and the liquid with them, salt, chili powder, thyme, and pepper. Bring to a full boil, reduce heat and simmer 5 minutes. Add the rice and tuna. Remove the jambalaya from the heat and let it stand 5 minutes. Fluff with fork and serve hot.

savory tuna loaf

Serves 4

3 slightly beaten egg whites
½ cup reconstituted instant dry milk
2 cups soft bread crumbs
¼ cup onions, finely chopped

1 tablespoon parsley, finely chopped
¼ teaspoon ground thyme
1 teaspoon salt
¼ teaspoon pepper
3 6½- or 7-ounce cans of tuna in vegetable oil

Combine the egg whites, milk, bread crumbs, onions, parsley, thyme, salt, and pepper in a mixing bowl and mix well. Add the undrained tuna and mix well. Put in a foil lined loaf pan and bake in a preheated moderate oven (350°F) 45 minutes. Lift the loaf from pan; pull the foil from its sides, and lift the loaf off of the foil with a wide spatula. Serve with your favorite fish sauce or with Green Pea Sauce.

green pea sauce

Yields 1 quart

1 10-ounce package frozen peas	1 teaspoon salt
¼ cup (½ stick) margarine	⅛ teaspoon white pepper
¼ cup all purpose flour	¾ cup instant dry milk
	1½ cups cold water

Cover the peas with water and cook uncovered for 12 minutes. Do not drain them. Melt the margarine in a saucepan, add the flour, salt, pepper, and instant dry milk. Cook this mixture over low heat, stirring constantly, for 1 minute. Add water gradually and cook, stirring constantly, until it is thickened. Add the peas and their liquid, and continue to cook just long enough to combine the liquid with the white sauce and to heat the sauce thoroughly. Serve hot over slices of tuna loaf or salmon loaf.

Texas tuna

Yields 6 sandwiches

1 12½-ounce can of tuna in vegetable oil	2 tablespoons vinegar
1 cup chopped onions	1 teaspoon salad mustard
1 cup catsup	½ teaspoon salt
⅔ cup water	⅛ teaspoon pepper
2 tablespoons sugar	6 toasted hamburger rolls

Drain the tuna, but reserve its oil. Break the tuna into large pieces.

Sauté the onions in the reserved oil. Add catsup, water, sugar, vinegar, mustard, salt, and pepper to the onions and simmer (uncovered) for about 20 minutes, stirring occasionally. Add the tuna and simmer for another 10 minutes, stirring occasionally. Put about ⅓ cup of tuna mixture on the bottom half of each roll. Cover with the top half and serve hot.

salmon burgers

Serves 6

1 1-pound can of salmon
½ cup chopped onions
3 tablespoons vegetable oil
⅓ cup salmon liquid
⅓ cup dry bread crumbs
3 slightly beaten egg whites

¼ cup chopped parsley
1 teaspoon ground mustard
½ teaspoon salt
½ cup dry bread crumbs
6 round buns

Drain the salmon, remove its skin and bones and reserve its liquid for later. Flake the salmon. Sauté the onions in oil until golden. Combine the onions (do not drain them), salmon liquid, ⅓ cup dry bread crumbs, egg whites, parsley, mustard, salt, and salmon. Shape into six cakes and roll each in ½ cup dry bread crumbs. Fry the cakes in a heavy frying pan containing about ⅛ inch of oil, which is hot but not smoking. Fry at a moderate heat. When the cakes are brown on one side, turn them carefully, and brown them on the other side. Cooking time is approximately 5 to 8 minutes. Drain on absorbent paper. Put salmon burgers in buns and serve them with your favorite sauce.

salmon loaf

Serves 6

1 1-pound can of salmon
3 tablespoons vegetable oil
3 tablespoons all purpose
   flour

1 teaspoon salt
⅛ teaspoon pepper
2 tablespoons parsley,
   minced

2 tablespoons instant dry
  milk
1 cup salmon liquid and
  water

2 cups bread crumbs
2 slightly beaten egg whites

Drain the salmon. Remove its skin and bones and reserve the salmon liquid. Put the oil in a saucepan. Combine the flour and instant dry milk and stir them into the oil until smooth. Gradually, add the salmon liquid and water. Cook and stir the sauce constantly, until the sauce is smooth and thickened. Add the salt, pepper, and minced parsley to the sauce. Combine the sauce, salmon, bread crumbs, and egg whites. Form this mixture into a loaf and bake it in an uncovered greased pan in preheated moderate oven (350°F) for 30 minutes, or until browned.

tartar sauce

Yields 1¼ cups

1 cup L C mayonnaise
2 tablespoons pickle relish
1 tablespoon onions, finely
  chopped

1 tablespoon parsley, finely
  chopped
1 tablespoon pimiento,
  chopped

Combine all the ingredients and chill until served.

chili sauce for fish

Yields 1½ cups

1 12-ounce bottle chili sauce
1½ tablespoon vinegar
1 tablespoon sugar

1 teaspoon Worcestershire
  sauce
2 tablespoons prepared
  horseradish

Combine all the ingredients and chill until served.

barbecue sauce for fish

Yields 1½ cups

1 cup catsup
1 tablespoon Worcester-
   shire sauce
½ teaspoon salt
⅛ teaspoon pepper
⅛ teaspoon monosodium
   glutamate (MSG)

2 teaspoons ground mustard
2 tablespoons lemon juice
¼ cup water
2 tablespoons onions,
   finely chopped
2 tablespoons fresh green
   peppers, finely chopped

Combine all the ingredients and chill until used.

FISH COOKERY CHART

Species	Type	Bake	Steam	Broil	Fry
Catfish	Lean	X		X	X
Cod	Lean	X	X	X	X
Flounder	Lean	X		X	X
Haddock	Lean	X	X	X	X
Halibut	Lean	X	X	X	X
Herring	Fat	X		X	X
Lake Perch	Lean				X
Mackerel	Fat	X	X	X	
Ocean Perch	Lean	X			X
Pike	Lean	X		X	X
Pompano	Fat	X		X	X
Red Snapper	Lean	X	X	X	
Salmon	Fat	X	X	X	
Shad	Fat		X		X
Smelts	Fat			X	X
Sole	Lean	X		X	X
Swordfish	Lean	X		X	X
Trout	Fat	X		X	X
Whitefish	Fat	X		X	X
Whiting	Lean		X	X	X

Note: Ordinarily I hate to use tables but they are necessary on some occasions. This one may help you organize your information and your thinking for the next time you go shopping.

Please remember that this table is only a guide. If you have some fish that you want to cook in a way different than that listed on the table, go right ahead — experiment and enjoy it. Cookbooks are meant to be guides to help you adapt your own cooking. It should be the beginning of a whole new world of enjoyment of food and cooking for both you and your husband.

chapter VI

poultry

The love for fried chicken is as American as the love for mom and apple pie. People may disagree on the second best way to prepare chicken but almost everyone agrees that fried chicken is the greatest. By changing your technique just a little bit, you can give your husband and family fried chicken as often as they want it. Fortunately both chicken and turkey are low in cholesterol and may be used freely on a low cholesterol diet. Pheasant may also be used but ducks and geese should be avoided since they are both very fat.

The first thing to remember when preparing poultry is to remove the skin and all visible fat with a sharp knife. Most fryers and broilers have very little fat but stewing chickens and roasters generally have great gobs of yellow fat, which must be removed. Giblets shouldn't be used in the low cholesterol diet, although there is no law against your cooking them and nibbling on them out in the kitchen while you are preparing dinner, or you can save them for your lunch when your husband isn't home.

Poultry, like all meat, is perishable so it is important to remember the following points:

Buy frozen or chilled poultry only from refrigerated cases.

Be sure the wrappers are not torn.

Store chilled poultry in the coldest part of the refrigerator and use it within two days.

Store frozen poultry at zero degrees or below. It should be wrapped in moisture resistant material and left solidly frozen until it is ready to be used.

CHICKEN

Fried Chicken

There are many excellent ways to prepare fried chicken, but Mrs. Pauline Bever's Fried Chicken is my family's favorite. It is crisp on the outside and tender on the inside — we think it just can't be beaten. Every summer we look forward to the time when Mrs. Bever comes to visit her daughter from her home in Florida and we can once again enjoy her charming company and her good fried chicken. She has one requisite for fried chicken which we hasten to supply: a heavy frying pan with a tight fitting lid.

I asked Mrs. Bever for her recipe for fried chicken and she told me that it is better to give general directions because it is a method more than an exact recipe. The quantity of chicken you prepare depends upon the number of people you want to serve and whether it is the main entree or you are taking it along with other entrees to a picnic. You probably have a favorite recipe for fried chicken. If you do, it is easy to adjust it for use on a low cholesterol diet. The important points to remember are to cut off all skin and fat, fry the chicken in vegetable oil instead of a saturated fat, and if you are used to dipping the chicken in whole eggs you should change to dipping it in egg whites. If you fry your chicken, then finish it by putting it in the oven with milk or cream over it, you should substitute liquid skim milk for the whole milk or cream. Other than those simple precautions, you can feel free to use any recipe you desire.

Another good way to prepare fried chicken is in the oven. You can safely coat the chicken an hour or so before you want to cook it, then keep it refrigerated until you are ready to pop it into the oven.

Chicken Cooked in a Sauce

Of course it is always good to be able to prepare any food in a variety of ways, and chicken is no exception. As we said before, most chicken recipes can be adjusted to fit a low cholesterol diet. For instance, the Chicken with Red Wine is not truly Coq Au Vin but it is a wonderful way of preparing chicken. I'm sure it will make a hit with your family. The Orange Chicken is wonderful for entertaining because it freezes so well. It is quite simple although it looks complicated. Chicken in Tomato Sauce has a spicy tomato taste, which most people find very appealing.

Roast Chicken

Roast chicken is cooked with the skin on, to be removed

from your husband's piece before serving him. The dressing for a low cholesterol diet should be cooked separately, so that it won't absorb any fat from the chicken. One way of doing this is to cook some dressing inside of the chicken for the rest of the family and some dressing in a separate pan for the low cholesterol diet. The dressing cooked in a separate pan is crisp, which many people prefer, or the separate dressing can be baked in an aluminum foil pouch in the same pan as the chicken.

Cathy Erickson is a good cook and hostess even though she has to plan her cooking around the numerous allergies in her family. Cathy puts her Brown Bag Chicken into the oven before Sunday school and it is all ready to serve after church. Her recipe is different because you don't remove the skin of the chicken before you cook it. The skin becomes rather hard and crisp and can be peeled off of your husband's piece of chicken very easily.

Stewed Chicken

Few women prepare stewed chicken these days. It was more suited to the use of stewing hens, which are no longer easily available. If you can't get a stewing hen, you can always substitute broilers or fryers. They aren't quite as flavorful but they cook a lot faster. Stewed chicken may be served several ways as long as it isn't prepared with butter, cream, or other saturated fats. The gravy can be thickened and vegetables added or that good rich broth can be used for cooking dumplings (see Chapter IV, Meats), noodles or spaetzles. We have always liked spaetzles but I never made them to suit us until Frances Sonitzky gave me her father's recipe and I learned that I should have been kneading the dough.

Broiled Chicken

Broiled chicken is always good, particularly in a low cholesterol diet because any fat remaining in the chicken will cook out while it is broiling. The fat can then be replaced by a sauce, margarine, or vegetable oil mixed with seasonings.

Leftovers

If you have any leftover chicken it should be refrigerated and kept for another meal. Leftover roast or stewed chicken is good for salads or sandwiches; it may be used for a casserole or chicken á la king. Now that you can buy precooked, frozen and canned chicken it is much simpler to serve.

TURKEY

Turkey is a versatile bird and it is a shame to restrict its use to Thanksgiving and Christmas. It is comparatively inexpensive — if anything can be called inexpensive these days — and lends itself well to the use of leftovers. The size turkey to buy depends upon the number of persons you are serving and whether or not you plan to make another meal of the leftovers. I like the little 8-pound turkeys for our family. An 8-pound turkey will provide a generous serving the first time around for six people with enough left over for another meal of turkey salad, sandwiches, or hash. However, if you have a larger family or want to freeze some turkey in addition to having a leftover meal soon, it is well to remember that you get a higher proportion of meat to bone in a 20- to 24-pound turkey.

Most turkeys are bought frozen these days. If you buy the fresh chilled turkeys they can be held in the coldest part of the refrigerator for five to six days. Make sure the wrappings are loose enough to allow some air circulation and remove the giblets when you buy the turkey. Cook them promptly and refrigerate them until you want to use them for yourself, but don't include them in giblet gravy or dressings for your husband's meal.

Stuffed turkeys are also available. They are satisfactory if you serve your husband only the turkey meat and none of the dressing. His dressing should always be cooked separately since dressing cooked inside the turkey will absorb the fat and juices that have cooked out of the turkey.

The following information refers to unstuffed turkeys since this is the type which is generally used for a low cholesterol diet. Stuffed turkeys may be used but with the above restriction as to the dressing.

If you are buying a turkey of under 12 pounds, allow ¾ to 1 pound of raw meat per serving. If you buy a heavier bird, allow ½ to ¾ pound (raw weight) per serving. The actual number of servings depends on the quality of the turkey, the correct cooking temperature, and skill of the carver. It is impossible to be exact regarding the number of servings but the table below will give you an approximate number of servings:

Ready-to-cook turkey (pounds)	Number of servings
6 to 8	6 to 10
8 to 12	10 to 20
12 to 16	20 to 32
16 to 20	32 to 40
20 to 24	40 to 50

Frozen turkeys, with the necks and giblets inside the body or neck cavities, must be thawed before cooking. Remove the giblets as soon as the turkey is thawed, cook them promptly and refrigerate them. The thawing method you use will depend upon the amount of time before you plan to cook the turkey. It can be thawed in the refrigerator or in cold water. Here is an approximate timetable for both methods of thawing:

Pounds	Refrigerator	Cold or Cool Water
6 to 8	1 to 1½ days	3 to 4 hours
8 to 12	1½ to 2 days	4 to 6 hours
12 to 16	2 to 2½ days	6 to 7 hours
16 to 20	2½ to 3 days	7 to 8 hours
20 to 24	3 to 3½ days	8 to 10 hours

Roasting Your Turkey

Turkeys of any size may be roasted. A turkey should be roasted in a shallow open pan to allow the heat to circulate around it. A rack at least ½-inch off the bottom of the roasting pan should be used to keep the turkey out of the juices and fat that gather in the bottom of the pan. There has been a great deal of discussion regarding whether the turkey should be roasted breast side up or breast side down. I think that it should be roasted breast side up; therefore I've included those directions in this book. If you are firmly convinced that it should be breast side down go right ahead and do it that way. The important point in the low cholesterol diet is to roast the meat or poultry until it is well done and as much fat is removed as possible. For best results follow these simple steps:

1. Preheat an oven to 325°F. Remember that in poultry cook-ing, as in meat cooking, low temperatures assure better flavor, appearance and more meat.
2. Rinse the thawed turkey with cold water, drain it, and pat it dry. Rub the cavity of the turkey lightly with salt. (It is advisable to bake the dressing separately so that the dressing won't absorb the fat and juices from the roasting turkey.)
3. Push the drumsticks under a band of skin at the tail or tie them together.
4. Place turkey on a rack, breast side up. Brush the skin with margarine or vegetable oil. Insert a roast meat thermometer so that the bulb of the thermometer is in the thickest part of the breast. Be sure that the thermometer does not touch any bone.
5. Put the pan and the turkey in the preheated oven. Do not cover the pan. Baste occasionally with margarine or vegetable oil. If the turkey becomes brown before it is completely cooked, place a loose tent of aluminum foil over it. When the turkey is two-thirds done, cut the band of skin or the cord at the drumsticks.
6. If a meat thermometer is not used, the turkey is done when the drumsticks move easily. The table following step 7 may be consulted to determine how long to roast your turkey. (It is best to plan to have your turkey out of the oven about 20 to 25 minutes before you plan to carve it. That gives the turkey time to set and it will carve more easily. It also gives you time to make the gravy and do other last minute tasks.)
7. When using a meat thermometer the turkey should be roasted until the thermometer reads 185°F.

Pounds	*Total Roasting Time (at 325°F)*
6 to 8	2 to 2½ hours
8 to 12	2½ to 3 hours

Pounds	Total Roasting Time
12 to 16	3 to 3¾ hours
16 to 20	3¾ to 4½ hours
20 to 24	4½ to 5½ hours

Turkeys of any size may be cooked on a rotisserie. However, the smaller turkeys work best, since most rotisseries are not built to handle a 20- or 24-pound turkey. The manufacturer's directions should be followed when cooking the turkey. Rub the body cavity with salt and push the drumsticks under the band of skin at the tail or tie them together. Fasten the neck skin to the back with a skewer. Flatten the wings over the breast and then tie a cord around the breast to hold them securely. Insert the spit rod through the center of the turkey from the tail end toward the front end. Insert the skewers firmly in place in the bird and screw them tightly. Test the balance, since only a well-balanced bird will rotate smoothly during the cooking period. Place the spit in the rotisserie. Brush the turkey with melted margarine or vegetable oil. Barbecue sauce may be used, if desired, during the last ¾ hour of cooking time. Follow the directions with your rotisserie and roast until done, or use these general directions:

Pounds	Rotisserie Cooking Time
6 to 8	2 to 2½ hours
8 to 10	2½ to 3 hours
10 to 12	3 to 3½ hours

Some people like to roast a turkey in aluminum foil. It does yield a very moist and tender turkey but it is not advisable to use this method when cooking turkey for the low cholesterol diet since it tends to cook the turkey in its fat and juices, which accumulate in the foil.

One of our favorite recipes for cooking turkey is a variation of the Greek recipe for Chicken Oregano from Chapter XII, Foreign Foods. We started doing it this way because we liked the Chicken Oregano so well. One time I went to buy a couple of chickens to prepare the recipe and they didn't have any whole chickens at the market. However, they did have a small (8-pound) turkey. My husband suggested we try that turkey prepared the same way. It was so delicious that we continue to prepare it in that manner.

Leftover turkey like any leftover meat or poultry should be frozen unless it is to be used within a couple of days. As soon as possible after serving, remove every bit of meat from the bones. Cool the meat and any gravy and stuffing promptly. Refrigerate, each wrapped *separately* and tightly, in the coldest part of your refrigerator. Use the gravy and stuffing within one or two days and be sure to reheat them thoroughly before serving. Serve the cooked turkey meat within two or three days after roasting. Small meal size portions, properly wrapped, may be frozen for future use. Never freeze an uncooked stuffed turkey or a roast, stuffed turkey — and *never* stuff your turkey the night before you roast it.

Leftover turkey is particularly good for sandwiches if your husband carries his lunch to work and has a refrigerator to keep his lunch cold until he eats it. It can be used for salad, hot turkey sandwiches, or any casserole dish calling for cooked chicken or turkey. (Equal amounts of precooked turkey may be used in any recipe that calls for precooked chicken.)

Boneless Turkey Roll or Roast

If you want to get your boneless turkey the easy way, you can buy one of the boneless turkey rolls on the market now. They come precooked or uncooked. Directions for thawing and/or cooking the rolls are generally printed on the package. They are more expensive than the bone-in turkeys but cost about the same per ounce of edible meat. The rolls should be left in their original wrapper and thawed for one or two days in the refrigerator or under running cool water. The wrapper should be removed before cooking but the string should be left in place until the turkey is done. For best results:

1. Preheat oven to moderate (350°F)
2. Rinse the defrosted, uncooked turkey roll (from which you have removed the wrapper) with cold water, drain it, and pat it dry. Rub it lightly with salt, pepper, and poultry seasoning, if the roast has not been preseasoned.
3. Place the roll on a rack in a shallow pan. Brush the entire roll with melted margarine or vegetable oil. Place it in a preheated

oven. Baste it occasionally with melted margarine or vegetable oil. If the roast becomes too brown, cover it with a loose tent of aluminum foil.

4. Roast it until a meat thermometer inserted in the center of the roll registers 170° to 175°F.

No turkey or chicken dinner would be complete without some good gravy. Therefore, this chapter ends with a recipe for a good rich brown gravy, which is acceptable on a low cholesterol diet.

Remember to caution your husband when he is carving the turkey to serve himself a piece without any skin. And keep in mind to do the same when you serve it from the kitchen.

Mrs. Bever's fried chicken

Cut-up frying chicken
Salt
All purpose flour

Vegetable oil
Cold liquid skim milk or water
Seasoning to taste

Remove all skin and fat from the chicken with a sharp knife. Wash the chicken and drain it well, but don't pat it dry.

Salt the chicken well and dredge it in flour. Pour enough oil in a heavy frying pan with a tight lid to have ⅔ inch of oil. Heat the oil until it is hot enough to sizzle but not hot enough to spatter and pop. Place the chicken carefully in the hot oil, but don't crowd it. Each piece of chicken should have room to brown properly. Cover the frying pan and cook over medium heat without turning the chicken until it is well browned on the bottom (about 12-15 minutes). Set the frying pan off the heat for a minute so the oil won't pop when you turn the chicken. Turn the chicken, return the frying pan to the heat, cover it tightly and let it cook until the other side is well browned (about 5 minutes). Remove the chicken to a hot platter.

Drain the oil from the frying pan until only about 2 or 3 tablespoons remain. Add 2 tablespoons of flour for each cup of gravy you want and stir until the flour is lightly browned. Add cold liquid skim milk or water, stir and cook over a medium heat until the gravy is smooth and thickened. Season to taste and serve hot.

This is a good basic recipe that can be easily varied by adding your favorite herbs to the breading mixture. The paprika gives color more than flavor so it is wise to include it even if you add other herbs.

oven fried chicken

Serves 4

2½ pounds cut-up frying
    chicken
½ cup cornflake crumbs
½ teaspoon salt
¼ teaspoon pepper
¼ teaspoon paprika
Vegetable oil as
    necessary

Wash the chicken, drain it, and remove all its fat and skin with a sharp knife.

Combine cornflake crumbs, salt, pepper, and paprika.

Brush the chicken thoroughly with oil, roll in the seasoned crumbs, and place on an oiled cookie sheet. (Be sure the cookie sheet has a slight rim around it.) Bake in a preheated moderate oven (350°F) for about 1 hour, or until tender and brown. Dribble a little oil over the chicken after half an hour in the oven.

chicken with red wine

Serves 4 to 6

2½ pounds chicken breasts,
    thighs, and legs
½ cup drained canned
    mushrooms
1 teaspoon salt
¼ teaspoon pepper
1 teaspoon Kitchen Bouquet
½ cup red table wine

2 tablespoons vegetable oil
½ cup chopped onions
¼ teaspoon monosodium glutamate (MSG)
½ teaspoon ground thyme

½ cup water and mushroom juice
2 tablespoons cornstarch
2 tablespoons water

Wash the chicken, drain it, and remove all its fat and skin with a sharp knife. Drain the mushrooms and reserve the juice. Combine the juice with enough water to yield ½ cup of liquid.

Sauté the chicken in oil in a heavy frying pan until very lightly browned. Remove chicken to a 2½-quart oven-proof casserole. Sauté the onions and mushrooms in the remaining oil until the onions are golden. Add monosodium glutamate, thyme, salt, pepper, kitchen bouquet, wine, and water and mushroom juice to the frying pan and mix well, stirring to remove any bits of crusted food in the pan. Pour the onion mixture over the chicken, cover the casserole and bake it in a preheated moderate oven (350°F) for 1 hour. Remove the cover, stir the chicken mixture, and continue to cook it uncovered for another 30 minutes. Remove the casserole from the oven. Remove the chicken to a platter. Combine the cornstarch with 2 tablespoons of water to form a smooth paste. Stir the cornstarch paste into the sauce, bring it to a boil, and cook until thickened, stirring constantly. Pour the sauce over the chicken and serve.

orange chicken

Serves 8 to 10

5 pounds chicken breasts and thighs
1 can mandarin oranges
½ cup (1 stick) margarine

Breading:
½ cup all purpose flour
¼ teaspoon paprika
¼ teaspoon ground thyme

Marinade:
¼ cup vegetable oil
¼ cup lemon juice
¼ cup orange marmalade

¼ teaspoon pepper
¼ teaspoon ground oregano
¼ teaspoon garlic powder
½ teaspoon salt

¼ cup sherry
¼ teaspoon ground thyme
¼ teaspoon salt
1 teaspoon leaf oregano
⅛ teaspoon pepper
¼ teaspoon garlic powder

Wash the chicken, drain it, and remove all its fat and skin with a sharp knife. Drain the oranges and discard the juice.

Combine the breading ingredients. Dredge the chicken in the breading and put it on a heavily greased cookie sheet with a rim. Put a slice of margarine on each piece of chicken. Bake the chicken in a preheated hot oven (400°F) for 30 minutes, decrease the heat to moderate (350°F), and continue to bake for 30 minutes longer, or until chicken is brown. Transfer the chicken to a shallow baking dish. (I use a 15-inch Corning Ware roaster.) Combine marinade ingredients and add them to the hot chicken. Let it stand at room temperature until the chicken is cool. Chicken may then be refrigerated a few hours or frozen until ready to use.

When ready to use, turn chicken over in the marinade. Scatter the orange sections over the chicken and bake it in a preheated moderate oven (350°F) until browned. The time will depend upon whether the chicken has been refrigerated or frozen: about an hour if the chicken was refrigerated and about 90 minutes if it was frozen.

chicken in tomato sauce

Serves 4 to 6

2½ pounds chicken breasts, thighs, and legs
3 tablespoons vegetable oil
½ cup chopped onions
½ cup chopped fresh green peppers

2 teaspoons salt
¼ teaspoon pepper
¼ teaspoon basil leaves
1 teaspoon oregano leaves
½ teaspoon monosodium glutamate (MSG)

2 cups tomatoes and juice
1 cup tomato sauce
½ teaspoon garlic powder

¼ teaspoon ground thyme
½ cup red table wine
  (optional)

Wash the chicken, drain it, and remove all its fat and skin with a sharp knife. Sauté the chicken in oil in a heavy frying pan until very lightly browned. Remove the chicken to a 2½-quart oven-proof casserole. Sauté the onions and green peppers in the remaining oil until the onions are golden. Add the tomatoes, tomato sauce, garlic powder, salt, pepper, basil, oregano, mono-sodium glutamate, thyme, and wine to the onions and simmer over a low heat for 15 minutes. (You may substitute chili powder for the spices in this recipe if you prefer.) Pour the sauce over the chicken, cover the casserole, and bake it in a preheated moderate oven (350°F) for 1 hour. Remove the cover, stir the chicken mixture, and continue to cook it uncovered for another 30 minutes.

roast chicken

Serves 6

1 4-pound roasting chicken
½ teaspoon salt
⅛ teaspoon pepper

1 small onion
½ teaspoon ground thyme
¼ cup (½ stick) melted
  margarine

Wash the chicken, drain it, and remove all the fat with a sharp knife, but do not remove the skin. Sprinkle the inside of the chicken with salt and pepper. Put the onion inside the chicken and then truss the chicken. Place the chicken on a rack in a roasting pan in the oven. Bake the chicken in a preheated moderate oven (350°F) for about 1¼ hours to 1½ hours or until the legs of the chicken will move easily. Combine the thyme with the melted margarine and use it to baste the chicken about every 15 minutes while it is baking.

fruit and bread dressing

Serves 4

½ cup chopped celery
¼ cup chopped onions
¼ cup (½ stick) margarine
½ teaspoon salt

¼ teaspoon ground sage
2 cups dry bread cubes
¾ cup syrup from fruit
     cocktail
¾ cup drained canned
     fruit cocktail

Sauté the celery and onions in margarine until tender but not brown. Add salt, sage, and the sautéed celery and onions to the bread cubes. (Do not drain the margarine. Add the fruit cocktail and juice.) Toss lightly and put it into a greased 8-inch square pyrex cake pan. Bake in a preheated moderate oven (350°F) for 35 to 45 minutes or until lightly browned.

bread dressing

Serves 4

½ cup chopped celery
½ cup chopped onions
¼ cup (½ stick) margarine
½ teaspoon poultry
     seasoning

½ teaspoon salt
⅛ teaspoon pepper
¼ cup lukewarm water
1 quart soft bread cubes

Sauté the celery and onions in margarine until tender but not brown. Add poultry seasoning, salt, pepper, and water to the sautéed vegetables and pour it over bread cubes. Toss the dressing lightly until well blended; stuff your poultry or bake it in a preheated moderate oven (350°F) 35 to 45 minutes, or until lightly browned.

Cathy's brown bag chicken

Serves 4

2½ pound whole fryer
½ teaspoon salt

1 teaspoon poultry seasoning
1 brown paper bag

Wash the chicken, drain it, and remove all the visible fat with a sharp knife. Sprinkle the inside of the chicken with salt. Sprinkle the outside of the chicken with poultry seasoning. This will seem like a lot of seasoning but it goes into the skin and gives it a delightful flavor.

Put chicken in a brown paper bag and tie it with a string, leaving the bag loose around the chicken. Place the bag in a shallow baking pan and bake it in a preheated slow oven (300°F) for 2 hours. (If the chicken is frozen it should be baked 3 hours instead of 2 hours, which allows time for church and Sunday school both for Cathy and her family.)

stewed chicken

Serves 6

1 4- to 5-pound stewing chicken
   Cold water as necessary
2 teaspoons salt

½ teaspoon white pepper
1 small onion
1 carrot
1 stalk celery with leaves

Wash the chicken, drain it, and remove all its fat and skin with a sharp knife. Cut it into serving pieces, if necessary.

Put the chicken in a heavy saucepan, add enough water to cover it, and add the remaining ingredients. Cover the pan and simmer 2 to 3 hours, or until tender. (The time will be much shorter if broilers or fryers are used.) Remove the chicken from the stock, cool the stock, and skim the fat from it. Remove the meat from the bones. Drain the vegetables from the stock and discard them. Return the boned chicken to the stock and reheat it.

The stock may be thickened using 1 tablespoon of flour (made into a paste with a cup of cold stock) for each cup of stock. Diced, cooked vegetables may be added if desired, or noodles or spaetzles cooked in the hot broth.

Mr. Sonitzky's spaetzles

Serves 4

1½ cups all purpose flour	3 drops yellow food coloring
½ teaspoon salt	2 egg whites
¼ cup water	Additional water, if necessary
1 teaspoon vegetable oil	

Combine the flour and salt in a small bowl. Mix ¼ cup water, oil, yellow food coloring, and egg whites together and pour into a well in the center of the flour. Stir to form a dough.

Turn the dough out on an unfloured bread board, kneading all of the excess flour into the dough to form a stiff dough, adding more water a few drops at a time, if necessary. Knead until smooth. Roll dough with a rolling pin until it is about ¼ inch thick. Cut into 6 portions. Pull or cut off bits of dough about the size of a fingernail and drop them on a lightly floured portion of the board. Cover with a cloth, to prevent them from drying out, until ready to cook them.

Drop them into boiling hot broth or salted water and cook them 10 to 15 minutes or until tender. Try to keep any excess flour out of the broth because it will cause the broth to foam up. Remove the cooked spaetzles from the broth with a slotted spoon. Serve hot with chicken or pot roast. Toasted crumbs may be added to the spaetzles if desired.

Many of the commercial noodles do not have enough egg yolk in them to cause your doctor to forbid them, but homemade noodles are such a treat that I couldn't resist including this recipe.

homemade noodles

Serves 6

2 cups all purpose flour
1 teaspoon salt
⅓ cup water
1 tablespoon vegetable oil

4 drops yellow food
   coloring
2 egg whites
   Additional water, if
   necessary

Combine the flour and salt in a small bowl. Mix ⅓ cup water, oil, yellow food coloring, and egg whites together and pour into a well in the center of the flour. Stir to form a dough.

Turn the dough out on an unfloured bread board, kneading all of the excess flour into the dough to form a stiff dough, adding more water a few drops at a time if necessary. Knead it until smooth. Roll the dough out on a lightly floured board ,to form a thin sheet. Cover the dough with a towel and let it stand for 20 minutes. Roll the sheet of dough as you would a jelly roll and cut into very thin strips. Unroll and lay them out to dry. You can use these noodles immediately or keep them in the refrigerator for about a week before you use them. They also freeze well.

Drop the noodles in boiling, salted water or broth, and cook them for about 20 minutes, or until tender. The time will vary with the thickness and width of the noodles. Drain and serve them hot as a side dish or in broth, if desired.

This recipe is good to serve for dinner when you are going to be gone in the afternoon. You can cook the chicken to the point where you add the rice and then refrigerate it until you are ready to use it.

chicken with rice and peas

Serves 6

3 pounds chicken breasts and thighs
3 tablespoons vegetable oil
2 cups chopped canned tomatoes and juice
1 cup hot water
2 chicken bouillon cubes
1 cup sliced onions

2 tablespoons chopped parsley
1 teaspoon salt
¼ teaspoon pepper
½ teaspoon basil leaves
½ teaspoon garlic powder
1½ cups long grain rice
1 10-ounce package frozen peas

Wash the chicken, drain it, and remove its fat and skin with a sharp knife.

Sauté the chicken in oil in heavy saucepan until lightly browned. Add the tomatoes, water, bouillon cubes, onions, parsley, salt, pepper, basil, and garlic powder. Cover and simmer it over a low heat for 20 minutes. Add the rice and simmer for 15 minutes, add the peas and simmer another 10 minutes, or until done and liquid is absorbed. (Add extra water at the end of the cooking if necessary.)

Serve hot in shallow soup bowls.

Speaking of rice, Margaret McColley serves this rice casserole with chicken or beef.

Margaret's rice casserole

Serves 4

1 cup long grain rice
1 package onion soup mix
2 tablespoons margarine

1 small can mushrooms
2¾ cups mushroom juice and water

Combine the rice, onion soup mix, and margarine in a 2-quart casserole, drain the mushrooms, reserving their juice, and add them to the casserole. Add enough water to the mushroom juice to yield 2¾ cups of liquid, then add the liquid to the casserole. Cover and bake for 1 hour in a preheated moderate oven (350°F). Remove the cover from the casserole and mix lightly. Continue to bake, uncovered, for another 15 minutes.

broiled chicken

Serves 4

4 1-pound broiler halves	½ teaspoon ground oregano
½ cup vegetable oil	1 teaspoon salt
½ teaspoon garlic powder	⅛ teaspoon white pepper
½ teaspoon ground thyme	¼ teaspoon monosodium glutamate (MSG)

Wash the chicken, drain it, and remove all the excess fat and skin with a sharp knife. Combine the remaining ingredients and mix well. Brush the broiler halves with the seasoned oil. Place them on a foil-lined broiler rack. Broil 6 to 8 inches from heat, turning and brushing with seasoned oil as necessary, until the chicken is brown and tender. This will take about 25 to 30 minutes depending upon the amount of heat.

chicken à la king

Serves 4

¼ cup all purpose flour	2 cups cooked, cubed chicken
⅓ cup instant dry milk	1 cup sliced mushrooms
1 teaspoon salt	¼ cup chopped pimiento
⅛ teaspoon white pepper	¼ cup sherry (optional)
3 tablespoons vegetable oil	3 cups cooked rice
2 cups chicken bouillon	1 tablespoon chopped parsley

Sift the flour, instant dry milk, salt, and pepper together. Heat the oil in heavy saucepan. Stir the flour mixture into hot oil until smooth. Gradually add the chicken stock to the flour mixture and cook them, stirring constantly, until thickened. Cook for 2 minutes longer, stirring constantly. Add the chicken, mushrooms, pimiento, and sherry; heat through. Serve over ¾ cup rice per serving. Garnish with parsley.

The cooking time and the amount of oregano are both correct. The turkey should be literally falling off the bones when it is done, with a good rich taste of oregano.

baked turkey oregano

1 8-pound oven-prepared turkey	2 tablespoons leaf oregano
½ cup vegetable oil	½ teaspoon monosodium glutamate (MSG)
½ cup lemon juice	Hot cooked rice
½ cup sherry	Chopped parsley
2 teaspoons salt	Melted margarine
¼ teaspoon pepper	

Prepare the turkey as for roasting. Put it on a rack in a shallow pan and bake in a slow (325°F) oven for 5 hours.

Combine the oil, lemon juice, sherry, salt, pepper, oregano, and monosodium glutamate to form a marinade. Mix the marinade well and use it to baste the turkey generously about every half hour during the roasting time. If there is any marinade left when the turkey is almost done, pour it into the body cavity of the turkey. Remove the turkey from the oven and remove any bones possible with your hands. Slice the rest of the turkey with a sharp knife.

Combine hot cooked rice with melted margarine and parsley and pile loosely in the middle of a platter. Place the turkey around it and serve both hot. (The amount of rice, margarine, and parsley will depend upon your family's likes and the number you are serving.)

roast turkey or chicken gravy

Ingredients	2 cups of gravy	4 cups of gravy (1 quart)
Vegetable oil	3 tablespoons	¼ cup
Flour	3 tablespoons	6 tablespoons
Liquid: cool broth, milk, or water	2 cups	4 cups

When the turkey is done, remove it to a warm platter. Allow about ¼ cup gravy per serving. Pour the drippings from the turkey into a bowl leaving all of the brown particles in the pan. Let the fat rise to the top of the drippings and then skim off as much fat as possible before using the drippings. Add enough liquid to the drippings to make the total amount that you need or save the drippings for another occasion and use cold milk or water. If you use cold milk be sure that it is liquid skim milk or reconstituted instant dry milk.

Pour the oil into the roasting pan. Put the roaster over a low heat, add the flour and cook and stir the oil and flour over the low heat until smooth and bubbling. Add the cool liquid all at once and cook, stirring constantly, until thickened and smooth. Scrape the brown particles from the pan while stirring the gravy to blend them into the gravy. Simmer gently for about 5 minutes. Season to taste and serve hot.

chapter VII
vegetables

Your husband is probably not too fond of vegetables but they are good for him. He can learn to enjoy them if they are prepared well. The whole trick is to spend some of the time and effort preparing vegetables that you used to spend on those rich desserts he is learning to live without.

Vegetables contain no cholesterol, and the American Heart Association in no way limits the kind and amount of vegetables in the low cholesterol diet. Even if your husband's doctor is limiting his caloric intake, chances are he is still allowed free rein on most vegetables. Even potatoes will not be high in calories if you don't cover them with sour cream or some other rich topping — and sour cream is a no-no anyway.

Broccoli, lettuce, tomatoes, potatoes, and cabbage are all good sources of vitamin C. The dark colored vegetables such as broccoli, carrots, fresh green peppers, sweet potatoes, and squash are rich sources of vitamin A.

It is a pity to serve only reheated, canned vegetables when there are so many attractive and tasty vegetables available to you. I'm not knocking canned vegetables. No one could deny their convenience, availability, and very good taste; but they are not the only vegetables. Branch out and serve some other types of vegetables as well.

Many interesting vegetables are available at the market. The frozen food shelves are an especially good source of new and interesting vegetable combinations. If you run out of ideas for vegetables to tempt your husband's appetite among the fresh and canned vegetables, you can always go to the frozen food counters for more inspiration. Remember, though, to read the ingredient list carefully because some of the prepared vegetables contain butter, bacon, eggs, or other restricted items.

Fresh vegetables, as already mentioned, contain no cholesterol, so it is a good idea to take advantage of them in season. When they are most plentiful, they are least expensive and best. There is nothing like vegetables fresh from the garden, but almost all vegetables are freely available now in the supermart. There is no reason why your husband shouldn't have whatever vegetable he prefers in all seasons, unless the doctor has given him instructions to the contrary. It is only when you add butter, cream, or cheese sauce that they present a problem. Your husband can continue to have creamed vegetables if he likes them. A good cream sauce can be made from instant dry milk, all purpose flour, and margarine or oil. The instant dry milk can be reconstituted and used as liquid skim milk or combined with the flour and used without reconstitution. It is probably best to try it both ways, then choose the method best for you.

It is a good idea to save the water in which peas, carrots or other vegetables have been cooked. Not only is this liquid rich in vitamins and flavor, it is a good base for soups or is delicious as the liquid in a cream sauce for the vegetable. It can be used in the recipes for White Sauce if you remember that either the liquid or the flour-fat mixture, called a roux, must be cool. When making a cream sauce, it is important to remember that a cool liquid should be added to a hot roux or a hot liquid to a cold roux. The liquid and the roux should not be the same temperature.

White Sauce recipes no. 1 and 2 may be prepared by cooking the roux ahead of time and allowing it to cool before adding the hot vegetable juice, but recipe no. 3 must have cool liquid. Therefore, the vegetables should be drained and the juice cooled in the refrigerator before the flour and seasonings are added. You can also use the common method of adding some flour and seasonings to water to form a paste, which is then added to the hot vegetables with their juice, and cooked until smooth. This last method also is tasty and certainly acceptable in a low cholesterol diet.

The White Sauce recipes may also be used for creamed dishes, such as creamed tunafish, creamed salmon and peas, or creamed chicken. If you are using the cream sauce for meat, fish, or poultry, you may want to add a tablespoon of sherry to the sauce for flavor. These sauces may also be used as the base for parsley or dill sauce, but you shouldn't add grated cheddar cheese to it; the cheese is forbidden.

Most vegetables with the exception of cauliflower, broccoli and a few others with a strong odor should be cooked in as little water as possible in order to preserve their vitamins and color. Frances Nielsen taught me an excellent method for cooking carrots, which I also use for green beans, asparagus, mushrooms, fresh green peppers, and onions.

Vegetable recipes are difficult to write because so many variations are possible for each recipe. For instance, in the Braised Carrot recipe, 5 cups of carrots or 3 cups of carrots will work as well as 1 quart of carrots, provided you adjust the seasonings accordingly. The recipe can also be varied by substituting ¼ cup chopped onion and ¼ cup chopped fresh green peppers for the ½ cup chopped onions. My husband likes it when I grate the carrots in long shreds, as though I were going to make carrot salad, and then cook them as directed above. It isn't advisable to stir them; turning them over with a pancake turner is much better. Cook them for 8 to 10 minutes. They have a wonderful, fresh garden flavor, which is worth the time it takes to grate that many carrots.

The above recipe is also good for frozen vegetables and the water or ice that clings to the frozen vegetables makes any additional water unnecessary. I have even used this recipe for chopped broccoli although you generally think of broccoli needing a great deal of water when it is cooked.

As you know, vegetable recipes are not as finely balanced as cake or pie recipes and often call for varying amounts to allow for variation in the size of the vegetables.

Some men feel deprived because they can no longer have vegetables prepared with bacon or salt pork. We can still give them the flavor of bacon because imitation bacon bits and bacon flavoring are now available. Both the bits and the flavoring are made with synthetic flavorings and are permissible on the low cholesterol diet. When you study a recipe such as baked beans, you see it is the fat in the meat that combines with the starch in the beans to produce a rich, smooth dish as much or more than it is the bacon flavor. Margarine or vegetable oil may be added to the baked beans to replace the bacon fat and the result is as rich and creamy as you will find anywhere.

In short, the most important point to remember about vegetables is to prepare them so your husband will want to eat them. You can prepare his favorite vegetables using margarine or oil instead of butter and adapting them to a low cholesterol recipe or you can experiment with new and different vegetable recipes to tempt his appetite.

Potatoes may be prepared in any manner as long as you don't use any saturated fats. Mashed potatoes prepared with margarine and liquid skim milk can be as rich and creamy as the ones prepared with whole milk and butter. The seasoning is important and, of course, a little bit of garnish helps too. You may think it will be hard to learn to fry potatoes in oil but remember that millions of women in this world cook with oil and would find our use of butter and lard most unusual. A thin cream sauce can be combined with precooked potatoes for escalloped potatoes. Once you've sprinkled them with paprika, your husband probably wouldn't even guess you had used the cream sauce recipe in this chapter instead of one made with butter.

If you want a thin white sauce, double the milk to 2 cups, and if you want a thick white sauce, increase the flour and margarine to 3 tablespoons each. Adjust seasonings to taste in both instances.

medium white sauce no. 1

Yields 1 cup

2 tablespoons (¼ stick) margarine
2 tablespoons all purpose flour

½ teaspoon salt
⅛ teaspoon white pepper
1 cup liquid skim milk

Melt the margarine in a heavy saucepan over a low heat. Add the flour, salt, and pepper, stir, and cook over the low heat until the mixture is smooth and bubbling, but do not let it brown. Remove it from the heat and add the milk all at once. Return it to the heat, cook, and stir it over a low heat until the sauce is smooth and thickened. (Stirring with a wooden spoon or a wire whisk gives me the best results.)

Variations

Veloute Sauce: Substitute 1 cup chicken or beef bouillon for the liquid skim milk.

Brown Sauce: Heat the margarine in a heavy saucepan over low heat until it is brown. Add the flour, salt, and pepper, cook, and stir it over a low heat until the mixture is well browned. Add 1 cup beef bouillon instead of the liquid skim milk, cook, and stir it over low heat until smooth and thickened.

medium white sauce no. 2

Yields 1 cup

2 tablespoons all purpose flour
¼ cup instant dry milk
½ teaspoon salt
⅛ teaspoon white pepper
1 tablespoon vegetable oil
1 cup cold water

Combine the flour, instant dry milk, salt, and pepper, and stir it until thoroughly mixed. Add the flour mixture to the oil in a heavy saucepan, stir, and cook it over a low heat until the mixture is smooth, but do not let it brown. Remove it from the heat and add the water all at once. Return the sauce to the heat, cook, and stir it over a low heat until the sauce is smooth and thickened.

medium white sauce no. 3

Yields 1 cup

1 cup liquid skim milk
2 tablespoons all purpose flour

½ teaspoon salt
⅛ teaspoon white pepper

Pour the milk into a jar. Add the flour, salt, and pepper. Tighten the lid on the jar and shake it until smooth. Pour the sauce into a heavy saucepan, cook, and stir it over a low heat until smooth and thickened. Continue to cook and stir it for 2 to 3 minutes longer, or until the raw taste of the flour has disappeared.

You need a heavy frying pan with a tight lid for this recipe. An electric frying pan is excellent, because the heat can be so well controlled.

Frances's braised carrots

Yields 4 servings

3 tablespoons vegetable oil
½ cup finely chopped onions
1 quart carrots, julienne or thinly sliced

1 teaspoon salt
¼ teaspoon monosodium glutamate (MSG)
⅛ teaspoon pepper

Preheat a frying pan to 275°F, add the oil and onions. Cook and stir the onions until they are limp but not brown. Add the carrots, salt, monosodium glutamate, and pepper. Cover the pan tightly and cook for about 15 minutes or until the carrots are tender, stirring occasionally. You may have to add a little water depending upon how tightly the lid of your frying pan fits and how much water is in the carrots.

This recipe is very good served with corn muffins and candied or baked sweet potatoes.

smothered cabbage

Serves 4 to 6

1 large head cabbage
½ cup chopped onions
1 teaspoon salt
3 tablespoons vegetable oil
½ cup hot water

⅛ teaspoon cayenne pepper
2 cups fresh green peppers, julienne
Imitation bacon bits (optional)

Clean and core the cabbage and chop it coarsely. Combine the cabbage, onions, and salt, and pour them into the oil, which has been heated in a heavy saucepan. Add the water to the saucepan and sprinkle the cabbage with cayenne pepper. Scatter green peppers over the cabbage, cover tightly, and cook over a low heat for 15 to 20 minutes, or until cabbage is tender. Add more salt, if necessary, and serve hot. Sprinkle with imitation bacon bits, if desired.

butternut squash

The woman who owns the vegetable stand where we shop in the country gave me this recipe, which is a method more than a recipe. She cuts the squash into two even halves, cleans out the seeds, salts the halves, and puts them (cut side down) on a cookie sheet. She bakes them in a preheated moderate (350" F) oven until they feel soft when you squeeze them. Serve them hot with dill vinegar and margarine and they are delicious. She also recommends this method for acorn squash.

butternut squash casserole

Serves 4 to 6

1 large butternut squash	¼ cup (½ stick) margarine
3 to 4 fresh tomatoes	Salt and pepper as
1 large sweet onion	necessary
1 large fresh green pepper	½ to 1 teaspoon leaf oregano

Clean the vegetables and slice them. Put about half of the squash in a well greased casserole. Cover with the sliced tomatoes, onions, and green peppers. Dot with margarine and sprinkle with salt, pepper, and oregano. Add the remaining squash to casserole, sprinkle it with seasonings, and dot it with the remaining margarine. Cover the casserole tightly and bake it in a preheated moderate (350°F) oven for 45 minutes. Remove the cover of casserole and continue to bake for about 30 minutes, or until squash is tender and lightly browned.

From Georgia DuBois who spent most of her married life overseas.

Georgia's eggplant

Serves 4 to 6

1 medium eggplant	2 cups canned tomatoes
5 tablespoons margarine	and juice
3 tablespoons all purpose	1 teaspoon salt
flour	1 tablespoon brown sugar
½ cup chopped fresh green	1 bay leaf
peppers	½ cup bread crumbs
½ cup chopped onions	1 tablespoon chopped
	parsley

Peel and dice the eggplant, and parboil it for 10 minutes. Drain the eggplant and place it in a greased 1½-quart casserole. Melt 3 tablespoons of margarine in a heavy frying pan, add the flour, cook, and stir it until well blended. Add the green peppers, onions, tomatoes and juice, salt, sugar, and bay leaf to the flour mixture. Cover and cook it for 5 minutes over a medium heat. Pour the tomato sauce over the eggplant. (Break up the tomatoes with your spoon if they are in large pieces.) Cover the eggplant with crumbs mixed with the parsley, dot with the remaining margarine, and bake in a preheated moderate (350°F) oven for 30 minutes.

baked beans

Serves 8 to 10

1 pound dry white beans	1 cup chopped onions
Cold water, as necessary	½ cup catsup
Hot water, as necessary	½ cup brown sugar
½ cup (1 stick) margarine	1 tablespoon salad mustard

Pick over and wash the beans thoroughly. Cover the beans with cold water, bring to a boil, boil 2 minutes, and turn off the heat. Cover the beans and let them stand for 1 to 1½ hours. Bring the beans to a boil, add hot water, if necessary, so that the beans are covered. Simmer the beans for 1½ hours or until they are just tender.

Heat the margarine in a heavy frying pan, add the onions, cook, and stir them over a low heat until the onions are lightly browned. Add the onions with all of the margarine in the frying pan, the catsup, brown sugar and mustard to the beans, and mix thoroughly. Pour the beans into a casserole and bake in a preheated moderate (350°F) oven for 3 to 4 hours. The cover should be removed during the last hour to allow the beans to brown. A little hot water may be added to the beans to keep them moist, if necessary.

Variations

Italian Style Baked Beans: Add 1 teaspoon leaf oregano and 1 teaspoon Italian seasoning to the beans before baking them.

Easy Baked Beans: Use 2 no. 2½-cans of vegetarian baked beans in tomato sauce instead of the beans. Do not drain the canned beans.

sweet-sour red cabbage

Serves 4 to 6

1 medium size head red cabbage	2 tablespoons flour
2 cups cold water	½ cup water
1 teaspoon salt	¼ cup vinegar
½ cup sliced onion	1 teaspoon salt
½ cup (½ stick) margarine	⅛ teaspoon pepper
¼ cup brown sugar	Bacon bits (optional)

Clean the cabbage, core and shred it. Put the cabbage with 2 cups cold water and 1 teaspoon salt in a heavy saucepan, cover and cook for 8 to 10 minutes.

Cook the onions in margarine until golden. Add the sugar, flour, water, vinegar, salt, and pepper to the onions. Cook and stir them until smooth and thickened. Drain the cabbage and add it to the thickened sauce; mix well. Heat the cabbage through. Garnish with bacon bits, if desired.

chapter VIII

salads and salad dressings

It is hard to believe that anything as tasty as a tossed green salad is also good for you. Yet salads add essential vitamins, minerals, and bulk to the menu and deserve a prominent place in everyone's diet. I've always heard that anything you like is generally illegal, immoral or fattening, but salads are none of these. They add color, texture, interest and eye appeal to a meal. Some tossed salads without dressing have only 10 or 15 calories. Of course, when you add a gooey sour cream dressing you've blown the whole thing — but that is another matter. The fact remains that a tossed green salad with a light dressing is wonderful.

If your husband says that he doesn't like salads it may be because he is tired of the same old hunk of lettuce with a drab dressing, which the waitress shoves in front of him at lunch. There is nothing wrong with lettuce as long as it is crisp and fresh, and served with an interesting dressing. But it can be pretty terrible if it is served wilted and soft with brown edges, which is frequently the case in a lunch room or snack counter.

Tossed green salad or tossed vegetable salad as it is sometimes called is one of the country's most popular salads and one of the best nutritionally. There are so many different types of lettuce and other salad greens that you'll always have a variety. The secret of a really good green salad is the freshness, crispness, and variety of the ingredients in it. Most vegetables owe their crispness to a high water content. Therefore, if wilted, they can be revived by soaking them in very cold water for a short time. After you have soaked and cleaned them, they should be drained well. If they are still wet you can pat them dry with a paper towel or dish towel. They should be stored until needed in the crisper of your refrigerator. If the crisper is full you can put them in a plastic bag or wrap them in clear plastic. They may also be stored in a plastic bowl or box in the refrigerator. There is a great variety of ingredients available for tossed salads and not all of them can really be called "greens." Some that you and your family might enjoy are: red and yellow tomatoes; head, bibb, and leaf lettuce; romaine, escarole, and curly or French endive; white, red, or Chinese cabbage; fresh red or green peppers or pimientos; julienne, diced, or grated carrots or kohlrabi; spinach leaves, tender dandelion greens, watercress, chives, or chicory; green onions, green onion tops, sweet onions, or Italian sweet onions; thinly sliced fresh mushrooms, cucumbers, radishes, cauliflower, or broccoli; pickled beets or pickled vegetable combinations; cooked leftover vegetables that have been marinated in dressing before combining them with other vegetables.

Fortunately, there are very few salad ingredients that should not be used in the low cholesterol kitchen. Olives and avocados are very high in calories and should be used sparingly, and coconut should not be used — but the sky is the limit for almost any other salad ingredient as long as it doesn't contain any saturated fat. This eliminates sour cream, cream cheese, cheddar and many other cheeses and egg yolks, but leaves a great many other ingredients. It is not advisable to use imitation sour cream unless you have read the list of ingredients or talked to the processor and know what kind of fat is used. We open this chapter with a recipe for Whipped Cheese, which may be used as a substitute for both sour cream and cream cheese in many salads and dips. It is even good as a topping for baked potatoes if you add a little chopped onions or chives to it. Try it in one of your own recipes that you haven't been able to use lately, or in a Frozen Fruit Salad.

Your vegetable salads should not be limited to tossed green salads. Many other salads using fresh and cooked vegetables can add interest to your meal. (They are also a sneaky way of adding vegetables to your family's diet.) Cole slaw, for instance, is a very good source of vitamin C; bean salads contain protein. Adding some grated carrot or diced fresh green peppers to a salad increases its vitamin A and, of course, not only do tomatoes add color and taste to a salad, but vitamin C as well. Today, you can even buy a tomato that has been canned by a special process so that it still retains most of its shape and texture for use in salads. Your use of vegetables in salads is no longer determined by the season. The markets now have a wide variety of fresh vegetables and greens available all year. Vegetables do not contain saturated fats and you can feel free to use any kind you like in salads. Just be careful to use a dressing made without any saturated fat. This chapter contains some of my favorite recipes, but don't limit yourself to these recipes. Use your own old favorites and any others you find interesting as well.

The latter part of this chapter includes recipes for the dressings included in the salads. Low cholesterol mayonnaise, which we call L C mayonnaise, and other salad dressings are included as basic recipes. This is one spot where you can improvise as long as you do not add any animal or saturated fat to the diet.

Have you discovered imitation bacon bits, those wonderful crunchy little morsels that taste and smell like bacon but are made from soy flour and artificial flavorings with vegetable oil? They are completely free of any saturated fats. They are grand for use as a garnish or to add flavor, and may be used in many ways: to garnish hot soup, to sprinkle on baked potatoes or in salads. You can even use them in Hot Potato Salad if you substitute oil for the bacon fat ordinarily used.

Main dish or luncheon salads are a great help in stretching the amount of meat, fish, or poultry the doctor says your husband can have at a time. They are delightful for the whole family for a leisurely lunch on Saturday or on a warm summer day because they can be prepared ahead of time and used when you desire.

I find that chicken, turkey, and veal salads can be pretty much interchanged. As a matter of fact it hasn't been too many years since the chicken salads served in some restaurants often contained a good bit of veal. Now that veal is more expensive than chicken I doubt that this is happening. I'm sure that turkey is still being used in chicken salads since you get more meat per pound from turkey than chicken, but it takes a real expert to tell the difference. The turkey meat is a little more coarse but since I like one as well as the other I never feel unhappy with someone who uses one for the other. One time when I was running a company cafeteria, a vice president discovered we were using turkey in our pot pies and calling them chicken pot pies. He insisted that we start calling them turkey pot pies. Do you know, I had many compliments on our new turkey pot pies. It was the same recipe and ingredients that we had been using for years but everyone thought they could detect a difference when only the name was changed.

I like to use canned or precooked frozen chicken for its convenience. Like all poultry, it should have all of the skin removed, for that is where the fat is.

Always be sure to refrigerate all salads unless they have a high vinegar content like pickled vegetables. Bacteria love all of those chopped mixtures and thrive if not refrigerated.

Some people insist that men do not like fruit salads. However, as a restaurant manager I found that men do like fruit salads and will eat them day after day. In fact, a great many men will order a fruit plate with cottage cheese for their lunch with a bowl of soup, a hard roll, and coffee or tea. Of course, whipped cream is out. The most popular fruit salads for men seem to be fruit and cottage cheese, mixed fruit, fresh or canned, and apple salads. Apple salads, such as a Waldorf Salad, are particularly good on a low cholesterol diet since research has found that the pectin in apples helps in the battle to control cholesterol. In other words, the first person to say, "An apple a day keeps the doctor away" knew more about diet than anyone realized at the time. Apple salads take many forms but of course the classic one is the simple Waldorf Salad.

A combination of fresh and canned fruits will add texture and sparkle to your menus. It is wise to concentrate on those fruits in season since this will combine the finest flavor with the lowest cost. The weekend newspaper advertisements will tell you which fruits are the least expensive and, therefore, which are in season. A walk through the fruit and vegetable section of the store will also help you plan your fruit salads. Sometimes it is better to actually see the fresh fruits, then decide what you want to use. Of course, you can always use canned fruit if the fresh fruit is too expensive or doesn't look good to you. Except for coconuts, which contain saturated fats, you are free to roam at will, pick up any of the items in the fruit and vegetable department that look good to you.

Fruit may be tossed with a light dressing or left plain in a

lovely arrangement, with everyone free to use the dressing he wants. Some of the most common combinations for fruit salads are:
Melons, in all combinations;
Grapefruit and oranges, together or with other fruits;
Fresh pineapple with strawberries, grapes, cherries, fresh strawberries, or peaches;
Apples with any combination of fresh or canned fruits;
Strawberries, alone or with oranges, grapefruit, grapes, or other fresh or canned fruits;
Grapes in a combination with other fresh or canned fruits;
Bing cherries with fresh pineapple or apples or citrus fruits;
Fresh or canned apricots filled with whipped cheese;
Fresh cranberries, oranges, and apples ground together (this was my grandfather's favorite and we always served it for holiday meals);
Sweet cabbage slaw with apples, pineapple, or peaches has always been a big favorite, some people like it with raisins or nuts.

Since there is such a variety of canned fruits for fruit salads, you should never be without the ingredients for a salad at a moment's notice. Canned fruits may include cherries, peaches, pineapple, grapes, pears, and cranberries or fruit cocktail. You can even buy mixed fruits for salads, which contain a good combination of fruits and can be served just as they come from the can.

No discussion of salads would be complete without mentioning gelatin salads, since they may be used freely on a low cholesterol diet. Sour cream and cream cheese should not be used in molded salads but whipped cheese makes a very good substitute for them in your molds. Cottage cheese may also be used in molded salads. It should be washed before you use it to get rid of the cream.

Fruits, nuts, and other salad ingredients have different effects in molded salads. Some of them float on the top and some of them sink to the bottom. If you want your fruit to be evenly distributed in the gelatin, it is best to let the gelatin get heavy — almost thickened — before you add the other ingredients. However, you can, if you desire, get a pretty layered effect by taking advantage of the fact that some things float and others sink in your gelatin molds.

Most commercial French and Italian style salad dressings will meet with your doctor's approval since they are made with oil, vinegar and spices. If you have any questions regarding the ingredients, check the labels to be sure of the contents. Sour cream or Roquefort dressings are out. Mayonnaise and salad dressings are borderline areas. Some doctors consider that there is not enough egg yolk in mayonnaise or salad dressing to worry about, since there is so much oil in both of them; other doctors think they should not be used. If your doctor feels your husband should not use them because of the egg yolks, you can use one of the recipes in this chapter, which are made with egg whites.

Not all dressings depend on eggs to hold the oil in suspension. Milk (evaporated skim milk or instant dry milk) may also be used as a base for cream dressings. One of the best recipes for salad dressing made with evaporated skim milk is prepared by Mrs. Gena LeVan. It was at her home that Gena's mother, Mrs. Bellina, first introduced me to the joys of Italian cooking. My husband and I were there for a week and Mrs. Bellina prepared a different Italian specialty each day — and each one of them was a masterpiece. Mrs. Bellina loved to cook and loved to see people eat heartily. She was very generous with her dinner invitations and she never knew how many people would sit down at the table when dinner was served. Friends were always dropping in around mealtime and Mr. Bellina felt free to ask guests without any more notice than the time to add an extra plate at the table. Mr. Bellina had a bakery and general store. Salesmen whom Mrs. Bellina liked were invited up for dinner if they happened in around mealtime. I'm sure many of them made it a point to be there at just the right time for one of her famous dinners.

You really don't need to make your own French Dressing since it is so readily available in the stores but I'm including some recipes, which I thought you might like to try. I'm not including a recipe for vinegar and oil dressing because most people make it just the way they like it. My husband always makes the Italian dressing at our house, which is quite appropriate since I'm only Italian by marriage. He does it by sprinkling vinegar and oil and salt and pepper on the tossed salad. The proportions vary with the taste of the person who mixes the salad but most people like about three or four times as much oil as vinegar or lemon juice.

whipped cheese

Yields 1½ cups

¼ cup reconstituted instant
   dry milk
1 cup rinsed cottage cheese

2 tablespoons lemon juice

Combine the instant milk, cottage cheese, and lemon juice in a blender and blend until smooth.

The fruits in this salad may be canned or fresh. Candied fruit that has been soaked in rum or brandy is nice for Christmas and, of course, green candied cherries are great for St. Patrick's Day.

frozen fruit salad

Serves 4

1 cup whipped cheese
1½ cups assorted fruits
2 tablespoons sugar

1 teaspoon vanilla
⅔ cup miniature
   marshmallows

Prepare the whipped cheese and blend it with the fruits, sugar, vanilla, and marshmallows. Freeze overnight or longer in a 1-quart mold or in individual molds that have been rinsed with cold water. Remove from freezer a half hour before serving. Unmold the salad on lettuce leaves and garnish it with low cholesterol mayonnaise.

creamy cole slaw

Serves 6

1½ teaspoons salt
¼ cup vinegar
½ cup L C mayonnaise

⅛ teaspoon white pepper
¼ cup finely chopped fresh
   green peppers

1 tablespoon chopped
  parsley
¼ cup sugar

1 cup shredded carrots
1 quart shredded cabbage

Combine the salt, vinegar, mayonnaise, parsley, sugar, and pepper in a bowl. Stir to mix well. Add carrots and cabbage and toss until well mixed. Refrigerate until ready to serve, at least 2 hours.

garden cole slaw

Serves 8 to 10

1½ quarts shredded cabbage
½ cup shredded carrots
¼ cup finely chopped fresh
  green peppers
¼ cup finely chopped onions
½ cup thinly sliced radishes
1½ teaspoons salt

¼ teaspoon coarsely ground
  black pepper
3 tablespoons sugar
¾ cup vegetable oil
¾ cup white vinegar
¾ cup ice water

Combine the cabbage, carrots, green peppers, onions, and radishes, and chill well. Just before serving combine salt, pepper, sugar, oil, vinegar, and ice water. Mix well. Pour over chilled vegetables and mix lightly.

Gena's sweet cole slaw

Serves 4

1 quart shredded cabbage
½ cup diced fresh green
  peppers
¼ cup diced pimientos
2 cups cold water
1½ tablespoons salt

1 cup sugar
½ cup white vinegar
½ cup water
1 teaspoon celery seed
2 cups thinly sliced celery

Combine the cabbage, green peppers, pimientos, cold water, and salt in bowl. Cover the bowl and place it in the refrigerator for 2 to 4 hours. Combine the sugar, vinegar, water, and celery seed in a saucepan and bring to a boil. Remove the pan from heat and cool it. Drain the cabbage mixture very well. Add the drained cabbage mixture and the celery to the cold syrup and refrigerate until served, at least 2 hours. This may be prepared a day in advance and keeps almost indefinitely.

pickled beet salad

Serves 4 to 6

2 cups julienne or sliced,
     drained, canned beets
½ cup sliced onions

½ cup French or Italian
     type dressing

Drain the beets. Combine the beets, onions, and dressing. Cover and refrigerate the salad overnight. Drain the beets and onions and serve them on a lettuce cup or in a bowl.

These may be used for antipasto, salad, relish or as a cold vegetable. It is wonderful to have a big container of them in the refrigerator for an emergency. One time we entertained a Japanese student unexpectedly and he didn't eat much else but he enjoyed several helpings of these vegetables. They may be canned, if desired, but they keep for several months in the refrigerator so I never bother to can them. The quantity and kinds of the vegetables may be varied as long as you are careful to use only vegetables that keep their individual character when they are pickled.

pickled vegetables

Yields about 1 gallon

1 quart julienne carrots
3 cups white vinegar

2 cups drained, canned
     green beans

3 cups sugar
2 tablespoons pickling
   spices
2 cups drained, canned
   wax beans

2 cups drained, canned
   kidney beans
2 cups julienne fresh green
   peppers
1 quart sliced onions

Cook the carrots until just barely tender, about 10 minutes. Drain carrots. Wash the kidney beans under running water and drain.

Put the pickling spices in a 6-inch square of white cloth, tie it into a bundle with white thread leaving room for the spices to expand a little. Combine the vinegar, sugar, and spice bag in a 6-quart kettle. Bring the mixture to a boil. Add the carrots, beans, peppers, and onions to the hot vinegar mixture. Bring the mixture to a boil, then remove it from the heat. Allow it to cool, then refrigerate it until ready to use, at least two or three days. Do not allow the mixture to boil again once you have added the onions and green peppers.

Italian bean salad

Serves 4 to 6

2 cups drained, canned
   green beans
2 cups drained, canned
   wax beans
1 cup chopped ripe olives
½ cup chopped onions

½ cup diced celery
½ cup diced fresh green
   peppers
1 cup Italian style salad
   dressing

Combine the beans, olives, onions, celery, green peppers, and salad dressing. Mix them gently. Refrigerate the salad overnight to blend the flavors. Drain and toss the salad lightly before serving.

corn salad

2 cups drained, canned
   whole kernel corn

¼ cup finely chopped
   onions

¼ cup chopped pimientos
½ cup chopped fresh green
    peppers

¼ cup diced cucumbers
¾ cup French dressing

Combine the corn, pimientos, green peppers, onions, and cucumbers. Add the French dressing and toss the salad lightly. Refrigerate it for 1 to 3 hours. Drain and toss the salad lightly before serving.

potato salad

Serves 6 to 8

3 cups diced, cooked
    potatoes
1 cup diced celery
¾ cup L C Mayonnaise
½ cup diced sweet pickles

1 tablespoon minced onions
1 tablespoon chopped
    chives or green onion
    tops
1 tablespoon white vinegar
1 teaspoon salt

Toss all the ingredients together lightly and chill well before using.

potato salad with whipped cheese

Serves 6 to 8

4 cups diced or sliced,
    cooked potatoes
½ cup diced celery
½ cup finely chopped onions
2 tablespoons chopped
    pimiento
1 tablespoon minced
    parsley

2 teaspoons salad mustard
1 teaspoon salt
¼ teaspoon pepper
2 tablespoons French
    dressing
¾ cup whipped cheese

Combine the potatoes, celery, onions, pimiento, parsley, mustard, salt, pepper, and French dressing. Toss the salad lightly and refrigerate for several hours to marinate the ingredients. Prepare the whipped cheese and fold it into the potato salad just before serving.

kidney bean salad

Serves 6 to 8

2 cups drained, rinsed, canned kidney beans	2 tablespoons chopped pimientos
½ cup chopped celery	2 tablespoons chopped sweet pickles
2 tablespoons finely chopped onions	¼ cup French dressing

Combine all the ingredients and chill well before using. Toss the salad lightly just before serving. L C mayonnaise may be used instead of the French dressing if a creamy salad is desired.

You can add nuts, fresh green peppers, apples, red cabbage, green onions, or many other ingredients to carrot salads. You can also vary these salads by your choice of dressing.

carrot and pineapple salad

Serves 4 to 6

2 cups shredded fresh carrots	1 cup drained crushed pineapple
¼ cup raisins	½ cup L C mayonnaise
¼ cup miniature marshmallows	

Toss all the ingredients together lightly and chill well before using.

hot potato salad

Serves 8 to 10

2 quarts cold, sliced,
   boiled potatoes
6 tablespoons vegetable oil
3 tablespoons white vinegar
3 tablespoons lemon juice
2 tablespoons finely
   chopped onions

1½ teaspoons salt
¼ teaspoon pepper
3 tablespoons chopped
   parsley
3 tablespoons imitation
   bacon bits

Layer the sliced potatoes in 3-quart greased casserole. Combine the oil, vinegar, lemon juice, onions, salt, and pepper and heat to simmering. Remove the oil mixture from the heat and pour it over the potatoes. Sprinkle the salad with the parsley and imitation bacon bits and heat it in moderate oven (350°F) for about 30 minutes, or until hot. Stir the salad lightly and serve hot.

chicken salad

Serves 4 to 6

3 cups diced cooked
   chicken
1½ cups chopped celery
½ cup chopped English
   walnuts

2 tablespoons lemon juice
1 teaspoon salt
¼ teaspoon white pepper
1 cup L C mayonnaise

Combine the chicken, celery, walnuts, lemon juice, salt, and pepper. Toss the salad gently to mix. Add the mayonnaise and mix lightly. Refrigerate it until well chilled.

tossed turkey salad

Serves 4 to 6

2 cups diced cooked turkey
1 cup chopped celery

1 cup drained pineapple
   tidbits

3 cups bite size pieces
  of lettuce

¼ cup chopped fresh green
  peppers
Salad dressing, as desired

Combine the turkey, lettuce, celery, and pineapple. Toss the salad gently to mix. Sprinkle the green peppers over salad. Serve with a choice of salad dressings.

veal and rice salad

Serves 6 to 8

2 cups cooked, diced veal
2 cups cold, cooked rice
1½ cups cold, cooked peas
1½ cups chopped celery
2 tablespoons chopped
  green olives

1 tablespoon finely
  chopped onions
1 cup L C mayonnaise
1 teaspoon salt
¼ teaspoon white pepper

Combine the veal, rice, peas, celery, olives, and onions, and toss lightly to mix. Combine the mayonnaise, salt, and pepper and add it to the veal mixture. Mix the salad lightly but thoroughly and chill well before serving.

chicken potato salad

Serves 6 to 8

4 cups diced, cooked
  chicken
4 cups diced, cooked
  potatoes
1 teaspoon onion powder
1 cup chopped celery
1 cup diced fresh green
  peppers

¼ cup sweet pickle relish
1 teaspoon salt
⅛ teaspoon white pepper
2 tablespoons vinegar
1 cup L C mayonnaise

Combine the chicken, potatoes, onion powder, celery, green peppers, and pickle relish. Combine the salt, pepper, vinegar, and mayonnaise, and add it to the chicken mixture. Mix the salad lightly but thoroughly and chill well before serving.

This recipe was my mother-in-law's favorite. I keep cubed beef in the freezer during the tomato season so that we can have it often. Wax beans may be substituted for the fresh tomatoes, but I really prefer the tomatoes.

tomato beef supper salad

Serves 6

3 cups cold roast or boiled beef, cut in ½-inch pieces
½ cup diced fresh green peppers
1 cup sliced sweet onions

1 cup French or Italian dressing
6 medium to large size fresh tomatoes

Combine the beef, peppers, onions, and dressing. Mix the salad well and let it marinate for 2 to 8 hours. Cut the tomatoes into wedges and add them to the meat mixture just before serving. Toss lightly and serve.

Variation
Tomato Veal Supper Salad: Substitute 3 cups cold roast veal cut in ½-inch pieces for the cold roast or boiled beef.

tuna macaroni salad

Serves 6 to 8

1 6-ounce package elbow macaroni

⅓ cup finely chopped onions

1 cup cubed mozzarella
cheese
1 7-ounce can tuna, drained
¼ cup sweet pickle relish

1 cup L C mayonnaise or
Gena's cream dressing
¼ teaspoon salt
¼ teaspoon white pepper

Cook the macaroni as directed on the package, drain, and rinse it with cold water. Combine the macaroni, cheese, tuna, pickle relish, and onions in a bowl. Combine the mayonnaise or dressing with salt and pepper; mix well and add to the tuna mixture. Toss the salad lightly and chill before serving.

Leftover broiled or steamed fish may be substituted for the salmon in this salad or for the tuna in the tuna macaroni salad.

salmon salad

Serves 4

1 1-pound can of salmon
1 cup chopped celery
⅓ cup L C mayonnaise or
cooked salad dressing
1 tablespoon lemon juice

2 tablespoons finely
chopped onions
¼ teaspoon salt
⅛ teaspoon white pepper

Drain the salmon. Remove the bones and break the salmon into bite size pieces with a fork. Combine the celery and salmon. Toss them lightly. Combine mayonnaise or salad dressing, lemon juice, onions, salt, and pepper. Mix the dressing well and add it to the salmon mixture. Toss the salad lightly and chill before serving.

Waldorf salad

Serves 4 to 6

4 cups cubed, unpeeled
red apples
2 cups chopped celery

⅔ cup chopped walnuts
⅔ cup L C mayonnaise

Combine all the ingredients and toss lightly. Chill the salad thoroughly and serve it in lettuce cups. Garnish each serving with a red maraschino cherry or finely chopped nuts, if desired.

fruit slaw

Serves 4 to 6

3 apples
2 bananas
½ cup French dressing

1 cup sliced celery
3 cups shredded cabbage
½ cup fresh orange sections

Core the apples but do not pare them. Slice the apples about ⅛ inch thick. Slice the bananas. Combine the apples, bananas, and French dressing. Add the celery, cabbage, and orange sections to the salad, and mix lightly. Refrigerate until served.

golden gate salad

Serves 4

2 tart red apples
⅓ cup golden raisins
½ cup seed dressing

⅓ cup slivered almonds
½ cup orange sections

Core the apples but do not pare them. Dice the apples. Combine the apples, raisins, and seed dressing. Marinate the salad in the refrigerator for 1 hour. Drain it and add the almonds and orange sections, refrigerate until served.

molded grapefruit salad

Serves 4 to 6

1 3-ounce package lime
   gelatin
1 cup boiling water
1 cup grapefruit juice
¼ teaspoon ground ginger

1 cup grapefruit segments
½ cup diced celery
1 cup washed cottage
   cheese or whipped
   cheese

Add the lime gelatin to the boiling water and stir until the gelatin is completely dissolved. Add the grapefruit juice and ginger. Chill the gelatin until cool and syrupy. Add the grapefruit segments, celery, and cottage cheese. Pour it into a 1½-quart mold, which has been rinsed with cool water. Chill the gelatin until firm.

molded cranberry salad

Serves 12

1 3-ounce package orange
   gelatin
1 3-ounce package lemon
   gelatin
2½ cups boiling water

1 16-ounce can whole
   canned cranberries
¾ cup drained, crushed
   pineapple
½ cup chopped walnuts

Add the orange and lemon gelatin to the boiling water and stir until completely dissolved. Chill the gelatin until cool and syrupy. Break up the cranberries with a fork and fold them into the gelatin. Add the pineapple and nuts. Pour into a 2-quart mold, which has been rinsed with cool water. Chill the gelatin until firm.

molded pineapple cheese salad

Serves 12

1 6-ounce package lemon
  gelatin
2 cups boiling water
1 cup cold pineapple juice
1 tablespoon vinegar

¼ cup chopped pimiento
2 cups washed cottage
  cheese
1½ cups drained, crushed
  pineapple

Add the lemon gelatin to the boiling water and stir until completely dissolved. Add the pineapple juice and vinegar. Chill the gelatin until cool and syrupy. Add the pimiento, cottage cheese, and crushed pineapple. Pour into a 2-quart mold, which has been rinsed with cool water. (This may also be prepared and served in a clear glass bowl.) Chill salad until firm.

golden cider salad

Serves 12

1 6-ounce package orange
  gelatin
3 cups hot cider or apple
  juice

1 cup chipped ice
3 cups drained, canned
  apricot halves
2 cups sliced bananas

Add the orange gelatin to the hot cider or apple juice and stir until the gelatin is completely dissolved. Add the chipped ice and stir until it is dissolved. Add the apricots and bananas. Pour the salad into a 3-quart mold, which has been rinsed with cool water. Chill the salad until firm.

The important thing to remember when preparing this mayon-naise is to beat it fast. Use the setting on your electric mixer for beating egg whites. The boiling water is a trick used by some French cooks to set the mayonnaise so that it will be more stable.

L C mayonnaise

Yields 2½ cups

2 egg whites
1 teaspoon sugar
1 teaspoon ground mustard
½ teaspoon salt
⅛ teaspoon white pepper
1 drop yellow coloring

1 cup oil
1 tablespoon white vinegar
1 cup oil
2 tablespoons white vinegar
or lemon juice
1 tablespoon boiling hot
water

Put the egg whites in a mixer bowl. Add the sugar, mustard, salt, pepper, and yellow coloring. Beat it until egg whites are foamy and well blended with the spices. Add 1 cup of oil a little at a time, beating constantly, then add 1 tablespoon vinegar, another cup of oil, 2 tablespoons of white vinegar or lemon juice, and finally the boiling hot water. Refrigerate until used. (The oil should be added just a teaspoon of oil at a time at first, but the more oil that has been added, the faster you can add the oil. At the end you can add the oil in a thin stream.)

To prepare in blender: Place the egg whites, sugar, mustard, salt, pepper, and yellow coloring in a blender. Cover and blend for about 2 seconds. With each of the following additions, briefly turn the blender on and off:

1 cup oil, 2 tablespoonsful at a time
1 tablespoon vinegar
1 cup oil, ¼ cup at a time
2 tablespoons vinegar or lemon juice
1 tablespoon boiling hot water

thousand island dressing

Yields 2¼ cups

1 cup L C mayonnaise
1 cup chili sauce
¼ cup pickle relish
1 tablespoon chopped
  pimiento
1 tablespoon chopped fresh
  green peppers
1 tablespoon chopped
  onions

Combine all the ingredients, stirring lightly to mix well. Keep it in refrigerator until used.

cooked dressing

Yields 2 cups

⅓ cup all purpose flour
1 teaspoon sugar
1 teaspoon salt
1 teaspoon ground mustard
¾ cup water
¼ cup white vinegar
½ cup (1 stick) margarine
2 slightly beaten egg whites

Combine the flour, sugar, salt, and mustard in a heavy saucepan. Add the water, vinegar, and margarine, and stir to mix. Cook over a low heat, stirring constantly, until the mixture boils. Boil for 1 minute. Remove the dressing from the heat and beat it into the egg whites, stirring or beating until well combined. Keep the dressing refrigerated until used.

Use this dressing for potato salad, meat or fish salad, or macaroni salad.

creamy French dressing

Yields 3 cups

1 egg white	¼ teaspoon garlic powder
1 teaspoon salt	¼ cup catsup
1 teaspoon paprika	½ cup white vinegar
½ teaspoon ground mustard	2 tablespoons lemon juice
¼ teaspoon white pepper	2 cups oil
½ teaspoon onion powder	

Put the ingredients in a mixer bowl in the order listed. Beat them at a high speed until creamy. Store the dressing in the refrigerator until served. Serve the dressing at room temperature and shake before using.

Gena's cream dressing

Yields 2 cups

2 teaspoons sugar	½ teaspoon ground mustard
½ teaspoon salt	½ teaspoon paprika
½ cup evaporated skim milk	3 tablespoons vinegar
⅛ teaspoon white pepper	1½ cups vegetable oil

Combine the sugar, salt, evaporated skim milk, pepper, mustard, and paprika. Add the vinegar and beat until well mixed. Gradually add the oil, beating constantly at a high speed. Refrigerate the dressing until served, at least 24 hours. This dressing may be thinned with evaporated skim milk, if desired.

creamy garlic dressing

Yields 2 cups

⅓ cup instant dry milk	¼ teaspoon onion powder
2 teaspoons sugar	⅓ cup water

½ teaspoon salt
⅛ teaspoon white pepper
1 teaspoon garlic powder

3 tablespoons vinegar
1½ cups vegetable oil

Combine the instant dry milk, sugar, salt, pepper, garlic powder, and onion powder in a mixer bowl. Add the water and beat slowly until well mixed. Add the vinegar and beat until well mixed. Gradually add the oil, beating constantly at a high speed. Refrigerate the dressing until used, at least 24 hours. This dressing may be thinned with reconstituted instant dry milk, if desired.

basic French dressing

Yields 2 cups

2 teaspoons salt
1 teaspoon sugar
½ teaspoon pepper

1 teaspoon paprika
½ cup vinegar
1½ cups vegetable oil

Combine all the ingredients in a covered jar and shake well. Shake the dressing again before using.

Lemon or orange juice may be used in place of the vinegar for fruit salads.

Basic French Dressing may be varied by adding chopped onions, chives, fresh herbs, celery seed, curry powder, or dill, for example.

Hattie's French dressing

Yields 1 quart

1 tablespoon paprika
1 teaspoon salt
2 cups water
1 cup catsup

1 cup vinegar
1¼ cups sugar
2 tablespoons vegetable oil

Combine the paprika, salt, and water and let it stand for 15 minutes. Add the catsup and let it stand for another 15 minutes. Beat it hard for 1 minute. Add the vinegar, sugar, and oil and beat well. Refrigerate the dressing until used. Serve the dressing at room temperature and stir before using.

seed dressing

Yields 1¾ cups

1 teaspoon salt
1 teaspoon ground mustard
1 teaspoon paprika
1 teaspoon celery or
   poppy seed

½ cup white corn syrup
¼ cup vinegar
1 cup vegetable oil
1 teaspoon onion powder

Combine all the ingredients in a mixer bowl. Beat the dressing until well blended and thick. Put it in covered container and chill for several hours before serving. Serve the dressing at room temperature and stir before using.

sweet sour French dressing

Yields 4½ cups

2 cups vegetable oil
2 cups sugar
1 tablespoon paprika
1 cup white vinegar
1 teaspoon onion powder
1 teaspoon Worcestershire
   sauce

1 teaspoon A-1 sauce
1 teaspoon celery seed
1 teaspoon salt
½ teaspoon monosodium
   glutamate (MSG)
   (optional)

Combine all the ingredients and mix well. The dressing should be prepared at least 24 hours before it is to be served to allow the

salads and salad dressings   155

flavors to mellow. It may be stored in the refrigerator, but should be allowed to return to room temperature before it is served.

lemon fruit dressing

Yields 1 cup

½ cup undiluted frozen
    lemonade concentrate

⅓ cup honey
2 tablespoons vegetable oil

Combine all the ingredients and beat them until smooth.

low calorie dressing

Yields 1⅔ cups

1¼ teaspoons plain gelatin
1½ cups tomato juice

2½ teaspoons dry salad
    dressing mix
2 tablespoons white
    vinegar or lemon juice

Combine the gelatin and tomato juice and let stand for 5 minutes to soften. Bring the tomato juice mixture just to a boil, stirring to dissolve the gelatin. Remove the gelatin from the heat. Add the salad dressing mix and the vinegar or lemon juice. Chill the dressing and stir it before serving.

Your own favorite comination of spices may be used instead of the salad dressing mix. I like to use Italian seasoning.

chapter IX
breads

Since good breads and rolls add greatly to a meal, it is heartening to discover that most breads can be made from ingredients that are acceptable on a low cholesterol diet. However, you will need to be cautious and maintain a vigilant watch on the ingredients in the breads you buy. Many of the breads and rolls that are sold in the stores contain whole milk solids, butter, whole eggs, and saturated fats. Some day in the future bakeries will probably become more responsive to the needs of their customers and advertise "low cholesterol breads." (Actually a great many rolls and breads are made from instant dry milk and without eggs and butter, but most bakeries don't advertise this fact because they feel the public might think their products are of inferior quality to those containing eggs and milk.) In the meantime, you will need to be very ingredient conscious whenever you go shopping. If the label tells you that the bread and rolls contain any forbidden foods, pass them up and continue searching until you find bread and rolls that contain the correct ingredients.

If you are fortunate enough to live in an area where French or Italian bread is available, you can feel free to use either of them. They are traditionally made from only the simplest ingredients: flour, water, salt, yeast, perhaps a very little oil, and maybe just a touch of sugar. The long crusty loaves or the shorter plump ones, fresh from the oven, have a marvelous texture and aroma. If you are unable to buy them, you might try making them. They are quite simple to make. The important thing to remember is to knead them long enough to develop the gluten in the flour, which gives them their characteristic texture. Also, remember that they should be served the day they are made if possible. Neither of them keep very well, which may explain why you see so many pictures of Italian and French people carrying home fresh loaves of bread.

As with everything else in life, you will get out of bread exactly what you put into it. The best bread will result from the freshest, purest ingredients. Yeast is a living organism that thrives on sugar but is slowed down by oil and salt. Therefore, it is best to allow the yeast mixed with a liquid and some flour and sugar to begin to grow well before you add the oil and salt. Yeast is available in two forms, active dry and compressed. Active dry yeast may be kept for several months in a cool dry place but compressed yeast will only keep for a week or so and must be refrigerated. Compressed yeast should be dissolved in lukewarm water (about 85°F) and active dry yeast should be dissolved in warmer water (about 110 to 115°F). Yeast batters thrive best in a draft-free spot with a temperature of about 85°F. I like to set bread to rise in the oven of my gas range where the pilot light keeps it gently warmed to the right temperature. However, any moderately warm spot free from drafts will do very well.

If you have some favorite breads recipes, it is not necessary to discard them for new ones. You can substitute vegetable oil for butter, lard, or shortening, use instant dry milk instead of whole milk, and use egg whites and a couple of drops of yellow food coloring instead of the whole eggs that you have been using. Vegetable oil should be substituted on an equal basis for saturated fats and the instant dry milk should be substituted for whole milk as directed in Chapter I. Remember that if you scalded the milk and then added the other ingredients you may need to use very hot water to reconstitute the milk in order to melt the ingredients added to the milk. It is also important to remember that yeast needs the correct temperature for survival whether it is dissolved in water, milk, or some other liquid. If you are using active dry yeast, this is particularly important. If it is dissolved in water that is not warm enough it will release certain enzymes, which may result in an inferior bread. If you've never made bread before, you might want to begin with the low cholesterol breads in this chapter.

Batter breads have been around a long time; our grandmothers called them no-knead breads. However, only in the past few years have they enjoyed a degree of popularity again. Batter breads do not have as fine a texture as the kneaded breads but they are easy to prepare. Remember never to let the bread rise above the side of the pan since the batter is very light and will probably fall if allowed to rise too high. Batter breads have a rougher crust and are darker than regular breads. They should be cooled out of the pan like other breads. Since you don't shape them by kneading, you may want to press the batter into the corners of the pans with your fingers or a spatula.

Since you can no longer buy sweet rolls without discussing the ingredients with the baker, the next step is to learn to make a good basic sweet dough at home. Once you have mastered the art of making the sweet dough, you will be surprised to see how easy it is to make the many variations.

Hot biscuits depend on baking powder and/or baking soda for leavening action. They are such an important part of the cuisine of some sections of the country that it would be hard to imagine meals without them. Many hot biscuit recipes can be adapted to a low cholesterol diet. A little different technique is often necessary but the final results are very appetizing.

Pancakes have come into their own in the last few years as you can see by the pancake houses scattered across the country. They are good and offer an amazing variety but not to someone on a low cholesterol diet. Pancake houses, and mixes, generally contain whole eggs and quite often butter or shortening — and those German pancakes are all eggs. If he likes pancakes it is better to prepare them at home with oil and egg whites instead of whole eggs and shortening.

I know that you hate to cook without those beautiful packaged mixes that require only water or milk and perhaps a couple of eggs to make a tempting cake or muffins or pancakes. It is regrettable but undeniably true that unsaturated fats become rancid too quickly to be used in packaged mixes. Therefore saturated or hydrogenated fats are used in mixes, which means that you can not use them on a low cholesterol diet. However, if you analyze the mixes, you realize that they are nothing more or less than flour, sugar, instant dry milk, salt, baking powder and/or baking soda, and perhaps some dried eggs and seasonings along with the saturated fats. For that reason you can prepare your own basic mixes, which you can keep on hand, adding the fat, egg whites and liquid when you prepare the recipes. Take, for instance, the Baking Powder Biscuits made with oil. You can make up a large amount of the dry ingredients and store them for future use. You might start out with six times the recipe:

Basic Recipe	*Large Quantity Mix*
1 cup cake flour × 6 =	6 cups cake flour
1 cup all purpose flour × 6 =	6 cups all purpose flour

4 teaspoons baking
   powder × 6 =
	24 teaspoons or
	   ½ cup baking powder

1 teaspoon salt × 6 =	6 teaspoons or 2 tablespoons salt
⅓ cup instant dry milk × 6 =	6/3 or 2 cups instant dry milk

Total scant 2½ cups   *Total 14¾ cups*

Sift and stir the ingredients together until they are very well blended. This blending is essential because you want to be sure to have a mixture that will give the same results every time.

You now have the ingredients for six batches of baking powder biscuits. When you add all of the ingredients in the basic recipe you have a total of a scant 2½ cups of dry ingredients. Therefore when you want to make baking powder biscuits you would use a scant 2½ cups of the mix plus ⅓ cup of oil and ¾ cup of ice water, then proceed as directed by the recipe to finish mixing and baking the biscuits.

This mix can be prepared and stored until the next time you want to make biscuits. It saves a great deal of time and will give you mixes that are economical and handy and that are approved for use in the low cholesterol diet.

Italian bread

Yields 2 loaves

2½ cups warm water	1 tablespoon salt
1 ounce compressed yeast	Yellow cornmeal
7 to 7½ cups all purpose	1 slightly beaten egg white
flour	1 tablespoon cold water

Combine the yeast and warm water in mixer bowl. Add 2 cups flour and beat thoroughly. Add the salt and 1 more cup flour and beat at a low speed until it is too thick to beat longer. Put the remaining flour on a breadboard, making a well in the center. Pour the batter in the well and knead it until the dough is smooth and elastic, taking up as much of the flour as necessary. The dough will be stiff and should use almost all of the flour. Let the dough rest, covered with a cloth, on a lightly floured breadboard for about 15 minutes. Knead the dough for about 10 minutes longer. Place the dough in a lightly greased bowl, turning the dough over so that it is greased on top. Cover it with a cloth, let it rise in a warm place until doubled in volume, punch it down and knead it for about 5 minutes longer. Return the dough to the bowl, cover it with a cloth, and let it rise again until doubled in volume. Turn the dough out on a lightly floured breadboard, knead it lightly, divide it into two equal portions, round each portion into a ball, cover them with a cloth, and let dough stand about 10 minutes.

Shape each dough half into a long thin loaf, tapering the ends. Place them diagonally, seam side on the bottom, on greased baking sheets sprinkled with cornmeal. Cut slits ⅛ inch deep, about 2 inches apart, on the top of the loaves. Combine the egg white and cold water, and brush the tops and sides of the loaves. Cover with a cloth and let rise again until doubled in volume. Bake in a preheated moderate oven (375°F). After 20 minutes brush the sides and tops again with the egg white mixture. Continue baking for another 20 minutes, a total of 40 minutes, or until loaves are golden brown. Turn out on a rack and cool.

white bread

Yields 3 loaves

3 cups warm water
½ cup instant dry milk
¼ cup sugar
1 ounce compressed yeast

9 to 10 cups all purpose flour
1 teaspoon salt
⅓ cup vegetable oil

Combine warm water, instant dry milk, and sugar and stir to mix well. Crumble the yeast and add it to the milk mixture. Mix it lightly and let stand for 5 minutes. Add 3 cups flour and beat the dough hard for 5 minutes. Add the salt and oil and continue beating for another minute. Add the remaining flour, beating it as long as possible and then use your hands to add the remainder of the flour. When almost all of the flour has been added put the remainder of the flour on a breadboard, turn the dough out on the board, and knead until it is elastic. Place the dough in a lightly greased bowl, turning the dough over so that it is lightly greased on top. Cover with a cloth and let it rise in a warm place until it is doubled in volume.

Turn the risen dough out on a lightly floured board, knead it lightly, and divide it into three portions. Round up each portion into a ball, cover them with a cloth, and let them stand for 15 minutes. Shape the balls into loaves and put each loaf into a greased loaf pan (9 × 5 × 3 inches). Cover the pans with a cloth and let the dough rise until doubled in volume. Bake in a preheated moderate oven (350°F) for 60 minutes, or until golden brown. Remove the loaves from the oven, turn them out onto a wire rack, brush with melted margarine, and cool.

French bread

Yields 2 loaves

2½ cups warm water
1 ounce compressed yeast
2 tablespoons sugar
7 to 7½ cups all purpose
    flour

1 tablespoon salt
2 tablespoons vegetable oil
    Yellow cornmeal
1 slightly beaten egg white
1 tablespoon cold water

Prepare according to directions for Italian bread adding the sugar with the yeast and the oil with the salt.

This recipe uses instant potatoes, but the taste is that of old fashioned potato bread. It makes particularly good shaped hamburger buns.

potato bread

Yields 3 loaves

1 ounce compressed yeast	1 cup instant dry potatoes
1 tablespoon sugar	3 tablespoons sugar
½ cup lukewarm water	¼ cup vegetable oil
4 cups hot water	1 tablespoon salt
1 cup instant dry milk	10 cups all purpose flour

Combine the yeast, 1 tablespoon sugar, and ½ cup lukewarm water, and let stand 5 minutes. Put the hot water in a mixer bowl, add the instant dry milk and instant potatoes, and beat until the potatoes are dissolved. Add 3 tablespoons sugar, the oil and salt, and beat to mix well. Add the yeast mixture and 4 cups flour, and beat hard for 5 minutes. Add the remaining flour, using as much as necessary to form a smooth elastic dough. Beat the flour in as much as possible, then use your hands to add the remaining flour. Turn the dough out on a lightly floured breadboard and knead for about 10 minutes. Put the dough in a lightly greased bowl, turning the dough over so that it is greased on top. Cover it with a cloth and let it rise in a warm place until doubled in volume.

Turn the risen dough out on a lightly floured board, knead it lightly, and divide it into three portions. Round each portion into a ball, cover them with a cloth, and let them stand for 15 minutes. Shape the balls into loaves and put each loaf into a greased loaf pan (9 × 5 × 3 inches). Cover the pans with a cloth and let the dough rise until it is doubled in volume. Bake for 1 hour in a preheated moderate oven (350° F), or until golden brown. Remove the loaves from the oven, turn them out onto a wire rack, brush them with melted margarine, and cool.

This bread is doubly good if you can find stone ground whole wheat flour. We buy ours at a little mill in Missouri and it really has a different flavor. Health stores in some cities are also a good source of stone ground flour.

whole wheat bread

Yields 4 loaves

4 cups warm water	6 cups all purpose flour
⅓ cup instant dry milk	2 teaspoons salt
½ cup light brown sugar	⅓ cup vegetable oil
1 ounce compressed yeast	6 cups whole wheat flour

Combine the warm water, instant dry milk, and brown sugar. Crumble the yeast and add it to the milk mixture. Let this stand for 5 minutes, then add 4 cups all purpose flour and beat hard for 2 minutes. Add the salt and oil and continue to beat hard for another 3 minutes. (Beating hard is very important because it develops the gluten in the flour. You must develop the gluten in the white flour as much as possible because whole wheat flour does not have much gluten and you need all of the gluten in the white flour to give you a good loaf of bread.) Add the remainder of the all purpose flour and the whole wheat flour, beating them as much as possible and then using your hands to add the remainder. When most of the flour has been added, put the remaining flour on a breadboard. Turn the dough out on the board and knead until it is elastic. Place the dough in a lightly greased bowl, turning the dough over so that it is greased on top. Cover with a cloth and let it rise in a warm place until it is doubled in volume.

Punch the risen dough down, and knead it for about 5 minutes. Return it to the bowl, cover with a cloth, and let it rise again until doubled in volume. Turn the dough out on a lightly floured board, knead it lightly, and divide it into four portions. Round each portion into a ball, cover the balls with a cloth, and let them stand for 15 minutes. Shape the balls into loaves, and put each loaf into a greased loaf pan (9 × 5 × 3 inches). Cover the loaves with a cloth, let them rise until doubled in volume, and bake them in a preheated oven: 10 minutes in a hot oven (425°F) to set the loaves; then 35 minutes in a moderate oven (375°F) to finish baking. Remove the loaves from the oven and turn them out onto a wire rack, brush them with margarine, and cool.

hot rolls

Yields 12 rolls

1¼ cups warm water	4 cups all purpose flour
⅓ cup instant dry milk	2 tablespoons vegetable oil
2 tablespoons sugar	2 egg whites
½ ounce compressed yeast	1 teaspoon salt

Combine the warm water, instant dry milk, and sugar, and mix well. Crumble the yeast, add it to the milk mixture and let stand 5 minutes. Add 1 cup flour and beat hard for 2 minutes. Add the oil, egg whites, and salt, and continue to beat for another 3 minutes. Add the remaining flour, beating in as much as possible, then use your hands to add the remainder. When most of the flour has been added, put the remainder of the flour on a breadboard, turn the dough out on the board, and knead until it is elastic. Place dough in lightly greased bowl, turning the dough over so that it is lightly greased on top. Cover the dough with a cloth and let it rise in a warm place until it is doubled in volume.

Turn the risen dough out on a lightly floured board, knead it lightly, and divide it into twelve equal portions. Roll each piece into a ball and place the balls in a greased 9-inch round cake pan. Cover the rolls with a cloth, and let them rise until doubled in volume. Bake the rolls in a preheated hot oven (400°F) for 15 to 20 minutes, or until golden brown. Remove the rolls from the oven and turn them out onto a wire rack, brush them with margarine, and serve warm if possible.

batter bread

Yields 2 loaves

2¾ cups warm water	2 teaspoons salt
⅓ cup instant dry milk	3 tablespoons vegetable oil

2 tablespoons sugar   6½ cups all purpose flour
1 ounce compressed yeast

Combine the warm water, instant dry milk, and sugar, and mix well. Crumble the yeast, add it to the milk mixture and let stand 5 minutes. Add the salt, oil, and 3 cups of the flour. Beat the dough until smooth, add the remaining flour and beat thoroughly. Cover the bowl with a cloth and let the dough rise until doubled in volume. Stir the risen dough down and beat it for 1 minute. Pour half of the batter into each of two greased loaf pans (9 × 5 × 3 inches) and spread evenly. Cover the batter with a cloth and let it rise until the batter reaches the top of the pan. Bake the bread in a preheated moderate oven (350°F) for 40 to 50 minutes, or until dark brown. Turn the loaves out onto a rack, brush them with melted margarine, and cool.

basic sweet dough

Yields 12 rolls

½ cup warm water
1 tablespoon instant dry
   milk
¼ cup sugar
1 ounce compressed yeast

2½ cups all purpose flour
½ teaspoon salt
3 tablespoons vegetable oil
2 egg whites

Combine the water, instant dry milk, and sugar, and mix well. Crumble the yeast, add it to the milk mixture, and let it stand for 5 minutes. Add 1 cup flour and beat for 1 minute. Add the salt, oil, and egg whites, and beat for 1 minute. Add the remaining flour, beating in as much as possible, then using your hands to add the remainder. Turn the dough out on a lightly floured breadboard. Knead until the dough is smooth and elastic and blisters appear on the surface. Place it in a lightly greased bowl, turning the dough over so that it is lightly greased on top. Cover it with a cloth and let it rise in a warm place until doubled in volume. Turn the dough out onto a lightly floured board and knead it for about 15 times. Shape and fill the dough according to your favorite method or use one of the following recipes.

cinnamon rolls

Yields 12 rolls

1 recipe basic sweet dough
¼ cup (½ stick) softened margarine

¼ cup light brown sugar
1 teaspoon cinnamon
2 tablespoons white sugar

Roll the basic sweet dough into a rectangular shape about 12 × 8 inches. Spread the dough with margarine, combine the sugars and cinnamon, and sprinkle them evenly over the margarine. Roll the dough up like a jelly roll, pinching the edges to seal it tightly. Cut the roll into twelve slices. Place the slices, just touching, in a greased pan. Cover them with a cloth and let them rise until doubled in volume. Bake them in a preheated moderate oven (350°F) for 20 minutes, or until lightly browned.

hot cross buns

Yields 9 buns

1 recipe basic sweet dough
½ teaspoon cinnamon
¼ teaspoon nutmeg
¼ cup currants
2 tablespoons finely chopped candied citron

Glaze:
¾ cup powdered sugar
1 tablespoon water
½ teaspoon vanilla

Prepare the basic sweet dough according to the earlier recipe adding the cinnamon and nutmeg with the first addition of flour and the currants and citron with the second addition. Divide the dough into nine equal portions. Shape each portion into a ball and arrange in a greased 9-inch square pyrex cake pan. Flatten each ball with the palm of your hand. Cover them with a cloth and let them rise until doubled in volume. Bake the buns in a preheated moderate oven (375°F) for 20 to 25 minutes, or until golden brown. Combine the glaze ingredients. Use half of the glaze on top of the rolls while they are still warm. Use the remainder to form a cross on each one.

raisin bran muffins

Yields 12 muffins

1½ cups all purpose flour
2 cups Bran Buds or All-Bran
1 tablespoon baking powder
½ teaspoon salt
1 cup washed and drained raisins

⅓ cup sugar
⅓ cup instant dry milk
⅓ cup vegetable oil
2 egg whites
1½ cups water

Place flour, bran baking powder, salt and raisins in mixer bowl. Mix at low speed about ½ minute to blend. Combine sugar, dry milk, oil, egg whites and water in bowl. Mix to blend well. Add liquid all at once to dry mixture. Mix at low speed only until flour is moistened. Fill muffin tins which have been greased with margarine or paper-lined about ⅔ full of batter. Bake them in a preheated hot oven (400° F.) for about 25 minutes or until muffins spring back when touched in the center.

baking powder biscuits (margarine)

Yields 10 to 12 biscuits

2 cups all purpose flour
3 tablespoons instant dry milk
4 teaspoons baking powder

1 teaspoon salt
3 tablespoons margarine
¾ cup water

Sift together the flour, instant dry milk, baking powder, and salt. Cut the margarine into flour mixture until it resembles a coarse meal. Add the water and stir with a fork to form a soft dough. Knead the dough about ten times on a lightly floured board. Pat or roll the dough to about ½ inch thick. Cut it with a floured 2-inch cutter. Put the biscuits on an ungreased cookie sheet and bake them in a preheated hot oven (400°F) for 15 to 20 minutes, or until golden brown. Serve warm.

baking powder biscuits (oil)

Yields 10 to 12 biscuits

1 cup cake flour
1 cup all purpose flour
4 teaspoons baking powder
1 teaspoon salt

⅓ cup instant dry milk
⅓ cup vegetable oil
¾ cup ice water

Sift together the flours, baking powder, salt and instant dry milk. Stir the oil into the ice water and add it all at once to the flour mixture. Stir the mixture with a fork to form a soft dough. Knead the dough about ten times on a lightly floured breadboard. Pat or roll the dough to about ½ inch thick. Cut the dough with a floured 2-inch cutter. Put the biscuits on an ungreased cookie sheet and bake them in a preheated hot oven (400°F) for 15 to 20 minutes, or until browned. Serve warm.

Variations:
Fruit Shortcake Biscuits: Add 2 tablespoons sugar with the flour and cut into 3-inch biscuits.
Drop Biscuits: Increase the water to 1 cup and drop on an ungreased cookie sheet.
Herb Biscuits: Add ¼ teaspoon each of ground oregano and ground thyme with the flour.
Spice Biscuits: Add ½ teaspoon ground cinnamon and ¼ teaspoon ground mace with the flour.

waffles

Yields 10 waffles

1 cup all purpose flour
1 cup cake flour
⅔ cup instant dry milk
2 tablespoons sugar
½ teaspoon salt

2 teaspoons baking powder
1⅔ cups water
⅔ cup vegetable oil
3 stiffly beaten egg whites

Sift the flours, instant dry milk, sugar, salt, and baking powder together into a mixing bowl. Add the water and oil to the flour mixture and beat it until smooth. Fold the egg whites into the batter, mixing only until smooth. Pour about ½ cup batter into a preheated waffle iron and bake until browned.

pancakes

Yields 14 4-inch pancakes

1 cup all purpose flour
⅓ cup instant dry milk
2 tablespoons sugar
2 teaspoons baking powder

½ teaspoon salt
2 egg whites
1 cup water
¼ cup vegetable oil

Sift the flour, instant dry milk, sugar, baking powder, and salt together into a mixing bowl. Add the egg whites, water, and oil, and mix together until well blended. Pour about ¼ cup batter onto a hot grill. Cook until bubbles form on the surface and the edge of the pancake is dry. Turn and cook about 2 minutes longer or until the pancake is nicely done on the underside.

Variations
Apple Pancakes: Add 1 cup chopped apples to the batter before baking.
Blueberry Pancakes: Drop 5 to 6 fresh blueberries onto the pancake before it is turned.

quick coffee cake

Yields 1 loaf

½ cup (1 stick) margarine
1 cup sugar
1 teaspoon vanilla
2 cups all purpose flour
1 teaspoon ground
    cinnamon
⅓ cup instant dry milk

2 teaspoons baking powder
1 teaspoon salt
¾ cup water
2 egg whites
½ cup raisins
½ cup chopped nuts

Cream the margarine and sugar together until light and fluffy, add the vanilla and stir to mix well. Sift together the flour, cinnamon, instant dry milk, baking powder, and salt. Combine the water and egg whites and mix well. Add the flour mixture and the egg white mixture to the creamed sugar and margarine. Mix only until all of the flour is moistened. Add the raisins and nuts to the batter and spoon it into a greased loaf pan (9 × 5 × 3 inches). Bake in a preheated moderate oven (375°F) for 1 hour or until browned. Remove the cake from the oven and cool on a wire rack.

Variation

Brown Sugar and Pecan Coffee Cake: Delete the raisins and nuts
    from the above recipe. Combine 2 tablespoons brown sugar,
    1 teaspoon ground cinnamon, and 1 cup chopped pecans.
    Put half of the batter in the loaf pan. Cover with the pecan
    mixture. Take a knife and swirl the pecan mixture through
    the coffee cake by drawing the knife through the batter to
    form a figure eight. Bake as directed above.

buttermilk doughnuts

Yields 18 to 20 doughnuts

1 cup cake flour
1 cup all purpose flour
1 teaspoon baking powder
½ teaspoon baking soda
½ teaspoon salt

½ teaspoon ground nutmeg
1 egg white
½ cup sugar
½ cup low fat buttermilk
1 tablespoon vegetable oil

Sift the flours, baking powder, soda, salt, and nutmeg together into a mixing bowl. Beat the egg white, sugar, buttermilk, and oil together and add them to the flour mixture. Stir the mixture to form a soft dough. Roll or pat the dough to about ½ inch thick on a lightly floured board. Cut with a doughnut cutter that has been dipped in flour. Fry in hot deep oil (375°F) for about 3 minutes on each side or until golden brown. Do not crowd the doughnuts. Remove them from the kettle and drain them on brown paper or paper towels. Dust the doughnuts with powdered sugar.

corn muffins

Yields 12 muffins

1⅓ cups all purpose flour
⅔ cup cornmeal
⅓ cup instant dry milk
1 tablespoon baking powder
1 teaspoon salt

2 tablespoons sugar
¾ cup water
2 egg whites
⅓ cup vegetable oil

Combine the flour, cornmeal, instant dry milk, baking powder, salt, and sugar, and stir until well blended. Combine the water, egg whites, and oil, and add them to the flour mixture. Stir only until the flour is moistened. Fill greased muffin tins about ⅔ full of batter and bake in a preheated hot oven (425°F) for 15 to 20 minutes or until golden brown.

hush puppies

Yields about 36 hush puppies

1½ cups cornmeal
½ teaspoon salt
¼ teaspoon baking soda

¼ cup finely chopped onions
¼ cup low fat buttermilk
⅓ cup water

Combine the cornmeal, salt, soda, and onions, and stir until well blended. Add the buttermilk and water to the cornmeal mixture. Stir only until the cornmeal is moistened. Drop by teaspoonsful into hot deep oil (375°F) and fry, turning once, until golden brown. Drain them on brown paper or paper towels and serve hot.

chapter X

cakes, cookies, and candies

Angelfood cake is lovely to look at, delightful to eat, and fits beautifully into a low cholesterol diet. It is easy to prepare from a mix or may be purchased at most bakeries. Of course, even food fit for angels can get pretty monotonous if it is the only dessert, so you probably have been looking around for other desserts to include in your menus. It is not generally wise to use cake mixes because most of them contain hydrogenated fats and/or egg yolk solids, which should not be included in a low cholesterol diet. For this reason, you may have to do some baking "from scratch" using recipes adapted for the low cholesterol diet.

An important thing to keep in mind is that generally it is not possible to convert recipes by substituting egg whites for whole eggs and oil or margarine for shortening. You need specially formulated recipes. I know of no simple formula for substituting oil or margarine for shortening or butter. A cake is a delicately balanced formula and all parts of it must be balanced. I ruined a lot of expensive ingredients and wasted a lot of time before I realized the truth of this. Sometimes you will get good results by substituting 2 egg whites for 1 whole egg along with margarine for butter but not always. I can only suggest that if you have a recipe that you hate to stop using, try it with egg whites and margarine before you stop using it. Sometimes they turn out well, depending upon the balance of the ingredients in the original recipe.

Chocolate can't be used but cocoa may and fortunately the substitution ratio for cocoa and chocolate is well established. To use cocoa in a recipe that originally used chocolate, substitute 3 tablespoons of cocoa for each ounce of chocolate. (You usually measure chocolate in 1 ounce squares.) When this substitution is used in a bakery or restaurant extra fat is added to compensate for the lost cocoa butter but this is not necessary when you are only making a small recipe for home use.

Of course, when making low cholesterol cakes, you still must follow the same careful instructions you did for your cakes using shortening, butter, and whole eggs. Some of the most important points to remember are:

1. Read the whole recipe through and be sure you understand it and have all of the ingredients before you start to work.

2. The temperature of the ingredients is very important. All ingredients should be at room temperature unless the recipe specifically states otherwise.

3. Measure exactly, use level measurements and don't vary them the first time you use a recipe.

4. Follow the recipe exactly the first time you use it. If you want to experiment — and I'm all for experimenting with recipes to develop your own version — do it after you have once prepared the recipe exactly as it is written. One of my family's favorite stories is about the time when I was fresh out of college and decided to make my boyfriend a birthday cake. I thought that there was too much liquid in the recipe so I changed it before I used it. Well, that cake was so hard that you couldn't even cut a piece off to soak in coffee. It really taught me a lesson I'll never forget. (The worst part of it was that it looked good so I frosted and served it before discovering what it was like. Then he started to cut it at the birthday party — only he just plain couldn't cut it.)

5. If you want to bake your cake in a different size pan than that shown in the recipe, fill the pan ⅔ full of batter. This is a good point to remember if you want to make cup cakes instead of a layer cake. The baking time will need to be varied with a different size pan, shorter for cupcakes and longer for larger cakes.

6. If you are baking a single cake, put it on the rack in the center of the oven. If you are baking layers, place them on the same rack in the oven if possible, being careful that the pans do not touch each other or the sides of the oven. (You need space for the hot air to circulate around the pans.)

7. Do not open the oven door until the time it should take to bake

the cake if finished. Do not remove your cake from the oven until it is done. Most cakes may be tested by touching the top of the cake near the center. If an indentation remains, the cake is not done and should be baked another 3 to 5 minutes, then tested again. Cakes should not be overbaked either since this will give you a dry cake, which is not very appealing.

8. When your cake is done remove it from the oven and handle it as follows: Angelfood cakes should be inverted until cooled. Do not allow the top of the cake to touch any surface. After the cake is cool, run a knife around the inside of the cake pan and remove the cake onto an inverted pan or a plate sprinkled with white sugar. Brush off loose crumbs and frost or serve with fruit or other toppings. Batter cakes should be cooled on a wire rack for 10 to 15 minutes. (This cooling period is to let the cake set so that it won't fall apart when you take it out of the pan.) Remove cake from the pan onto a wire rack or brown paper sprinkled with white sugar. Frost if desired.

Cakes freeze beautifully. They may be frozen for future use before they are frosted or they may be frosted and then frozen. I like to freeze them first and then wrap them and store them in the freezer. Be careful about the type of frosting you use since an egg white based frosting, such as a seven-minute frosting, does not freeze well, but most powdered sugar frostings freeze beautifully.

Since angelfood cake is such a basic for the low cholesterol diet, this chapter opens with a good recipe for it. The mixes for angelfood cake are so good and so plentiful that few people make them from scratch, but it is a good idea to have a tested basic recipe to use if the need arises.

Another basic type of cake is the white cake, which is decorated and used for birthdays, served plain with fruit for shortcake, used for pineapple upsidedown cake, or made into cupcakes. It is commonly called "butter cake" but since we don't use butter we will make ours with margarine. One thing that cannot be emphasized too often is that when you are buying margarine you must read the list of ingredients. The first of the ingredients should read vegetable oil, soybean oil, cottonseed oil, corn oil or safflower oil. As you know, the ingredients are listed in the order of their quantities on the wrapper and therefore whatever ingredient is listed first is the one which is used in the greatest quantity in that product. Almost all the new soft margarines are good to be used and so are many others, but read the label or you may be defeating your own purpose in using the margarine.

Have you ever tried making a Wacky Cake? Your husband and family will love it and it is tailor made for a low cholesterol diet. This recipe has been around for a long time under various names — Crazy Cake, Wacky Cake, Hurry Up Cake — and all of the names are descriptive. My sister has been making it ever since she first learned to cook and it is very good even if it is a bit unconventional. Many books direct you to combine the dry ingredients in the cake pan, make separate holes for the liquid ingredients, then stir the batter and bake it in the same pan. However, you will find that it is simpler to combine the dry ingredients, then add the liquid, and you get the same results.

Many men feel that no cake can really beat a good chocolate cake. If your husband is one of those men, you can probably make him happy with one of the two recipes in this chapter.

You have probably noticed that some recipes call for sifted flour and others do not mention sifting the flour. Sifted and unsifted flour measure differently so be sure to follow the directions in the recipe. A recipe will not call for sifted flour unless it is important to sift the flour before mixing it with the other ingredients.

You have probably also noted that many recipes call for slightly beaten egg whites. This means to separate the eggs and take a fork and beat the egg whites just a little bit so they are slightly foamy and no longer in one mass.

I think that some of the best cooks in the world are to be found in little towns in the USA. My own heritage is midwestern and I tend to find that food the most satisfying and familiar. Although I enjoy and give due credit to the cooking of all sections of the country, I find that my recipe files are crowded with recipes that mean home to me. One of the cakes I remember best from my childhood in Kamrar, Iowa, is the Applesauce Cake made by my mother's good friend Mrs. Margaret Kennedy.

Remember the Burnt Sugar Cake that your mother used to make in the thirties and forties? Somehow or other you never seem to see it anymore. I guess cakes go out of style like dresses and furniture but this is such a good cake that it would be a shame to forget it. I found my mother's recipe handwritten in an old cookbook. With a few adaptations, it is as good as ever and your husband will probably remember his mother making this cake also.

Most people think that a good cake deserves a good frosting. Of course, plain cake served with fresh or frozen fruit is a very good dessert but there is something about a tall, gorgeous frosting that makes even a simple cake an occasion. Many frostings may be used on a low cholesterol diet since very few of them contain sour cream or other saturated fats. Margarine can be easily substituted for butter in the famous butter cream frostings made with powdered sugar, which we call powdered sugar frosting because who ever heard of a margarine cream frosting. Coconut should not be used because of the saturated fat in it but chopped nuts, candied fruit, raisins, and bright colored candies may all be used to add a little interest to the frostings.

My mother's Hot Water Frosting is one of the simplest frostings to prepare. It has the virtue of being quick as well as delicious. However, it is best to use it on a cake which is to be eaten within a day or so since it does not hold up as well as some of the powdered sugar frostings and it cannot be frozen. As a matter of fact, none of the marshmallow type frostings freeze well. If you plan to freeze your cake it is always best to use a powdered sugar frosting.

A good Powdered Sugar Frosting recipe is always dependable. You can vary it in many ways and add many things to it to make it interesting — in fact, it is a good basic frosting. You probably make a very good one now and if it doesn't use butter or cream you can continue to use it. However if it depends on butter you will want to substitute margarine for the butter and if it uses cream then perhaps you will want to switch to one of the ones in this chapter.

It is always a good idea to have some cookies on hand for packing a lunch or snacking. Very few things are cozier than a cup of tea or a glass of milk and some cookies or you might want to serve them with wine the way the Italians do. You can buy a few cookies which are made without saturated fat and egg yolks such as meringues but you have to be careful since most cookies are made with butter or shortening and whole eggs. Remember not to buy those coconut macaroons, which look so good, since they contain coconut. The ingredients should be checked if you buy packaged cookies and it is not wise to buy cookies at a bakery unless you have discussed the ingredients with the baker. Remember also when you are reading the ingredients list that chocolate chips contain cocoa butter and should not be used, although cocoa may be.

There are many attractive cookie jars these days but I recommend putting flowers in your cookie jar and keeping your cookies in the freezer (or at least your reserve supply). If you are using your cookies for packing lunches you can wrap them in individual portions in aluminum foil before you freeze them. If you use them for snacking they can be kept in a plastic container with a tight cover in the freezer, which is just about as handy as a cookie jar and keeps the cookies a lot fresher.

Cookies are like cakes inasmuch as you can't easily substitute oil and egg whites for butter or shortening and whole eggs. Margarine can be substituted for butter but you need special recipes for cookies made with oil. I hate to think of all of the ingredients I ruined before I finally came up with some cookies that I considered acceptable — the ones in this chapter.

When I was a teenager in Iowa our neighbor Mrs. Blanche Echleberger made the most wonderful old-fashioned cookies. I still remember how the fragrance of those baking cookies filled the air. I had tried to use a couple of her recipes, which were published in a church cookbook, but she made them with eggs and sour cream and I never could come up with an adaptation that I thought did justice to the original recipes. When my mother went out to Iowa to visit last spring she saw Mrs. Echleberger and told her about my struggles with her recipes. Mrs. Echleberger said that she no longer makes those rich cookies herself but she did have a recipe for her old Molasses Cookies that fit into a low cholesterol diet. They are big and round, not too sweet but spicy and awfully good alone or with a glass of milk or a dish of fruit or gelatin. I was so pleased to get the recipe.

If you like a crisper cookie without ginger the Cinnamon Crisps will fill the bill. They are an adaptation of one of Mrs. Echleberger's recipes, which I developed from her molasses cookie recipe.

If your husband has a sweet tooth, he will probably appreciate some fudge. This chapter has two good basic recipes, which can be varied by adding marshmallows, nuts, raisins, or dry cereal. Different flavorings, such as peppermint or run, may also be added for variety.

Cracker Holton always makes dozens and dozens of cookies and pounds and pounds of candy every year at Christmastime. She packs the candy and cookies in boxes (with the help of her family) for many of her friends. Cracker Holton makes a great variety of cookies but she concentrates on only two or three varieties of candy. The most unusual one is, I think, her recipe for Date Nut Candy, which she gave me last year.

Mary Boineau is allergic to chocolate and it is a real affliction for anyone who likes candy as well as she does. She also likes the taste of burnt sugar so I developed a candy with the texture of fudge and her favorite flavor.

angelfood cake

Yield 1 10-inch cake

1¾ cups egg whites (about 12 egg whites)	1½ teaspoons cream of tartar
1¼ cups sifted cake flour	1 cup sugar
¾ cup sugar	½ teaspoon almond flavoring
½ teaspoon salt	1 teaspoon vanilla

Let the egg whites warm to room temperature in a mixer bowl. Sift the flour and ¾ cups sugar together twice. Beat the egg whites with the salt and cream of tartar at a high speed until soft peaks are formed. Add 1 cup sugar gradually, beating it at a high speed to form a meringue. Add the almond flavoring and vanilla to the meringue and mix lightly. Remove the beater from the bowl and add the flour mixture, a quarter at a time, folding it in gently with a wire whisk or rubber scraper. Fold only until the flour mixture is blended into the meringue. Push the batter into an ungreased 10-inch tube pan. Cut gently through the batter to remove air pockets.

Bake in a preheated moderate oven (375°F) for 30 to 35

minutes or until the cake springs back when touched in the center. Invert the cake on a funnel and let it hang until it is completely cold. Carefully loosen the cake from the pan with a spatula and remove it to a cake plate. Serve plain with fresh or frozen fruit or frost with a light frosting, if desired.

This recipe may be doubled or even tripled for a large party. It can be baked in layer pans or in a flat oblong cake pan. Be sure to fill the greased and floured pans ⅔ full of batter and bake it longer for a thicker cake.

white birthday cake

Yields 2 9-inch layers

2¼ cups cake flour
2½ teaspoons baking powder
⅓ cup instant dry milk
¼ teaspoon salt
½ cup (1 stick) softened margarine

1 cup sugar
1 teaspoon vanilla
4 egg whites
⅔ cup lukewarm water

Sift the flour, baking powder, instant dry milk, and salt together twice. Cream the margarine until light and add the sugar gradually, creaming them together until very light and fluffy. Add the vanilla and blend well. Add the egg whites one at a time, beating well after each addition. (Beat about 5 minutes altogether.) Add all of the flour mixture and all of the water to the creamed mixture and mix at a low speed for 2 minutes. Scrape the mixture from the sides and bottom of the bowl and continue to beat for another minute. Pour half of the batter into each of two greased and floured 9-inch cake pans and bake in a preheated moderate oven (350°F) for about 35 minutes, or until the cake springs back when touched in the center.

Variation

Nut Cake: Add ½ cup chopped nuts to cake batter and blend lightly just before the batter is poured into pans.

walnut applesauce cake

Yields 1 10-inch tube cake

2 cups sugar
1 cup (2 sticks margarine)
2½ cups applesauce
2 cups all purpose flour
1½ cups graham flour
1 tablespoon baking soda
1 teaspoon ground cinnamon
1 teaspoon ground nutmeg
2 cups light seedless raisins
2 cups chopped English or
    black walnuts

Cream sugar and margarine together until light and fluffy. Add applesauce and beat 1 minute at medium speed. Stir flours, soda, cinnamon and nutmeg together to blend. Add flour mixture to creamed mixture and beat 4 minutes at medium speed. Add raisins and nuts and mix lightly.

Spread batter in a 10-inch tube pan which has been well greased with margarine. Bake in a preheated moderate (375° F.) oven for 1 hour and 15 minutes or until a cake tester comes out clean. Cool 15 minutes in the pan and then turn out on a wire rack to cool completely. The cake may be served without frosting or frosted with a simple powdered sugar frosting.

This recipe may be doubled and baked in an 11- × 14-inch pan if your family eats lots of cake or if you want to frost it and take it along to a party or a picnic.

wacky cake

Yields 1 9-inch square cake

1½ cups all purpose flour
3 tablespoons cocoa
1 cup sugar
1 tablespoon vinegar
1 teaspoon vanilla
1 cup cold water

½ teaspoon salt   ⅓ cup vegetable oil
1 teaspoon baking soda

Sift the flour, cocoa, sugar, salt, and soda together in a mixer bowl.
Add the vinegar, vanilla, water, and oil to the flour mixture. Beat
the batter at a moderate speed for 2 minutes. Pour the batter into
a greased and floured 9-inch square pyrex cake pan and bake it
in a preheated moderate oven (350°F) for 40 minutes, or until
the cake springs back when touched in the center.

chocolate cake

Yields 2 9-inch layers

½ cup (1 stick) margarine   ½ cup cocoa
1½ cups sugar   1 teaspoon baking powder
1 teaspoon vanilla   1 teaspoon baking soda
3 egg whites   ¼ teaspoon salt
2 cups cake flour   2 tablespoons vinegar
¼ cup instant dry milk   ¾ cups water

Cream the margarine until light and fluffy. Add the sugar and
continue to cream until light and fluffy. Add the vanilla and mix
well. Add the egg whites and mix well. Sift together the flour,
instant dry milk, cocoa, baking powder, soda, and salt. Combine
the vinegar and water. Add all of the flour mixture and all of the
vinegar mixture to the batter and beat it at a moderate speed for
2 minutes. Scrape down the bowl and beat the batter for another
minute. Pour half of the batter into each of two greased and floured
9-inch cake pans. Bake in a preheated moderate oven (375°F)
for 30 to 35 minutes, or until cake springs back when touched in
the center.

cocoa buttermilk cake

Yields 1 9-inch square cake

2 cups all purpose flour   ½ cup water
1½ cups sugar   ⅓ cup vegetable oil

2 tablespoons instant dry milk
1 teaspoon baking soda
1 teaspoon baking powder
¼ cup cocoa
¾ cup low fat buttermilk
2 slightly beaten egg whites
1 teaspoon vanilla

Sift the flour, sugar, instant dry milk, soda, and baking powder together into a mixing bowl. Combine the water, oil, and cocoa in a small saucepan. Stir and heat to boiling over a low heat. Boil for ½ minute, then add the cocoa mixture to flour mixture and mix until smooth. Add the buttermilk, egg whites, and vanilla, and beat for about 2 minutes at a medium speed or until smooth. Pour the batter into a greased 9-inch square pyrex cake pan and bake in a preheated moderate oven (350°F) for 30 to 35 minutes, or until cake springs back when touched in the center.

A poppyseed filling is generally available in Polish or Bohemian neighborhoods in our area. It is a combination of ground poppyseeds with sugar and other ingredients. I really don't know if there is any acceptable substitute but it is such a good recipe that I am including it in the hopes that you can get the filling and thus enjoy this very good cake.

Frances Nielsen's poppyseed cake

4 egg whites
⅔ cup oil
2 cups sugar
1½ cups poppyseed filling
1 14½ ounce can of evaporated skim milk
3 cups all purpose flour
1½ teaspoons baking soda
1 teaspoon baking powder

Combine the egg whites and oil and beat together until thick. Add the sugar and beat at a medium speed for 1 minute. Add the poppyseed filling and beat at a medium speed until well mixed.

Add evaporated skim milk, flour, soda, and baking powder. (Pour the milk right out of the can.) Beat for 4 minutes at a medium speed. Scrape the bottom of the bowl and then beat the batter for another minute. Pour the batter into a well-greased 10-inch tube pan and bake it in a preheated moderate oven (375°F) for 1 hour. Let the cake cool and then turn it out onto a cake plate and frost.

This cake may also be baked in three 9-inch layer cake pans. If baked this way it is good filled with a tart jelly and frosted with a powdered sugar frosting.

This is good served warm with applesauce or cold with a whipped milk or marshmallow topping.

gingerbread

Yields 1 9-inch square gingerbread

1 cup light molasses	2¼ cups all purpose,flour
1½ cups boiling water	⅓ cup instant dry milk
1 teaspoon baking soda	1 tablespoon baking powder
½ cup (1 stick) margarine	
1 cup sugar	½ teaspoon salt
2 slightly beaten egg whites	1 teaspoon ground ginger
	2 teaspoons ground cinnamon

Combine the molasses, boiling water, and soda in a bowl, stir well to mix, and let cool to lukewarm. (You need a bowl for this because it is going to foam up and take a lot more room than you have in a measuring cup.)

Cream the margarine and sugar together until light. Add the molasses mixture and blend well. Add the egg whites and blend well. Sift the flour, instant dry milk, baking powder, salt, ginger, and cinnamon together into the mixer bowl and beat at medium speed for 2 minutes. Pour the batter into a greased 9-inch square pyrex pan and bake it in a preheated moderate oven (375°F) for

35 to 40 minutes, or until gingerbread springs back when touched in the center.

Mrs. Kennedy's applesauce cake

Yields 1 10-inch tube cake

2 cups sugar	3½ cups all purpose flour
¾ cup vegetable oil	1 tablespoon cocoa
2 cups applesauce	1 teaspoon ground cinnamon
1 tablespoon baking soda	½ teaspoon ground cloves
1 cup washed and drained raisins	½ teaspoon ground allspice
1 cup chopped nuts	

Combine the sugar and oil in a mixing bowl. Combine the applesauce and soda and add them to the sugar mixture. Beat them at a medium speed for 1 minute. Add the raisins and nuts. Sift the flour, cocoa, cinnamon, cloves, and allspice together into the mixing bowl and beat at a medium speed for 2 minutes. Pour the batter into a greased and floured 10-inch tube cake pan and bake in a preheated moderate oven (350°F) for 70 minutes. Let the cake cool in the pan and then remove onto cake plate or rack.

burnt sugar cake

Yields 1 9-inch square cake

½ cup sugar	2 egg whites
1 cup boiling water	2¾ cups sifted cake flour
¾ cup (1½ sticks) margarine	1 tablespoon baking powder
1 cup sugar	¼ teaspoon salt
1 teaspoon vanilla	⅓ cup instant dry milk

Melt ½ cup sugar in a heavy saucepan, stirring it constantly with a wooden spoon until it is a rich caramel color. Remove the caramel from the heat and add the boiling water. Return the caramel to the heat and continue to stir over a low heat until the sugar and water are thoroughly mixed and there are no lumps of caramelized sugar left in the pan. Set aside to cool.

Cream the margarine, 1 cup sugar, and vanilla together until light and fluffy. Add the egg whites to the creamed mixture and beat them at a medium speed until well blended. Sift the flour, baking powder, salt, and instant dry milk together. Add the flour mixture alternately with the caramelized sugar mixture to the creamed mixture. Beat at a moderate speed for about 2 minutes or until well blended. Pour the batter into a greased and floured 9-inch square pyrex cake pan and bake in a moderate oven (350°F) for 30 to 35 minutes, or until cake springs back when touched in the center.

A Burnt Sugar Cake wouldn't be complete without a luscious calorie filled frosting to go with it.

burnt sugar frosting·

Frosts 1 9-inch square cake

¾ cup sugar	¼ teaspoon cream of tartar
¾ cup boiling water	¼ teaspoon salt
2 egg whites	¼ cup sugar

Melt ¾ cup sugar in a heavy saucepan, stirring it constantly with a wooden spoon until it is a rich caramel color. Remove the caramel from the heat and add the boiling water. Return the caramel to the heat and continue to stir it over a low heat until the sugar and water are thoroughly mixed and there are no lumps of caramelized sugar left in the pan. Continue to cook the sugar syrup over a low heat until it forms a soft ball in cold water or until it registers 238°F on a candy thermometer.

Beat the egg whites with the cream of tartar and salt until foamy. Gradually beat ¼ cup sugar into the egg whites to form a meringue. Beating constantly at high speed, gradually pour the hot syrup over the meringue. Continue beating until the frosting is completely cool and stiff. (This frosting does not freeze well.)

This is an adaptation of Savarin dough and may also be used as a basis for Babas Au Rhum.

rum cake

Yields 1 9-inch tube or Bundt cake

1 cup warm water	4 slightly beaten egg whites
1 ounce compressed yeast	3 cups all purpose flour
¼ cup sugar	¼ cup instant dry milk
½ teaspoon salt	¾ cup (1½ sticks) softened margarine

Combine the water, compressed yeast, and sugar in a mixing bowl. Let it stand for about 5 minutes to develop the yeast. Add the salt and egg whites and blend. Add the flour and instant dry milk and beat hard for 8 minutes. (This beating must be done by hand because it is too stiff a dough for a mixer unless you have one with a dough hook — and you must really beat it to develop the gluten in the flour.) Cover the bowl and let the batter rise until doubled in volume. Beat the softened margarine into the batter until well blended. Pour the batter into a well-greased 9-inch tube or Bundt cake pan. Cover the dough and let it rise until almost doubled in volume. Bake the cake in a preheated 400°F oven for 10 minutes, reduce the heat to 350°F and continue to bake for another 40 minutes or until golden brown.

Remove cake onto a wire rack and let it stand until lukewarm. Pour the rum syrup into bottom of pan in which cake was baked. Put cake back into pan and let it stand for about 30 minutes to absorb the syrup.

This cake is traditionally served with whipped cream but that is now out. So serve it with sweetened whipped instant dry or evaporated skim milk. The cake is best slightly warmed with the whipped topping very cold — umm it is really good.

rum syrup

1¼ cups sugar	½ cup water
½ cup white corn syrup	¼ cup rum

Combine the sugar, syrup, and water in a heavy saucepan. Stir over a low heat until the sugar is dissolved. When it looks clear, wash down sides of the pan with a brush dipped in cold water. Put the lid on the saucepan and simmer for 5 minutes so that the steam will dissolve any remaining sugar crystals. Remove the lid, raise the heat and boil for 5 minutes without stirring. Cool slightly, add the rum and pour into the bottom of cake pan.

Variation

Chocolate Fudge Cake: Prepare basic recipe using 2½ cups of flour and ½ cup cocoa. Add the cocoa with the flour. Slice the cake and serve with the cocoa sauce instead of soaking the cake with rum syrup.

cocoa sauce

Yields 1⅘ cups

½ cup brown sugar	½ cup cocoa
½ cup sugar	2 tablespoons (¼ stick)
½ cup white corn syrup	margarine
½ cup water	1 teaspoon vanilla

Combine the sugars, syrup, water, and cocoa. Simmer over a low heat for 5 minutes. Remove the mixture from the heat, add the margarine and vanilla and serve warm.

Mom's hot water frosting

Frosts 1 9-inch layer or cake square

1　egg white
¾　cup sugar
¼　teaspoon cream of tartar

1　teaspoon vanilla
¼　cup boiling water

Combine the egg white, sugar, cream of tartar, and vanilla in a mixer bowl. Start the mixer at high speed and gradually add the boiling water to the egg white mixture. Whip until it stands in stiff peaks and is cool.

It is worth taking the time and effort to cook the syrup for this recipe, which makes a really impressive frosting for a cake. Try it for your next birthday cake and see how everyone thinks it is the greatest.

marshmallow frosting

Frosts 1 9-inch layer cake

⅔　cup sugar
½　cup water
1　tablespoon white corn
　　syrup
3　egg whites

1　teaspoon cream of tartar
⅓　cup sugar
1　teaspoon vanilla

Combine ⅔ cup sugar, water, and corn syrup in a heavy saucepan. Stir over a low heat until the sugar is dissolved. Raise the heat and cook without stirring until a few drops form a soft ball in cold water or until it registers 238°F on a candy thermometer. Beat the egg whites with the cream of tartar until foamy. Gradually beat ⅓ cup sugar into the egg whites to form a meringue. Beating constantly at high speed, gradually pour the hot syrup over the meringue. Continue beating until the frosting is completely cool and stiff. Add the vanilla.

powdered sugar frosting

Frosts 1 9-inch layer cake

½ cup (1 stick) softened margarine
3 cups sifted powdered sugar
¼ teaspoon salt
1 tablespoon instant dry milk
2 to 3 tablespoons water
1 teaspoon vanilla

Cream the softened margarine until light and fluffy. Combine the powdered sugar, salt, and instant dry milk together and gradually beat them into the margarine. Add water as necessary and beat until light. Add the vanilla. This frosting may be kept in the refrigerator for quite a long time or it may be used on a cake to be frozen since it freezes very well.

Sue Myers' cocoa fudge frosting

Frosts 1 9-inch layer cake

1 pound package powdered sugar
½ cup cocoa
½ cup (1 stick) softened margarine
1 teaspoon vanilla
2 tablespoons water
¼ cup white corn syrup

Combine the powdered sugar, cocoa, margarine, and vanilla in a mixer bowl. Combine the water and syrup and heat them to simmering, but do not boil. Add the hot syrup to the sugar mixture and beat at a low speed for 3 minutes or until smooth and glossy. (It is best to use this frosting while it is still warm. It will spread when it is cool but it won't be as glossy.)

sugar cookies

Yields 2½ dozen 3-inch cookies

3 egg whites
⅔ cup vegetable oil
2 teaspoons vanilla
1 teaspoon grated lemon rind

¾ cup sugar
2 cups all purpose flour
2 teaspoons baking powder
½ teaspoon salt

Combine the egg whites, oil, vanilla, and lemon rind and mix well. Beat the sugar into the egg whites until the mixture is thick. Combine the flour, baking powder, and salt and sift together into sugar mixture. Mix well. Drop the batter by teaspoonsful about 2 inches apart onto ungreased cookie sheet. Press each cookie flat with the bottom of a glass that has been moistened with water and dipped into sugar. Bake in a preheated hot oven (400°F) for 8 to 10 minutes or until lightly browned. Remove from cookie sheet onto wire rack while still warm.

oatmeal cookies

Yields 2½ dozen cookies

½ cup (1 stick) margarine
½ cup brown sugar
¼ cup white sugar
2 slightly beaten egg whites
1 teaspoon vanilla
¾ cup all purpose flour

½ teaspoon baking soda
½ teaspoon salt
1 cup rolled oats
½ cup chopped nuts
½ cup washed and drained raisins

Cream the margarine and sugars together until light and fluffy. Add the egg whites and vanilla and mix well. Sift the flour, soda, and salt together into a mixing bowl, and blend well. Add the oatmeal, nuts, and raisins and mix well. Drop the batter by teaspoonsful onto a lightly greased cookie sheet. Bake in a pre-heated moderate (375°F) oven for about 10 to 12 minutes or until lightly browned. Remove from cookie sheet while still warm.

shortbread cookies

Yields 4 dozen

1 cup softened margarine
1½ cups sugar

2½ cups sifted all purpose flour
½ teaspoon butter flavoring

Cream the margarine until light and fluffy. Add the sugar and continue to cream until light and fluffy. Add the flour and butter flavoring and mix with a spoon until well combined. Cover and refrigerate for 4 to 6 hours. Divide the dough into two parts and keep them refrigerated until ready to roll and cut. Roll half of the dough at a time about ⅓ inch thick on a lightly floured board. Cut with a 2-inch cutter. Place the cookies, about 1 inch apart, on ungreased cookie sheets. Bake in preheated cool oven (300°F) for about 25 minutes or until golden. Remove the cookies from cookie sheets onto wire rack while still warm.

Cheerio bars

Yields 16 bars

3 tablespoons margarine
½ pound marshmallows
4 cups Cheerios

½ cup coarsely chopped nuts
½ teaspoon salt

Combine the margarine and marshmallows in the top of a double boiler, and melt them over hot water, stirring occasionally. Remove them from the heat and add the cheerios, nuts, and salt. Put the Cheerio mixture into a greased 8-inch square pyrex cake pan. Pat the mixture out evenly and chill for about 30 to 45 minutes or until set. Cut the bars in squares, 4 × 4 inches.

chocolate nut cookies

Yields 2½ dozen 3-inch cookies

¼ cup (½ stick) margarine
1 cup sugar
1¾ cups all purpose flour
¼ cup cocoa
1 teaspoon soda

¼ teaspoon cinnamon
⅛ teaspoon salt
½ cup reconstituted instant milk
½ cup chopped pecans

Cream the margarine and sugar together until light and fluffy. Sift the flour, cocoa, soda, cinnamon, and salt together into a mixer bowl. Add the reconstituted instant milk and pecans and mix until well blended. Drop the batter by tablespoonsful onto a lightly greased cookie sheet. Bake in preheated moderate oven (350°F) for 10 to 12 minutes. Remove the cookies from the cookie sheet while they are still warm.

pecan balls

Yields 4 dozen cookies

1 cup margarine
⅓ cup sugar
1 tablespoon water
1 teaspoon vanilla

2 cups sifted all purpose flour
1 cup chopped pecans
1 cup powdered sugar

Cream the margarine and sugar until light and fluffy. Add the water and vanilla and mix well. Add the flour and pecans and mix well. Chill the dough for 3 to 4 hours. Shape the dough into balls by the tablespoonful. Bake them on an ungreased cookie sheet in a preheated slow oven (325°F) for about 20 minutes. Cool slightly and roll in powdered sugar.

pecan macaroons

Yields 3 dozen cookies

4 egg whites
1 cup sugar

1 teaspoon vanilla
1 cup finely ground pecans

Beat the egg whites at a high speed until stiff. Add the sugar gradually, beating to form a meringue. Add the vanilla and nuts and mix well by hand but do not beat again. Drop by tablespoonsful onto a greased cookie sheet. Bake in a preheated slow oven (225°F) 45 minutes. Remove the cookies from the cookie sheet and cool on wire rack.

These cookies are good for lunches. They're hearty and spicy. They'll appeal to the men in your life and the women too.

applesauce raisin cookies

Yields 3 dozen cookies

½ cup (1 stick) margarine
½ cup brown sugar
½ cup sugar
1 cup applesauce
2 cups sifted all purpose
   flour
1 teaspoon ground
   cinnamon

½ teaspoon ground nutmeg
1 teaspoon baking soda
2 teaspoons baking powder
2 cups rolled oats
1 cup washed and drained
   raisins

Cream the margarine and sugars until light and fluffy. Add the applesauce to the creamed mixture. Sift the flour, cinnamon, nutmeg, soda, and baking powder together and add to the applesauce mixture. Add the rolled oats and raisins. Drop by tablespoonsful onto a lightly greased cookie sheet. Bake in a preheated moderate oven (375°F) for about 10 to 12 minutes. Remove the cookies from the cookie sheet while still warm onto wire rack.

Mrs. Echleberger's molasses cookies

Yields about 4 dozen 3-inch cookies

1 cup (2 sticks) margarine	1 tablespoon baking soda
1 cup sugar	1 teaspoon ground ginger
1 cup molasses	1 teaspoon ground
5½ cups all purpose flour	cinnamon
	1 cup boiling water

Cream the margarine with the sugar until light and fluffy. Add the molasses and mix well. Sift the flour, soda, ginger, and cinnamon together and add to the creamed mixture alternately with the water. Mix at a low speed for about 4 minutes to form a soft dough. Roll the dough about ¼ inch thick on a lightly floured board. Cut the cookies with a 3-inch cutter and bake on a lightly greased cookie sheet in a preheated moderate oven (350°F) for 15 minutes. Remove the cookies from the pan while warm onto a wire rack.

cinnamon crisps

Yields 3 dozen 3-inch cookies

1 cup (2 sticks) margarine	1 tablespoon baking soda
1 cup sugar	1 teaspoon ground
1 cup molasses	cinnamon
4½ cups all purpose flour	¾ cup boiling water

Cream the margarine with the sugar until light and fluffy. Add the molasses and mix well. Sift the flour, soda, and cinnamon together, add to the creamed mixture alternately with the water, and mix at a low speed for about 4 minutes to form a soft dough. Roll the dough about ¼ inch thick on a lightly floured board. Cut the cookies with a 3-inch cutter and bake on a lightly greased cookie sheet in a preheated moderate oven (350°F) for 15 minutes. Remove the cookies from the pan while warm onto a wire rack.

date squares

Yields 36 squares

¾ cup pitted dates
1½ cups water
¾ cup sugar
1 cup (2 sticks) margarine
2 cups brown sugar

2¼ cups rolled oats
2½ cups all purpose flour
1½ teaspoons baking soda
1 teaspoon salt
2 teaspoons vanilla

Combine the dates, water, and sugar in a heavy saucepan and cook over low heat, stirring constantly, until thick. Remove the dates from the heat and cool.

Combine the margarine, brown sugar, rolled oats, flour, soda, salt, and vanilla and mix until it has a crumbly texture. Divide the oatmeal mixture in half. Spread half of the mixture evenly over the bottom of a greased 13- × 10-inch cake pan. Pour the date mixture into pan and spread over oatmeal mixture. Spread remaining half of oatmeal mixture over the filling, and pat down so that it is smooth on top. Bake the squares in a preheated moderate oven (350°F) for 25 to 30 minutes, or until lightly browned. Cut into 6-inch squares while still warm.

Frances Sonitzky's cocoa fudge brownies

Yields 12 brownies

⅔ cup all purpose flour
½ teaspoon baking powder
½ teaspoon salt
1 tablespoon instant dry milk
6 tablespoons cocoa

1 cup sugar
⅓ cup vegetable oil
½ cup water
2 well-beaten egg whites
¾ cup chopped nuts

Sift the flour, baking powder, salt, instant dry milk, cocoa, and sugar together into mixing bowl. Add the oil and water and beat at a medium speed until smooth. Fold the egg whites and nuts into the batter and pour it into a greased 9-inch square pyrex cake pan. Bake the brownies in a preheated slow oven (325°F) for 35 to 40 minutes, or until firm to the touch. Cut the brownies into 4-inch squares while warm but not hot.

brownie cupcakes

Yields 16 cupcakes

¾ cup cocoa
2 tablespoons instant dry milk
1½ cups sugar
1½ cups all purpose flour
½ teaspoon baking powder
4 egg whites
1 tablespoon vanilla
⅔ cup vegetable oil
1½ cups chopped pecans

Sift the cocoa, instant dry milk, sugar, flour, and baking powder together into a mixing bowl. Combine the egg whites, vanilla, and vegetable oil, and beat with rotary beater until well blended. Add the egg white mixture and nuts to the flour mixture and stir only until well blended (do not beat). Spoon the batter into foil-lined cupcake pans and bake them in a preheated moderate oven (350°F) for 30 to 35 minutes. (You can also spread the batter out into a 10- × 13-inch pan and bake about the same length of time.)

cocoa fudge

Yields 2½ pounds

4 cups sugar
½ cup cocoa
½ cup instant dry milk
½ cup (1 stick) margarine
¾ cup water
¼ teaspoon salt
2 teaspoons vanilla

Combine the sugar, cocoa, instant dry milk, margarine, water, and salt in a heavy saucepan, and mix lightly. Simmer the fudge over a low heat until it registers 238°F on a candy thermometer or forms a soft ball in cold water. Remove the fudge from the heat and add the vanilla. Cool the fudge until the bottom of the saucepan feels lukewarm to your hand. (If you beat the fudge while it is hot, the candy will be grainy.) Beat the candy until it loses its gloss and then pour it quickly into a well-greased pan. Cut the fudge when cool.

Mrs. Edwin Myers' white fudge

Yields 2½ pounds

4 cups sugar	½ cup (1 stick) margarine
¾ cup instant dry milk	1 teaspoon vanilla
1½ cups water	¼ cup candied cherries
¼ teaspoon salt	¼ cup chopped nuts

Combine the sugar, instant dry milk, water, salt, and margarine in a heavy saucepan, and mix lightly. Simmer the candy over a low heat until it registers 238°F on a candy thermometer or forms a soft ball in cold water. Remove the fudge from the heat and add the vanilla. Cool the fudge until the bottom of the pan feels lukewarm to your hand. Beat the candy until it begins to lose its gloss, add the cherries and nuts, and mix lightly, then pour quickly into a well-greased pan. Cut the fudge into squares when cool. It may be refrigerated or frozen until served.

Cracker Holton's date nut candy

Yields 5 to 6 pounds

3 cups sugar	1 tablespoon margarine
2 cups chopped pitted dates	⅔ cup instant dry milk
¾ cup water	2 to 3 pounds powdered
1 cup chopped nuts	sugar

Combine the sugar, dates, and water in a heavy saucepan and cook over a low heat, stirring constantly, until it registers 240°F on a candy thermometer. Remove the dates from the heat and cool to lukewarm. Add the margarine and nuts, mix well, and cool until it can be handled. Combine the instant dry milk with 1 pound powdered sugar. Put sugar milk mixture on a breadboard and add the cooked mixture. Knead the sugar mixture into the cooked mixture as you would add flour to a bread dough. Continue to knead and add powdered sugar until the candy will no longer easily absorb the sugar. Roll the candy into rolls about 1 inch thick and about 6 inches long. Refrigerate the candy until well chilled, cut into serving size pieces, and wrap each piece individually. If you want to do so you can wrap a whole roll and tuck it into a package of cookies or candy.

Mary's burnt sugar candy

Yields 1¾ pounds

1 cup sugar
1 cup boiling water
2 cups sugar

½ cup (1 stick) margarine
⅛ teaspoon salt
¼ cup instant dry milk

Cook 1 cup sugar in a heavy saucepan over a low heat, stirring constantly, until it is dark and liquid. Add the boiling water and stir constantly over a low fire until the sugar is dissolved in the water. Add 2 cups sugar, margarine, and salt and cook over low heat until it registers 238°F on a candy thermometer or forms a soft ball in cold water. Remove the candy from the heat and stir the instant dry milk into it. Cool it until the bottom of the saucepan feels lukewarm to your hand. Beat the candy until it begins to lose its gloss, then pour it quickly into a well-greased pan. Cut the candy when cool.

200

chapter XI

pies and puddings

Pies are not usually included in a low cholesterol diet — or most other diets, for that matter, because they are high in calories. If your husband's doctor has not told him to lose weight, a recipe or two would be useful to have, in case he gets a sudden yearning for pie. There is an amazing variety of pies and most of them can be prepared for a low cholesterol diet once you have mastered the art of making a good pie crust with oil or margarine instead of hydrogenated fat.

It is not wise to buy a frozen pie or a pie from a bakery unless you are sure of the ingredients, since pie crust is generally made with lard or hydrogenated fats. I've never found a bakery or frozen pie that could be used, but we shouldn't rule out the possibility. There is always the hope that some alert baker will prepare a crust that you can serve with confidence. Remember that it should be made with vegetable oil or with a margarine that contains a high percentage of vegetable oil. Be sure that it does not use *hydrogenated* vegetable oil as a main ingredient, because once it has been hydrogenated the vegetable oil is no longer an unsaturated fat.

When you are making crusts with vegetable oil or margarine you should still follow the same guidelines you'd use in preparing any good crust.

1. It is important to follow the recipe exactly. Use too much oil or margarine and you'll have a greasy crust, which will be too soft to handle. Use too much flour, salt or water and you'll have a tough crust.
2. Temperature is very important. The water should be cold and the dough should not be allowed to stand in a warm room after it is prepared. Refrigerating the dough after it is mixed is desirable.
3. The dough should never be stretched to fit the pie tin. The dough

will go back to its original size while it is baking and the crust will not fit the pan.

4. Bent or warped pie tins should never be used.
5. The top crust of a fruit or meat pie should always have slits in it to allow steam to escape.
6. Pie shells that are to be baked before filling should be pricked with a fork. This is not necessary if the pie shell is to be filled and then baked.
7. A cooked filling should be allowed to cool before it is poured into a pie crust and baked.
8. Meringue should always touch all of the inside of the crust to prevent it pulling away from the sides of the crust while it is baking.
9. It is important to use the correct baking temperature. If the temperature is too low, the crust will be tough. If the temperature is too high, the crust will brown without cooking in the center.
10. The dough should be handled as little as possible when it is rolled and shaped to fit the pan. Handling it too much will toughen it. Don't limit your pie crust recipes to the traditional type. Try some of the interesting ones in this chapter.

A good thing to remember when your husband asks for pie is that a deep-dish fruit pie with a crisp top crust is very good and has much less crust per person than the traditional pie. They can also be made in little individual casseroles or baking cups. Have you noticed how many people leave the bottom crust on their pie? I'm sure they would be very happy to have a deep dish pie and trade that bottom crust for a lot more filling. You can use a casserole for a deep dish pie or a 9- or 10-inch square pyrex cake pan. Use twice as much filling as you do for a 9-inch pie and the same amount of crust you would use for a 9-inch pie shell. Put the filling in the cake pan. Form the pastry into a square, flute the edges so that the crust is just inside the edge of the cake pan, and bake it at the temperature designated by the original pie filling. Or you can bake little pastry rounds and put them on top of a dessert dish of pudding. The taste is like that of a pie but with a lot less calories.

Fruit pies may be used freely on a low cholesterol diet as long as they are made with one of the crusts in this chapter and without the addition of butter, cream, or other saturated fats — and as long as your husband's doctor isn't telling him to lose weight. Therefore we will concentrate on some pies that are traditionally made with whole eggs. Lemon Meringue Pie and Pumpkin Pie are two favorites, which your husband may have been missing lately. Another holiday pie that should not be used unless you are very sure of the ingredients is mincemeat pie. Mincemeat quite often contains beef fat for flavor and richness. Many people like to serve this pie warm with hard sauce or to add some brandy to the filling before baking it. These pies freeze very well and can be prepared and frozen, then brought out on the day you want to serve them and baked fresh for the holidays. The recipe in this chapter makes a very good Mincemeat, which may be used freely. It will be enough for three or four pies depending upon how thick you like to make your pies.

There are a few recipes for fruit pies that should be included in any recipe book. However, the recipes in this chapter are only a sample of the many fruit pies that may be used in the low cholesterol kitchen. Use your own collection of recipes, with the crusts in this chapter, as long as they do not contain cream, butter, or other saturated fats.

It is not wise to buy a prepared cream pie or to use a packaged pudding mix unless you are sure that the ingredients do not contain any egg yolks or saturated fats. However, if your husband likes cream pies you can use the recipes in this chapter or their variations. Remember that coconut is forbidden but nuts, bananas, pineapple, and other fruits and flavorings may be used.

I have a theory about puddings. I think that they were developed by housewives who wanted to give their families a good, wholesome, inexpensive dessert. Have you ever noticed how many recipes are available for puddings that use only minimal amounts of eggs, cream, and butter? They were the desserts served to the family; the cakes and elaborate desserts were saved for company. So many of them are simple to prepare and use ingredients that are generally on hand in the kitchen. They are extravagant with fruits and nuts, which were probably used in season, and they are very scant on things like cream, butter, and eggs. That may have been the case when the puddings were first made. A great many of them can be used to add an interesting dessert to a low cholesterol meal. The Cocoa Fudge Pudding was a standard dessert in my dormitory when I was in college and I am sure that they are still serving it to the present generation of students. It is rich and gooey, so you would expect it to be full of eggs and butter but it isn't.

There are so many fruit puddings that it is hard to know which ones to choose, especially in the fall with its amazing variety of apples. It is a good idea to feature fruit puddings in the low cholesterol diet and particularly apple puddings, since research seems to indicate that the pectin in apples helps to keep the cholesterol count low. There are so many good apple puddings that I hardly know where to start, but Ozark Pudding is one of the most famous.

My cousin Betty Sniffin knows that we like rhubarb very well. So when we are there she always prepares it in a variety of ways. One glorious year we were there in the spring when the rhubarb is at its best so she gave us a big box of it. We brought it home with us and froze it and enjoyed it for several months. The Rhubarb Squares are a favorite of the many ways she prepares it.

Fruit gelatin is an attractive way to end a meal and it doesn't contain any saturated fats unless you top it with whipped cream. Fresh pineapple is about the only fruit that you can't use with gelatin (an enzyme in the pineapple keeps the gelatin from getting hard). If you are using canned fruits, using the juice as part of the liquid is a good way to add to the flavor of the gelatin. Or course, it also adds calories to the gelatin. There is an almost endless variety of fruit and gelatin combinations that can be used. I'm sure your family has its own favorites and unless they include cream cheese, whipped cream or any other foods with saturated fats, you can continue to use them. One of the easiest gelatins to prepare combines frozen strawberries and strawberry gelatin with bananas.

It is nice to have something to take the place of whipped cream for a topping on puddings, gelatin, or shortcake. Whipped milk may be used or Marshmallow Topping, which keeps very well in the refrigerator for a few days or in the freezer for several months.

You can flavor it as you did whipped cream. One of our favorites is a tablespoon of orange marmalade and 2 tablespoons of rum per quart of topping.

Ice cream should not generally be used because of its high butterfat content. However, if you live in an area where a substitute ice cream made with vegetable oil is available, you can use it as long as your husband can afford the calories. Sherbets and ices are good and generally available. You can also make a frozen custard at home that is very good. There are freezers available at most hardware and department stores, with or without a motor, which have complete directions for freezing ice cream. The same directions may be used for freezing custard. The taste of the frozen custard that you lick off of the dasher when you finish the freezing process is a memory of childhood.

Lena Studley, who lived near my family when I was a child, made the most wonderful ice cream. I can taste it yet. The list of ingredients she used, rich cream and lots of eggs, could never be used on a low cholesterol diet. She used the cream and eggs because they gave a creamy texture to the ice cream by preventing the formation of ice crystals in the ice cream as it was freezing. You can also prevent the formation of ice crystals by adding egg whites, gelatin, or margarine as we have done in the recipes in this chapter. Stirring or beating the ice cream as it is freezing also helps to break up any large ice crystals, so don't neglect this important step.

In addition to the fruit puddings and pies in this chapter, fruit should also be served as a sauce or fresh for dessert. Baked apples are good, but don't forget that spiced peaches, baked pears, dried fruit compote and many other fruit combinations have a place in the low cholesterol diet. Fruit may be used for snacking; it is good for breakfast or dessert, and it is good for you. You can't beat a combination like that.

margarine pastry

Double crust 8- or 9-inch pie:
1½ cups all purpose flour

Single crust 8- or 9-inch pie:
1 cup all purpose flour

¾ teaspoon salt
¾ cup (1½ sticks)
   margarine
½ cup cold water,
   approximately

½ teaspoon salt
½ cup (1 stick)
   margarine
⅓ cup cold water,
   approximately

Sift the flour and salt together into a mixing bowl. Cut the margarine into the flour until it resembles coarse meal. Add the water and mix lightly but thoroughly. Form the pastry into a ball and refrigerate for at least 15 minutes before using.

If you are making a double crust pie use a little more than half of the dough for the bottom crust. Roll the crust out on a lightly floured board, fit bottom crust into the pan, pat out any air bubbles, and fill. Roll the crust out for the top and cover the filling. Cut slits in the top crust to allow steam to escape. Trim ½ inch beyond the edge of the pan. Seal the edges and flute. Bake according to directions with filling.

For a pie shell to be baked before filling, prick the dough in several places. Be sure you have not stretched the dough or it will go back to its original size before it finishes baking. Bake in a preheated hot oven (425°F) for 12 to 15 minutes, or until lightly browned.

oil pastry

Double crust 8- or 9-inch pie:
   1¾ cups all purpose flour
   1 teaspoon salt
   ½ cup vegetable oil
   3 tablespoons cold water

Single crust 8- or 9-inch pie:
   1 cup plus 2 tablespoons
      all purpose flour
   ½ teaspoon salt
   ⅓ cup vegetable oil
   2 tablespoons cold water

Sift the flour and salt together into a mixing bowl. Add the oil and mix thoroughly with a fork. Sprinkle the water on top of the dough and mix well. Press the dough firmly into a ball. If it is too dry to form a ball, add 1 to 2 more tablespoons oil.

If you are making a double crust, use a little more than half of the dough for the bottom crust and a little less than half of the dough for the top crust. Flatten the larger portion slightly and roll out between two aluminum-foil circles. Peel off the top piece of foil. Put the pastry in a pie tin, foil side up. Peel off top piece of foil, pat out any air bubbles, and fill. Roll out the remaining pastry as you did the bottom crust. Put the top crust over a pie filling and cut slits in it to allow steam to escape. Trim ½ inch beyond the edge of the pan. Seal the edges and flute. Bake according to directions of the filling.

For a pie shell to be baked before filling, prick the dough in several places. Bake in a preheated hot oven (425°F) for 12 to 15 minutes, or until lightly browned.

rum pastry

Double crust for 8- or 9-inch pie:
- 1¾ cups all purpose flour
- 1 teaspoon baking powder
- ½ teaspoon salt
- 1 tablespoon sugar
- ¾ cup (1½ sticks) margarine
- 2 tablespoons rum
- 4 tablespoons cold water

Single crust for 8- or 9-inch pie:
- 1 cup plus 2 tablespoons all purpose flour
- ½ teaspoon baking powder
- ¼ teaspoon salt
- 2 teaspoons sugar
- ½ cup (1 stick) margarine
- 1 tablespoon rum
- 3 tablespoons cold water

Combine the flour, baking powder, salt, and sugar, and sift together into a mixing bowl. Cut the margarine into the flour until it resembles a coarse meal. Add the rum and water to the flour mixture and mix lightly but thoroughly.

Use a little more than half of the pastry for the bottom crust and a little less than half for the top crust. (This pastry does not need to be refrigerated unless it is too soft and warm to be handled easily, in which case it should be refrigerated until it is firm enough to handle.) Roll the crust out on a lightly floured board. Fit the bottom crust into the pan, pat out any air bubbles, and fill. Roll the crust out for the top and cover the filling. Cut slits in the top crust to allow steam to escape. Trim ½ inch beyond the edge of the pan. Seal the edges and flute. Bake according to directions of the filling.

For a pie shell, prick the dough in several places if it is to be baked before it is filled. Be sure that you have not stretched the dough or it will go back to its original size before it finishes baking. Bake in a preheated hot oven (425°F) for 12 to 15 minutes or until lightly browned.

Be sure to chop the nuts rather than grinding them. If you grind them you release the oil in the nuts and your results won't be as good because oil doesn't work well with a meringue.

nut meringue crust

Yields 1 9-inch pie crust

1 egg white
¼ cup sugar

1½ cups finely chopped nuts

Beat the egg whites at a high speed until stiff. Add the sugar gradually while beating at a high speed to form a meringue. Fold the chopped nuts into the meringue and spread evenly in a greased 9-inch pie tin, smoothing the meringue up around the sides of the pan. Bake in a preheated moderate oven (350°F) for about 10 minutes, or until lightly browned.

Cool for a few minutes so that it will be easier to handle, then gently remove the crust from the pan and cool it on a wire rack. Fill with a cream filling or fresh berries topped with marshmallow topping.

cornflake crust

Yields 1 8- or 9-inch crust

1½ cups cornflake crumbs
½ cup (1 stick) melted
　　margarine

⅓ cup sugar
1 teaspoon cinnamon

Combine all the ingredients and mix well. Press the mixture firmly against the sides and bottom of a pie tin. Bake for 10 minutes in a preheated moderate oven (350°F). Cool before adding the filling.

Brazil nut crust

Yields 1 8- or 9-inch crust

1½ cups ground brazil nuts
¼ teaspoon nutmeg

2 tablespoons sugar

Combine all the ingredients and mix well. Press the mixture firmly against the sides and bottom of a pie tin. Bake for about 10 minutes in a preheated moderate oven (350°F), or until lightly browned. Cool before adding the filling.

Graham cracker crust

Yields 1 8- or 9-inch crust

1½ cups Graham cracker
      crumbs
3 tablespoons sugar

⅓ cup (⅔ stick) melted
   margarine

Combine the cracker crumbs and sugar in a mixing bowl and mix well. Add the melted margarine and mix well. Press the mixture firmly against the sides and bottom of a pie tin. Bake for 10 minutes in a preheated moderate oven (350°F). Cool before adding the filling.

lemon meringue pie

Yields 1 9-inch pie

1½ cups sugar
⅓ cup cornstarch
2 cups water
4 drops yellow food
   coloring
¼ cup (½ stick) margarine
¼ cup lemon juice

1 tablespoon grated lemon
   rind
1 prebaked 9-inch pie shell
3 egg whites
¼ teaspoon cream of tartar
6 tablespoons sugar
½ teaspoon vanilla

Combine the sugar, cornstarch, water, and yellow food coloring, and stir until smooth. Cook them over a medium heat, stirring constantly, until thick. Continue to cook for 1 minute. Remove the mixture from the stove and add the margarine, lemon juice, and rind. Stir until the margarine is melted, then pour into the prebaked pie shell.

Combine the egg whites and cream of tartar and beat until frothy. Add the sugar gradually and beat at a high speed to form a meringue. Spread the meringue on the pie, being careful to seal the meringue to the edges of the crust so that it will not shrink. Bake the pie in a preheated hot oven (400°F) for 8 or 10 minutes, or until the meringue is lightly browned.

pumpkin pie

Yields 1 9-inch pie

2 cups canned pumpkin
1 cup sugar
1½ cups water
1⅓ cups instant dry milk
1 tablespoon pumpkin pie spice
2 egg whites
½ teaspoon salt
1 9-inch unbaked pie shell

Combine the pumpkin, sugar, water, instant dry milk, pumpkin pie spice, egg whites, and salt. Mix until well blended and pour into an unbaked pie shell. (Be sure that the shell is built up around the edges because this is a deep, generous pie. If you want a more shallow pie, use a 10-inch pie shell.) Bake the pie in a preheated hot oven (425°F) for 50 to 55 minutes, or until a knife will come out clean when dipped in the center.

mincemeat

Yields 3 to 4 quarts

2 quarts chopped green
  tomatoes
1 orange
2½ quarts chopped, firm
  apples
1 tablespoon salt
1 pound seeded raisins

3½ cups brown sugar
2 teaspoons ground
  cinnamon
1 teaspoon ground cloves
1 teaspoon ground ginger
1 teaspoon ground nutmeg
½ cup cider vinegar

Wash and drain the tomatoes, orange, and apples. Core, chop, and measure the tomatoes and mix with the salt. Let the tomatoes stand for 1 hour, drain, cover with boiling water, and let stand for 5 minutes before draining well. Grate the rind of the orange, remove and discard its peel. Chop the pulp and mix with the rind. Prepare and measure the apples. Mix all the ingredients and simmer over a low heat until the tomatoes and apples are tender. Cool and refrigerate until used, or else put into a pie shell and bake in a very hot oven (450°F) for 45 minutes, or until browned.

strawberry chiffon pie

Yields 1 9-inch pie

1 1-pound package frozen
  strawberries
2 tablespoons lemon juice
  Water as necessary
1 3-ounce package straw-
  berry gelatin

⅓ cup instant dry milk
2 cups drained, sieved
  cottage cheese
1 9-inch Graham cracker
  pie shell

Thaw and drain the strawberries, reserving the syrup. Combine the lemon juice, water, and syrup to form 1 cup liquid, and heat to boiling. Stir the gelatin into the hot liquid until thoroughly dissolved. Chill to a jelly-like consistency. Sprinkle the instant dry milk over the gelatin and beat until fluffy and doubled in volume. Fold the sieved cottage cheese and strawberries into gelatin mixture. Pour into the pie shell and chill for at least 1 hour before serving.

glazed strawberry pie

Yields 1 9-inch pie

1 quart fresh strawberries
1 cup sugar
3 tablespoons cornstarch
1 tablespoon margarine
1 9-inch Graham cracker crust

Wash and hull the strawberries. Crush 2 cups of the berries and add enough water to yield 2 cups. Combine the crushed berries with the sugar and cornstarch. Cook over a low heat, stirring constantly, until thick and clear. Slice the remaining berries, add them to the mixture, and continue to cook for 1 minute longer. Add the margarine and cool, then pour into the crust. Chill the pie before serving.

old-fashioned apple pie

Yields 1 9-inch pie

5 cups pared, sliced, tart apples
1 cup sugar
1 tablespoon all purpose flour
¼ teaspoon ground nutmeg
½ teaspoon ground cinnamon
Pastry for a 9-inch 2 crust pie
2 tablespoons margarine

Put the apples in a mixing bowl. Combine the sugar, flour, nutmeg, and cinnamon, and mix into the apples. Arrange the apples in a pie tin over the bottom crust, and sprinkle with any remaining sugar mixture. Dot with the margarine and cover with the top crust. Cut slits in the top crust to allow steam to escape. Trim ½ inch beyond the edge of the pan. Seal the edges together and flute. Bake in a preheated hot oven (425°F) for 40 to 45 minutes, or until crust is browned.

fresh berry pie

Yields 1 9-inch pie

4 cups fresh berries
1½ cups sugar
⅓ cup all purpose flour

½ teaspoon cinnamon
   Pastry for a 9-inch
     2 crust pie
2 tablespoons margarine

Wash and prepare the berries for a pie. Combine the sugar, flour, and cinnamon, and mix lightly through the berries. Pour the berries into a pastry-lined pan. Dot with the margarine and cover with the top crust. Cut slits in the top crust to allow steam to escape. Trim ½ inch beyond the edge of the pan. Seal the edges together and flute. Bake in a preheated hot oven (425°F) 35 to 45 minutes or until juice begins to bubble through slits and crust is browned.

Other canned fruits may be used instead of the cherries in this recipe by substituting their fruit and juice for the cherries and juice and adjusting the sugar to the sweetness of the fruit. If you use blueberries or boysenberries, add 2 tablespoons lemon juice with the filling just before you pour it into the pie tin.

canned cherry pie

Yield 1 9-inch pie

3½ cups drained, pitted
      cherries

½ cup cherry juice
   Red food coloring

1 cup sugar
¼ cup all purpose flour
¼ teaspoon cinnamon
¼ teaspoon nutmeg

(optional)
Pastry for 9-inch 2 crust
pie
1 tablespoon margarine

Drain the cherries well, reserving ½ cup juice. Combine the sugar, flour, cinnamon, nutmeg, reserved cherry juice, and red food coloring in saucepan. Cook over a low heat, stirring constantly, until thickened. Add the cherries to the thickened mixture and mix lightly. Pour into a pastry-lined pan. Dot with the margarine and cover with the top crust. Cut slits in the top crust to allow steam to escape. Trim ½ inch beyond the edge of the pan. Seal the edges together and flute. Bake in a preheated hot oven (425°F) for 35 to 45 minutes, or until juice begins to bubble through slits and crust is browned.

double chocolate cream pie

Yields 1 9-inch pie

2½ cups water
1 cup instant dry milk
1 cup sugar
2 slightly beaten egg whites
¼ cup cornstarch
½ teaspoon salt
¼ cup cocoa

¼ cup (½ stick) margarine
2 teaspoons vanilla
3 egg whites
¼ teaspoon cream of tartar
¼ cup sugar
1 tablespoon cocoa
2 tablespoons sugar

Combine the water, instant dry milk, 1 cup sugar, 2 egg whites, cornstarch, salt, cocoa, and margarine in a heavy saucepan. Simmer over a low heat, stirring constantly, until thickened. Stir and cook for 2 minutes longer. Remove the filling from the heat, add the vanilla, cool slightly, and pour into the pie shell.

Combine 3 egg whites and cream of tartar and beat until frothy. Add ¼ cup sugar gradually, and beat at a high speed to form a meringue. Combine 1 tablespoon cocoa and 2 tablespoons sugar and fold into the meringue. Spread the meringue on the pie being careful to seal the edges of the meringue to the edges of the crust so that it will not shrink while baking. Bake in a preheated hot oven (400°F) for 8 to 10 minutes, or until meringue is lightly browned.

banana cream pie

Yields 1 9-inch pie

2¼ cups water
1 cup instant dry milk
¾ cup sugar
2 slightly beaten egg whites
¼ cup cornstarch
½ teaspoon salt
4 drops yellow food coloring

2 tablespoons margarine
2 teaspoons vanilla
2 large bananas
1 prebaked 8-inch pie shell
2 egg whites
¼ teaspoon cream of tartar
¼ cup sugar

Combine the water, instant dry milk, ¾ cup sugar, 2 egg whites, cornstarch, salt, and yellow food coloring in a heavy saucepan. Simmer over a low heat, stirring constantly, until thickened. Stir and cook for 2 minutes longer. Remove from heat, add the margarine and vanilla and stir lightly until the margarine is melted. Cool, add the sliced bananas, and pour into the pie shell.

Combine 2 egg whites and cream of tartar, and beat until frothy. Add ¼ cup sugar gradually, and beat at a high speed to form a meringue. Spread the meringue on the pie, being careful to seal the meringue to the edges of the crust so that it will not shrink while baking. Bake the pie in a preheated hot oven (425°F) for 8 or 10 minutes, or until meringue is lightly browned.

cocoa fudge pudding

Serves 6 to 8

1 cup sifted all purpose flour	½ cup water
¾ cup sugar	2 tablespoons vegetable oil
2 tablespoons cocoa	1 teaspoon vanilla
2 teaspoons baking powder	1 cup chopped walnuts
½ teaspoon salt	¾ cup brown sugar
2 tablespoons instant dry milk	¼ cup cocoa
	1¾ cups hot water

Sift the flour, sugar, 2 tablespoons cocoa, baking powder, salt, and instant dry milk together into a mixing bowl. Add the water, oil, and vanilla, and mix until smooth. Stir the walnuts into the batter and pour it into a greased 8-inch square pan. Combine the brown sugar, ¼ cup cocoa, and 1¾ cups hot water, and pour over the top of the batter. Bake in a preheated moderate oven (350°F) for 45 minutes or until the cake portion springs back when touched in the center. It may be served slightly warmed or chilled.

(This recipe may be doubled and baked in a 13- × 10-inch cake pan if your family really goes for pudding.)

This pudding may be baked ahead of time and reheated in a slow oven if you expect to be busy at the last minute. You can serve this pudding plain, but a hard sauce really adds something to it.

Frances Sonitzky's date pudding

Serves 9

1 teaspoon baking soda	1 tablespoon softened margarine
1 cup chopped dates	

1 cup boiling water
1 cup sugar
1 cup cake flour

1 cup chopped English
  walnuts
2 slightly beaten egg whites

Sprinkle the soda over the dates. Add the boiling water and let it stand until cool. Combine the sugar and flour. Add the margarine and mix until smooth. Add the dates to the flour mixture and mix lightly. Add the egg whites and nuts and mix well. Pour into a greased 9-inch square pyrex cake pan and bake in a slow oven (300°F) for 40 minutes. Serve with hard sauce.

hard sauce

⅓ cup (⅔ stick) margarine
1 cup sifted powdered sugar

1 teaspoon vanilla
⅛ teaspoon salt

Cream the margarine until light colored and smooth. Add the powdered sugar and beat until light and fluffy. Add the vanilla and salt and mix well. Serve well-chilled over a hot pudding.

Some people consider cheese cake to be a cake but it has always seemed to me to be more of a pudding so we will include it in this section. But wherever you include it, it is wonderful.

pineapple cheese cake

Serves 8

¾ cup Graham cracker
  crumbs
3 tablespoons sugar
2 tablespoons (¼ stick)
  melted margarine
1 tablespoon vegetable oil
1 3-ounce package
  pineapple gelatin
1 cup boiling water

1½ pounds washed cottage
  cheese
¼ cup sugar
½ teaspoon salt
1 cup crushed pineapple
  with juice
1 tablespoon water
2 teaspoons cornstarch

Combine the Graham cracker crumbs, 3 tablespoons sugar, margarine, and oil. Mix well and press firmly onto bottom of an 8-inch springform pan and chill.

Add the gelatin to the boiling water and stir until the gelatin is thoroughly dissolved. Combine the cottage cheese, ¼ cup sugar, and salt, and mix until well blended. Pour the cottage cheese mixture into the gelatin mixture and blend well. Pour the cheese mixture into the crust and chill until firm. Combine crushed pineapple, water, and cornstarch. Stir and cook the pineapple over a low flame until thickened and clear. Remove from the heat and cool for 15 minutes. Spread the pineapple mixture over the cheese mixture and chill for at least another hour before serving.

Ozark pudding

Serves 9

3 egg whites
1 cup plus 2 tablespoons
   sugar
¾ cup all purpose flour
1½ teaspoons baking powder

¼ teaspoon salt
1 cup chopped apples
½ cup chopped nuts
1 teaspoon vanilla

Beat the egg whites until frothy and add the sugar gradually, beating at a low speed. Sift the flour, baking powder, and salt together into the egg white mixture and blend well. Fold the apples, nuts, and vanilla into the pudding and pour into a greased and floured 9-inch square pyrex cake pan. Bake in a preheated moderate oven (350°F) for 30 to 35 minutes. Serve warm with cold milk.

blueberry betty

Serves 6

4 cups day-old bread cubes
¾ cup (1½ sticks) melted
   margarine

2 cups fresh or frozen
   blueberries
2 tablespoons lemon juice

¼ cup sugar   ½ cup brown sugar
1 teaspoon ground allspice

Combine the bread cubes, margarine, sugar, and allspice and mix lightly but well. Sprinkle the berries with lemon juice and brown sugar. Alternate layers of bread cubes and blueberries, with bread cubes on the bottom and on the top, in a greased 9-inch square pyrex cake pan. Bake in a preheated moderate oven (350°F) for 20 to 30 minutes, or until bubbly. Serve warm or chilled.

raspberry crisp

Serves 6

1 quart fresh raspberries   ⅓ cup flour
⅓ cup white sugar   ⅓ cup brown sugar
¼ cup (½ stick) margarine   ¾ cup rolled oats

Put the raspberries in bottom of a 9-inch square pyrex cake pan and sprinkle with the white sugar. Mix the margarine, flour, brown sugar, and rolled oats until it resembles a coarse meal. Sprinkle the flour mixture over the raspberries and bake in a preheated moderate oven (350°F) for about 30 minutes, or until lightly browned. Serve warm or chilled.

rhubarb squares

Serves 12

6 cups washed rhubarb   ½ teaspoon salt
2 tablespoons water   2 cups rolled oats
2 cups sugar   1⅓ cups brown sugar
⅓ cup cornstarch   1 cup (2 sticks) melted
2 cups flour   margarine
1 teaspoon baking soda

Cut the rhubarb into about 1-inch pieces. Combine the rhubarb and water in a heavy sauce pan. Cover it and cook over low heat until the rhubarb is soft. Stir the sugar and cornstarch together and add to the rhubarb; cook and stir until thickened. Sift the flour, soda, and salt together. Add the rolled oats, brown sugar, and melted margarine and mix with your hands until it is the texture of coarse meal.

Put ⅔ of the crumb mixture into the bottom of a 10- × 13-inch cake pan. Spread the rhubarb sauce over the crumb layer and top with the remaining crumbs. Bake the squares in a preheated moderate oven (350°F) for 30 to 35 minutes, or until lightly browned.

Try to get Rome Beauty apples for this recipe if it is at all possible. Other baking apples will make a good apple dumpling but for a really superb dumpling you need Rome Beauty apples, which keep their shape while they are baking.

baked apple dumplings

Serves 4

Pastry for a 2 crust
  9-inch pie
½ cup sugar
½ teaspoon ground
  cinnamon

½ teaspoon ground mace
4 medium size Rome
  Beauty apples

Make the pastry as directed in this chapter and cut it into four circles about 8 inches in diameter.

Combine the sugar, cinnamon, and mace, and mix well. Peel and core the apples and roll them in the sugar mixture. Put an apple on each circle and put ¼ of the remaining sugar mixture in the center of each apple. Bring the pastry up around the apples and seal. Prick each dumpling on the top with a fork and bake them in a preheated moderate oven (375°F) for about 40 to 45 minutes, or until pastry is browned and crisp. Serve warm with cold milk or lemon sauce.

lemon sauce

1 tablespoon cornstarch	1 cup water
½ cup sugar	2 tablespoons lemon juice
1 teaspoon grated lemon peel	2 tablespoons margarine
	⅛ teaspoon salt

Combine the cornstarch, sugar, lemon peel, and water, and stir until smooth. Stir and cook over a low heat until thick and transparent. Cook for 2 minutes longer, stirring constantly. Remove the sauce from the heat and add the lemon juice, margarine, and salt. Stir until the margarine is melted. Serve warm with dumplings.

apple crumb pudding

Serves 6

2 cups canned applesauce	1 teaspoon ground nutmeg
1½ tablespoons lemon juice	2 teaspoons ground cinnamon
1 tablespoon grated lemon peel	½ cup chopped walnuts
1½ cups Graham cracker crumbs	½ cup washed and drained raisins
¼ cup (½ stick) melted margarine	

Combine applesauce, lemon juice, and lemon peel and mix well. Combine Graham cracker crumbs, margarine, nutmeg, cinnamon, walnuts, and raisins. Put a third of the crumb mixture in the bottom of a greased 1½-quart casserole. Cover with a half of the applesauce mixture. Cover with a third of the crumbs. Add the remaining applesauce mixture. Cover with the remaining crumbs and bake in a preheated moderate oven (350°F) for about 25 minutes, or until lightly browned. Serve warm or well chilled.

apple cranberry crisp

Serves 6

2 cups fresh cranberries
3 cups unpeeled sliced
   apples
¾ cup sugar
½ cup (1 stick) melted
   margarine

1 cup rolled oats
½ cup all purpose flour
½ cup sugar
½ cup washed and drained
   raisins

Combine the cranberries, apples and ¾ cup sugar in a 2-quart casserole. Combine margarine, rolled oats, flour, sugar, and raisins and spread over the fruit layer. Bake in a preheated moderate oven (350°F) for about 25 minutes, or until lightly browned.

strawberry banana gelatin

Serves 6

1 3-ounce package
   strawberry gelatin
1½ cups boiling water

1 10- or 12-ounce package
   frozen strawberries
2 large bananas

Add the gelatin to the boiling water and stir until completely dissolved. Add the frozen strawberries and stir gently until the strawberries are defrosted. Peel the bananas and slice them into the gelatin mixture. Pour the gelatin and fruit into a bowl or individual dessert dishes and chill for about 30 minutes, or until firm.

It is very important to cook the sugar syrup to the correct temperature. I very strongly recommend a candy thermometer. However, if you do not have a thermometer, cook the syrup until it forms a soft ball in cold water as you do when you are making fudge.

marshmallow topping

Yields about 2 quarts

1 cup sugar
½ cup water
4 egg whites

⅛ teaspoon salt
1 teaspoon vanilla

Combine the sugar and water in a heavy saucepan and stir to dissolve the sugar. Cook over a moderate heat for about 10 minutes or until the syrup has reached a soft ball stage on a candy thermometer (238°F). While the syrup is cooking, combine the egg whites and salt and beat at a high speed until it forms soft peaks. Pour the hot syrup slowly into the egg whites while beating at a high speed. Add the vanilla and beat at a moderate speed for another 5 minutes, or until topping is cool. Put the topping into a clean container, cover tightly, and refrigerate until needed if it is not to be used right away.

Other fruit juices may be substituted for the orange and grapefruit juice, if you desire. Cranberry juice is particularly good.

orange grapefruit sherbet

Yields about 2 quarts sherbet

2 cups sugar
1 cup water
2 egg whites
2 tablespoons sugar
1 tablespoon grated orange
    peel

1 cup orange juice
¾ cup grapefruit juice
¼ cup lemon juice
4 drops yellow food
    coloring

Combine 2 cups sugar and water in a saucepan. Bring to a rolling boil and boil 5 minutes. Beat the egg whites in a large mixer bowl until foamy. Add 2 tablespoons sugar and continue to beat until stiff peaks are formed. Add the hot syrup gradually to the egg whites while beating at a high speed to form a meringue. Gradually add the orange peel and fruit juices while beating at a moderate speed. Add the yellow food coloring, mix lightly and pour into shallow metal pan. (I use a 13- × 10-inch cake pan.) Place in a freezer for about 30 minutes. Mix well with a spoon. Continue to freeze and mix every 30 minutes until the sherbet is too stiff to mix easily. (The sherbet will divide into layers at first but don't worry about it.) Allow the sherbet to freeze completely. Pack in a plastic container with a tight lid and leave it in the freezer until ready to serve.

If you like a harder texture for your sherbet, prepare it the day before you want to use it and give it 24 hours to ripen in the freezer.

strawberry sherbet

Yields about 1 quart sherbet

1   12-ounce package frozen
      strawberries
1   3-ounce package
      strawberry gelatin
⅛   teaspoon salt

1   cup boiling water
1   cup strawberry juice
      and water
1   cup evaporated skim milk

Thaw the frozen strawberries. Drain the strawberries and reserve their juice. Dissolve the strawberry gelatin and salt in the boiling water. Stir to dissolve the gelatin. Combine the strawberry juice with enough water to yield 1 cup, add it to the gelatin, and chill until slightly syrupy. Add the milk gradually, stirring constantly, and pour into shallow metal pan. Add the strawberries and mix lightly. Place the sherbet in the freezer and freeze quickly until firm around the edges. Beat hard with a spoon. Return to the freezer and freeze until firm. Pack in a plastic container with a tight lid and leave in the freezer until ready to serve.

If you are going to freeze this in a mechanical freezer, do not add the strawberries until the sherbet is starting to get firm.

frozen pineapple milk dessert

Yields about 3 cups

1½ cups instant dry milk
¼ cup water
2 tablespoons lemon juice
¼ cup sugar

2 tablespoons vegetable oil
1 cup crushed pineapple and juice
¼ teaspoon almond flavoring

Combine the instant dry milk, water, lemon juice, and sugar, and beat at a high speed until thick and foamy. Add oil gradually while beating at a high speed. Add the pineapple and almond flavoring. Pour into a shallow metal pan and freeze until slushy. Stir with a spoon to distribute the pineapple. Return to the freezer and freeze until firm.

Double this recipe if you want a larger amount for a crowd and be sure to allow larger servings or they will be coming back for more.

frozen vanilla custard

Yields about 1½ quarts

3 cups water
⅛ teaspoon yellow food coloring
½ cup (1 stick) margarine
¾ cup sugar
¼ teaspoon salt

2 tablespoons all purpose flour
1 cup instant dry milk
1 cup cold water
3 slightly beaten egg whites
1½ tablespoons vanilla

Combine 3 cups water, yellow food coloring, and margarine in a saucepan and heat until the water is simmering and the margarine is melted.

Combine the sugar, salt, flour, instant dry milk, and 1 cup cold water, and stir until smooth. Add the smooth mixture to the simmering water, return to a simmer, stirring constantly, and continue to cook and stir for about 3 minutes. Remove from the heat and gradually stir about a cup of the hot mixture into the egg whites. Then blend the egg white mixture into the hot mixture in the saucepan. Continue to cook for about 1 minute more, stirring constantly. Remove from heat, add the vanilla and chill thoroughly. (It is very important that the custard be thoroughly chilled.) Freeze according to the directions with the freezer, pack it well, and ripen for 3 to 4 hours before serving, in the ice cream freezer or another freezer.

If you want to add fruits or nuts or crushed peppermint candy, it should be done after the ice cream is frozen and before it is packed to ripen.

frozen chocolate custard

Yields about 1¾ quarts

1 tablespoon unflavored gelatin	6 tablespoons cocoa
¼ cup cold water	1⅓ cups instant dry milk
3 cups water	⅛ teaspoons salt
½ cup (1 stick) margarine	1 cup cold water
1 cup sugar	2 tablespoons vanilla

Soak the gelatin in ¼ cup cold water. Combine 3 cups water and margarine in a saucepan and heat until the water is simmering and the margarine is melted.

Combine the sugar, cocoa, instant dry milk, salt, and 1 cup water, and stir until smooth. Add the smooth mixture to the simmering water, return to a simmer and cook, stirring constantly, until smooth. Remove the mixture from the heat, add the gelatin and vanilla and stir until the gelatin is melted. Chill the custard thoroughly. (It is very important that the custard be thoroughly chilled.) Freeze according to the directions with the freezer, pack it well, and ripen for 3 to 4 hours in either a freezer or the ice cream freezer.

If you want to add fruit or nuts or crushed peppermint candy, it should be done after the ice cream is frozen and before it is packed to ripen. The flavorings may also be varied by using other extracts instead of the vanilla or with the vanilla.

Peanut butter contains carbohydrate which will thicken a sauce if it is cooked so that if you like a thinner sauce, the peanut butter should be added with the margarine after the sauce has been cooked instead of with the sugar.

cocoa peanut butter topping

Yield 1¾ cups

½ cup white sugar
½ cup brown sugar
½ cup white corn syrup
½ cup cocoa
½ cup water

½ cup peanut butter
2 tablespoons instant dry milk
2 tablespoons (¼ stick) margarine
2 teaspoons vanilla

Combine the sugars, syrup, cocoa, water and peanut butter and simmer over a low heat for 5 minutes. Remove from the heat and add instant dry milk, margarine, and vanilla. Stir until the milk and margarine are absorbed into the sauce. Serve slightly warm or chilled.

coffee rum topping

Yields about 2 cups

1 cup sugar
1½ cups hot, double strength coffee

2 tablespoons arrowroot
2 tablespoons cold water
¼ cup light rum

Melt the sugar in a heavy saucepan, stirring constantly with a wooden spoon, until it is a rich caramel color. Remove the caramel from heat and add the hot coffee. Return it to the heat and continue to stir over a low heat until sugar and coffee are thoroughly mixed and there are no lumps of caramelized sugar left in the pan. Mix the arrowroot (cornstarch may be used instead of arrowroot but it won't be as clear and transparent) and water and stir until smooth. Stir the arrowroot mixture into the hot coffee mixture and continue cooking, stirring constantly, until the sauce is thick and smooth. Remove the sauce from the heat, add the rum, and serve warm. This sauce will keep in the refrigerator for a long time but should be slightly warmed each time that it is served.

butterscotch sauce

Yields about 2 cups

1½ cups brown sugar
½ cup white corn syrup
¼ teaspoon salt
½ cup water

2 tablespoons instant dry milk
¼ cup (½ stick) margarine
1 teaspoon vanilla

Combine the sugar, syrup, salt, and water and simmer over a low heat for 5 minutes. Remove it from the heat and add the instant dry milk, margarine, and vanilla. Stir until the milk and margarine are absorbed into the sauce. Serve warm.

chapter XII

foreign foods

We have a heritage of recipes from generations of housewives who immigrated to this country. It would be a shame to lose this heritage of ours — especially the recipes from countries that cooked with oil and used more vegetables and fruits than meat for economic reasons. These recipes are often just the thing for the low cholesterol diet.

Consult friends of cultural backgrounds different from yours. Try cookbooks that contain foreign recipes. You will probably find that your friends have recipes made with ingredients readily available in this country, which fit very well into the low cholesterol diet. Italian, Greek, Spanish, Chinese, and Japanese recipes are particularly popular and suitable for your use. If you or your husband have a cultural background with a cuisine all its own, you can probably collect a good supply of recipes from your mother or other members of your family.

I'm certainly no authority on Italian cooking in Italy but here in this country many of the good Italian recipes include a basic meat and tomato sauce. My husband is an excellent cook (better than I am in many instances) and my family and friends all think Chuck's recipe for Meat and Tomato Sauce (spaghetti sauce) is superb. He used to make the sauce to serve me and my friends long before we were married and it never failed to draw compliments. It took me quite awhile to get him to write down the exact ingredients, but finally I persuaded him to make a special batch and to write down every bit of spice and every step in the recipe. We like to make a big batch of it so it can be frozen if there is any left over. It is such a good feeling to have several containers of it in the freezer for unexpected guests. The sauce is very mildly spiced and you may want to add more oregano to it if you are serving it with spaghetti or mostaccioli. If your husband has been hungry for spaghetti and meat sauce but hasn't been able to have it because most of the spaghetti sauces are so rich and greasy, this would be a good one for you to try. If you don't want to freeze it, it will keep very well in the refrigerator for a week or so.

Meat and Tomato Sauce is very good served over spaghetti or other pasta. Prepare the spaghetti according to directions on the package, drain it and toss it with just enough of the sauce to give it color and prevent it sticking together. Put a generous serving of sauce on top of the spaghetti and pass some extra sauce. Serve it with a tossed green salad, Italian bread, a glass of red table wine and fruit for dessert — and you have a truly good low cholesterol meal. You can even cut down on the meat in the sauce if your doctor is strict about the amount of meat in your husband's diet or use a mushroom sauce made with tomatoes and spices to serve over the spaghetti for a meatless meal.

One of the most popular and tasty dishes made with meat and tomato sauce is Lasagna. It is not as difficult to make as you might think and it can be used on a low cholesterol diet without too much adaptation. Since you can use mozzarella cheese, it is only a question of leaving out the parmesan cheese and making sure the meat and tomato sauce has been cooked according to the basic principles of low cholesterol cooking. Remember not to make the lasagna too thick. If you are having a crowd of people increase the number of pans of lasagna rather than making it thicker. The amount of oregano in the recipe depends upon how well you and your family like oregano. I like it so well that my mother says she is surprised that I don't use it on ice cream, so be generous or scant with the oregano as you want. You can make several pans of lasagna at once if you like, freeze them, then bake a pan as you need it. It is a good idea to defrost the lasagna before you bake it but it can be baked from a frozen state if time is short. Just increase the baking time to an hour and a half instead of an hour, and it will be well done. You can also use different sized pans to make lasagna. If you want to freeze smaller portions you can use the individual foil pans. Freeze the amount that you think your family would eat at one time. In short, lasagna is a very versatile dish to prepare and like minestrone soup depends upon the cook so have fun with it. Don't forget to allow it to stand about 15 minutes before you serve it because it needs that time to get firm and will not be as good if it is served directly from the oven.

Rice is used a great deal in northern Italy and in that manner their cooking is somewhat akin to the cuisine of both China and Japan. Both Chinese and Japanese cooking are beginning to have a great deal of popularity in this country because of their attractive appearance and delicious taste. Many oriental recipes are not only delicious but easily fit into a low cholesterol diet. Who knows, you may even gain quite a reputation as a gourmet cook without anyone suspecting that it is all because you are keeping your husband healthy.

Chinese cooking offers a wide range of recipes for you to use on a low cholesterol diet. Many of their recipes are prepared with oil and they are very talented at making a little bit of meat go a long way. Their method of cooking vegetables until they are tender crisp is not only good but very good for you. Sweet and Sour Pork cooked in the Chinese manner has gained a lot of popularity in this country. It is particularly good because it enables you to use pork, since you cook it until all of the fat is cooked out of it but the flavor remains.

Japanese cooking seems to be gaining in popularity in many parts of this country. Most of the Japanese recipes fit very well into a low cholesterol diet because they are long on vegetables and fish and use vegetable oil for cooking. A recipe which most people seem to like is Sukiyaki, which has as many different versions as our beef stew. I've included a recipe that uses vegetables available in this country.

Just as I knew very little about Italian cooking until I met my husband, I also knew very little about Greek cooking until I met Vi Kliner. Vi is of Greek ancestry and is accomplished in Greek cooking as well as American. She and Frances Nielsen, who taught me so much about so many different styles of cooking, are the sort of friends that I would wish for any woman. If you aren't lucky enough to have friends who will share their recipes with you, go to the local library, read magazine articles, buy cookbooks with recipes for foreign foods. Most of the recipes in this chapter were collected from friends over the years. They do not pretend to be exact duplicates of the original recipes but they are good, they use ingredients readily available in this country, and they are spiced and prepared to suit American tastes. When I was deciding which recipes to use for this chapter I called Vi; she gave me some of her recipes that you might like to try in your own kitchen.

We have a new Spanish cousin-in-law, who was born in Spain of Spanish parents and grew up in Bordeaux, France. To help Dora feel at home in this country we explored Spanish and French recipes — and found quite a few that fit into my husband's low cholesterol diet. Spanish food is not as spicy as we had anticipated. It adapts well to a low cholesterol diet because the Spanish cook with oil and use a great many fresh fruits and vegetables.

British and Scandinavian cooking are both such an integral part of our American cuisine that it is hard to say where one ends and the other begins. They do, however, have many recipes that are not widely used in this country and it may be interesting to explore their cooking further as a source of additional recipes for your low cholesterol kitchen. I collected from various friends and relatives, but the recipes are only a sampling of the many available. For instance, Shirley Ruda from London makes a delicious Frosted Tea Cake. She made one and brought it when she came to visit my mother one day. We all thought it was so good that I asked her for the recipe. It was very easy to adapt for a low cholesterol diet. The only change necessary was to use egg whites instead of whole eggs.

Breakfast is a real problem in a low cholesterol kitchen. One answer to that problem is to give your husband a toasted English muffin with a bit of jam or jelly with his orange juice and coffee. The recipe for English muffins is from Virginia Ballantine. She makes them often and serves them to her family to enjoy for their breakfast.

Betty Eggebrecht is of Irish ancestry even though her name doesn't sound like it. She makes Irish Soda Bread for special occasions. Her boys and anyone else lucky enough to taste it love it. She made it for her sons when they were growing up; now their wives and children come home and still want some of her good soda bread to celebrate their homecoming.

Beatrice Eskew found Cornish Pasties served in the mining country of upper Michigan just as they are in England. These pasties freeze well and can be kept until she needs them.

I could never forget my Welsh grandmother's cookies. They are a national Welsh dish and I enjoyed them again on my first trip to Wales. I was attending the International Home Economics Association meeting in Bristol and one of the highlights of the trip for me was a tour of Cardiff with tea at the College of Domestic Science on Llantrisant Road. The tea was wonderful and I was delighted to discover again these cookies, which are supposed to be the same as those burned by King Alfred the Great. It seems that he took refuge in a Welsh cottage and while his hostess was preparing a place for him to hide she asked him to watch the cakes on the hearth. He was evidently thinking of greater things and let the cakes burn, for which he was soundly scolded. The Welsh generally bake these on a griddle like English muffins but I think you will find that it is easier and the results better if you bake them in the oven.

By no means could a complete collection of the many low cholesterol recipes to be found in foreign cooking be included in one chapter. We have not even mentioned many countries, which could provide an almost unlimited number of new and different recipes. It is only a very small collection of recipes but I hope it will inspire you to start your own collection of foreign recipes. As a final bit of encouragement to start your own collection, this book closes with an adaptation of an East Indian recipe. The original was so hot that it burned my tongue. This is milder but if you want, you can increase the pepper and add a little curry powder for a more authentic taste.

mushroom sauce

Yields about 1 quart

1½	pounds fresh mushrooms	⅛	teaspoon cayenne pepper
3	tablespoons vegetable oil	1	cup tomato juice
1	large can plum tomatoes	2	beef bouillon cubes
¼	teaspoon basil leaves		Salt and pepper to taste
1	teaspoon garlic powder		

Wash and slice the mushrooms. Cook the mushrooms in oil in a heavy saucepan over a moderate heat for 5 minutes. Crush the tomatoes and add them to the mushrooms. Add the basil, garlic powder, pepper, tomato juice, and bouillon cubes to the tomato mixture. Cover and simmer about 1 hour over a low heat, stirring occasionally. Uncover and add salt and pepper to taste. Cook uncovered over a low heat until the sauce is reduced to the proper thickness.

This recipe can be easily doubled if you want to freeze some of it. Chuck sometimes cooks double the amount in a 12-quart stainless steel pot, which is marvelous for soups and sauces. It should be prepared the day before you intend to serve it to allow the spices time to mellow (and to make it easier for you the day you intend to serve it). Be sure to use ground meat that has had the fat removed before it was ground or else drain off all of the fat after the meat is browned.

Chuck's meat and tomato sauce

Yields about 3 quarts

2 finely chopped garlic cloves
¼ cup finely chopped onions
3 tablespoons vegetable oil
1½ pounds ground round of beef or veal
2 6-ounce cans of tomato paste
1 29-ounce can of tomato puree

1 46-ounce can of tomato juice
½ teaspoon ground allspice
1 teaspoon ground oregano
⅛ teaspoon ground cloves
¼ teaspoon ground cumin
½ teaspoon paprika
½ teaspoon ground thyme
¼ teaspoon ground basil
Salt to taste
Pepper to taste

Sauté the garlic and onions in the oil in a heavy saucepan. Add the meat and brown, stirring frequently. Add the tomato paste, tomato puree, tomato juice, and spices. Simmer over a low heat (do not cover the pan) for about 4 hours, adding salt and pepper to taste after about 3½ hours. Do not shorten the cooking time since it needs a long slow cooking time to develop the flavor and do not allow it to cook too fast. It needs to simmer slowly. (Add more tomato juice if the sauce becomes too thick.)

lasagna

Serves 6 to 8

½	pound lasagna noodles	1½	teaspoons salt
2	pounds ricotta cheese or 2 pounds washed cottage cheese	½	pound shredded mozzarella cheese
3	egg whites	1	quart Chuck's Meat and Tomato Sauce
¼	cup chopped parsley	1½	tablespoon oregano leaves
¼	teaspoon white pepper		

Cook the noodles according to directions on the package. Drain and cover the noodles with cold water so they will separate easily.

Combine the ricotta cheese, egg whites, parsley, pepper, and salt, and mix lightly but thoroughly. (This mixture should be at room temperature when it is used so that it will spread easily.)

Combine the lasagna ingredients in layers in a 13- × 10- × 2½-inch baking pan as follows:

1. 1 cup sauce
2. ⅓ noodles
3. ½ ricotta mixture
4. ⅓ mozzarella cheese
5. 1 cup sauce
6. ⅓ oregano
7. ⅓ noodles
8. ½ ricotta mixture
9. ⅓ mozzarella cheese
10. 1 cup sauce
11. ⅓ oregano
12. ⅓ noodles
13. 1 cup sauce
14. ⅓ mozzarella cheese
15. ⅓ oregano

Bake the lasagna in a preheated moderate oven (350°F) for 1 hour. Remove it from the oven and allow it to stand 15 minutes to become firm before it is served.

Risotto Milanese goes very well with chicken and is luscious warmed up for breakfast the next morning.

risotto Milanese

Serves 6 to 8

½ cup finely chopped
    onions
3 tablespoons vegetable oil
2 cups long grain rice

Pinch of saffron
2 to 3 quarts hot chicken
    broth
Salt to taste

Sauté the onions in the oil in heavy saucepan until golden. Add the rice and saffron to the onions and continue to cook and stir until the rice is translucent. Cover the rice with hot chicken broth and simmer, stirring occasionally until rice absorbs broth. Continue to cook the rice, adding 1 cup hot broth at time and stirring occasionally for 26 minutes. (Some people like to use white wine for part of the hot chicken broth, but we prefer it with chicken broth.)

sweet sour pork

Serves 6

1½ pounds pork tenderloin
1 tablespoon vegetable oil
1½ cups water
3 chicken bouillon cubes
2 cups pineapple chunks
1 cup pineapple syrup

½ cup vinegar
⅓ cup soy sauce
¼ cup cornstarch
½ cup light brown sugar
1 cup julienne fresh green
    peppers
1 cup fresh tomato wedges

Remove all the visible fat from the pork with a sharp knife and cut the meat into about ¾-inch cubes. Brown the pork in vegetable oil in heavy saucepan. Add the water and bouillon cubes, cover and simmer for 30 minutes, or until pork is tender. Chill the pork and juice and remove the fat.

Drain the pineapple and reserve 1 cup juice for sauce.

Combine the pineapple syrup, vinegar, soy sauce, cornstarch, and light brown sugar and stir to form a smooth paste. Add the sauce to the meat and broth and cook over a low heat, stirring constantly, until sauce is thickened. Add the green peppers and cook for 10 minutes over a low heat, stirring occasionally. Add the pineapple and tomatoes and continue to cook over a low heat for about 5 minutes or until pineapple and tomatoes are hot. Serve over rice.

chicken and tomatoes

Serves 4

1½ pounds chicken breasts	1 tablespoon soy sauce
1 tablespoon soy sauce	1 tablespoon cornstarch
1 tablespoon sherry	¼ teaspoon salt
1 tablespoon cornstarch	1 tablespoon sugar
¼ cup vegetable oil	½ cup chicken broth
1 cup sliced onions	2 cups tomato wedges

Remove all the bones, skin, and fat from the chicken with a sharp knife. Cut the chicken into 1-inch cubes. Combine 1 tablespoon soy sauce, sherry, and 1 tablespoon cornstarch. Dredge the chicken in the soy mixture and sauté in oil in heavy frying pan for about 10 minutes or until tender. Add the onions to the chicken and continue to cook for about 2 minutes longer. Remove the chicken and onions from the frying pan with a slotted spoon. Drain the oil from pan. Add 1 tablespoon soy sauce, 1 tablespoon cornstarch, salt, sugar, and chicken broth to the pan and cook over a low heat, stirring constantly, for about 2 minutes or until thickened. Add the chicken and onions and tomatoes. Heat thoroughly and serve hot.

beef with green string beans

Serves 2 to 3

½ pound round of beef	1 tablespoon sherry
2 tablespoons soy sauce	2 tablespoons vegetable oil
1 tablespoon sugar	1 pound frozen green beans
1 tablespoon cornstarch	1 teaspoon salt

Remove all the visible fat from the beef with a sharp knife. Cut the beef into thin slices, about ¼-inch thick. (Beef will cut more easily if it is chilled until it is almost, but not quite, frozen.)

Combine the soy sauce, sugar, cornstarch, and sherry, and mix well. Dredge the beef in the soy sauce mixture, then brown it in the hot oil in a heavy frying pan. Add the frozen green beans to the meat. Cover tightly and cook over a low heat for about 15 minutes, or until the beans are tender crisp. (You will not need to add any water if the lid of the pan is tight since the frozen green beans will have enough moisture clinging to them.) Add salt to the beans just before serving, if necessary. Serve hot.

Do not try to increase the amounts in this recipe. It is better to prepare this much and then divide it among four people, then prepare another batch and give them a second helping rather than to crowd the pan.

sukiyaki

Serves 2

½ cup soy sauce	½ cup julienne fresh green
¼ cup beef broth	peppers
1 teaspoon sugar	½ cup thinly sliced celery

½ pound thick cut beef or
    veal round steak
1 tablespoon vegetable oil
½ cup sliced onions

½ cup drained, canned
    mushrooms
¼ cup sliced green onions
    Salt to taste

Combine the soy sauce, beef broth, and sugar to form a sauce.

Remove all the visible fat from the meat with a sharp knife. Cut the meat into thin slices across the grain. (The meat will slice more easily if it has been chilled.)

Brown the meat in the oil in a heavy frying pan. Add the onions, green peppers, celery, and sauce. Cook and stir over a medium heat for 5 minutes. Add the mushrooms and green onions and cook for an additional 2 minutes. Add salt to taste and serve over hot rice.

Try serving this stew to your husband when he says that he is hungry for pork. It really is delicious. You can substitute white potatoes for the sweet potatoes but it isn't nearly as good.

pork and sweet potato stew

Serves 6

1½ pounds pork tenderloin
2 tablespoons vegetable oil
1½ cups water
2 chicken bouillon cubes
1 tablespoon soy sauce
¼ teaspoon ground ginger

1 teaspoon salt
1 tablespoon cornstarch
2 tablespoons water
4 cups drained, canned
    sweet potatoes
½ cup sliced fresh green
    onions

Remove all the visible fat from the pork with a sharp knife and cut into 1-inch cubes. Brown the pork in the oil in heavy saucepan. Add 1½ cups water, bouillon cubes, soy sauce, ginger, and salt. Cover the pan and simmer for 30 minutes, or until the pork is tender. Chill the pork and juice and remove the fat.

Reheat the pork and juice to simmering. Combine the cornstarch and water and stir until smooth. Add them to the pork and stir over a low heat until thickened. Add the potatoes and onions and continue to heat until the potatoes have been thoroughly heated.

Vi's oriental green beans

Serves 6

2 pounds fresh green beans
½ cup chopped green onions
⅓ cup vegetable oil
2 cups canned tomatoes
    and juice
1 teaspoon salt
⅛ teaspoon pepper
6 small, peeled potatoes

Wash the green beans, remove their strings, and cut them into serving size pieces. Sauté the beans and onions in the oil in a heavy saucepan until the onions are golden. Add the tomatoes, salt, and pepper and simmer over low heat for 1 hour. Add the potatoes and continue cooking for about 20 minutes, or until the potatoes are done. Serve hot.

Vi's chicken oregano

Serves 4

2 pounds chicken breasts,
    thighs or legs
¼ cup lemon juice
1 teaspoon salt
⅛ teaspoon pepper
¼ cup vegetable oil
1 teaspoon leaf oregano

Wash the chicken, drain it, and remove all the fat and skin with a sharp knife. Sprinkle the chicken with the lemon juice, salt, and pepper, and let it marinate in the refrigerator for 1 hour.

Place the chicken, flesh side up, in an oiled shallow baking dish.

Pour any remaining marinade over the chicken. Pour the remaining oil over the chicken, sprinkle it with oregano, and bake it in a preheated moderate oven (350°F) for 1¼ to 1½ hours, or until the chicken is lightly browned and tender.

Vi's Greek okra

Serves 4 to 6

1   pound fresh or frozen
   okra
2   tablespoons vinegar
1   cup chopped onions

¼   cup vegetable oil
2   cups canned tomatoes
   and juice
1   teaspoon salt
⅛   teaspoon pepper

Wash and trim the okra. Sprinkle it with the vinegar and let it stand for 5 minutes. Sauté the okra and onions in the oil in a heavy frying pan until the okra turns a darker green and the onions are transparent. Combine the okra and onions with the salt, pepper, and tomatoes in a 1½-quart casserole. Bake it, uncovered, in a preheated moderate oven (350°F) for 1 hour.

Dora's stuffed tomatoes

Serves 6

6   medium size ripe
   tomatoes
2   tablespoons chopped
   onions
2   tablespoons chopped
   fresh green peppers
2   tablespoons vegetable oil
1   cup cooked rice

1   tablespoon chopped
   parsley
2   tablespoons beef or
   chicken broth
½   teaspoon salt
⅛   teaspoon pepper
2   tablespoons dry bread
   crumbs

Remove center of the tomatoes and remove some of the pulp but do not cut through the bottom skin of the tomatoes. Sauté the onions and green peppers in the oil until the onions are golden. Add the rice, parsley, broth, salt, and pepper to the onions, and mix well. Stuff the tomatoes with the rice mixture. Put 1 teaspoon crumbs on top of the filling in each tomato. Place the tomatoes in a shallow baking dish, with a bit of water in the bottom of the pan. Bake them in a preheated slow oven (325°F) for 25 to 30 minutes or until tomatoes are soft but still hold their shape.

gazpacho (cold soup)

Serves 4

1 cup minced, peeled cucumbers
3 cups minced, peeled tomatoes
3 tablespoons minced pimientos
¼ cup minced onions

3 tablespoons vegetable oil
3 tablespoons vinegar
2 crushed garlic cloves
1 cup ice water
Salt to taste
Pepper to taste

Combine the minced cucumbers, tomatoes, pimientos, and onions with their juices. Drain the juices from the vegetables and combine the juices with the oil, vinegar, garlic, and ice water. Beat the sauce well to mix. Pour the sauce over the vegetables, mix well, and season to taste. Chill and serve.

sangria

Yields 2 quarts

1 quart good red table wine
¼ cup lemon juice
½ cup orange juice
1 lemon

1 orange
Sugar as desired
1 quart ginger ale

Combine the wine, lemon juice and orange juice. Slice the orange and lemon into thin slices and add them to the wine. Add sugar to taste, depending upon the sweetness of the wine. Refrigerate the wine until well chilled. Add the ginger ale and serve over ice cubes in tall glasses or serve well chilled in wine glasses.

Basque fried chicken and potatoes

2 pounds chicken breasts, thighs or legs	2 cups thinly sliced potatoes
¼ cup vegetable oil	Salt to taste
	Pepper to taste

Wash the chicken, drain and remove the fat and skin with a sharp knife. Rub the chicken well with the oil so that it has a thin coating of oil. Brown the chicken slowly over a medium heat in a heavy frying pan. When the chicken is lightly browned, add the potatoes. Distribute the potatoes well, and season them with salt and pepper. Partially cover the pan and continue cooking the chicken over a low heat for 20 to 30 minutes, or until the potatoes and chicken are both tender. Turn the potatoes carefully two or three times while cooking or else shake the pan to loosen the potatoes from the bottom of the pan. (If you had any oil left after rubbing it on the chicken, add the oil, while the potatoes are cooking, to the bottom of the frying pan.)

peppers and onions

Serves 4

4 fresh green peppers	1 minced clove of garlic
1 cup sliced onions	Salt to taste
2 tablespoons vegetable oil	

Hold each pepper on a fork over an open flame until the skin is charred. Hold the pepper under running water and rub to remove the charred skin. Remove the seeds and stems from the peppers and slice them. Sauté the peppers, onions and garlic in the oil in a heavy frying pan slowly for 10 to 15 minutes, or until peppers and onions are just tender, stirring occasionally. Serve them hot with a steak or hamburgers.

Shirley's frosted tea cake

Serves 12

2 cups sugar	Frosting:
2 cups all purpose flour	½ cup (1 stick) margarine
1 cup (2 sticks) margarine	¼ cup cocoa
¼ cup cocoa	⅓ cup reconstituted instant
½ cup water	dry milk
¾ cup low fat buttermilk	1 pound package powdered
2 slightly beaten egg whites	sugar
1 teaspoon baking soda	1 teaspoon vanilla
1 teaspoon vanilla	1 cup chopped nuts

Sift the sugar and flour together into mixing bowl. Combine 1 cup margarine, ¼ cup cocoa, and water in a small saucepan, stir, and heat to boiling over a low heat. Boil for ½ minute and then add the cocoa mixture to the flour mixture and mix until smooth. Add the buttermilk, egg whites, soda, and 1 teaspoon vanilla, and beat for about 2 minutes at a medium speed, or until smooth. Pour the batter into a greased 10- × 13-inch metal cake pan and bake it in a preheated moderate oven (375°F) for 30 to 35 minutes, or until the cake springs back when touched in the center.

Combine ½ cup margarine, ¼ cup cocoa, and milk in a saucepan, stir, and heat to boiling over a low heat. Boil for ½ minute, then add the powdered sugar and 1 teaspoon vanilla to the cocoa mixture, and beat until smooth. Mix the nuts into the frosting and spread on the warm cake.

English muffins

Yields about 2 dozen muffins

1 cup hot water	½ ounce compressed yeast
2 tablespoons sugar	¼ cup instant dry milk
1 teaspoon salt	6 cups all purpose flour
¼ cup vegetable oil	Cornmeal as necessary
1 cup warm water	

Combine the hot water, sugar, salt, and oil, stir to dissolve the sugar, and cool to lukewarm. Put 1 cup warm water in a mixing bowl. Add the yeast and stir to dissolve. Stir the instant milk into the flour and add half of the mixture along with all of the sugar mixture to the yeast and water. Beat well for about 3 minutes. Add the remaining flour and knead the dough until smooth on a lightly floured board. Return the dough to the bowl, cover it with a cloth, and let it rise in a warm place until doubled in volume.

Punch down dough and divide it in half. Sprinkle a board heavily with cornmeal. Roll out each half of the dough until it is about ¼ inch thick. Cut into rounds with a 3-inch cookie cutter. Cover the rounds and let them rise for 30 minutes. Bake them on a slightly greased medium-hot skillet or griddle, cornmeal coated side down. Brown them well, about 15 minutes, then turn and bake them 15 minutes longer. Toast the muffins and serve them hot.

Irish soda bread

Yields 1 loaf

3 cups sifted all purpose flour	1 teaspoon salt
⅔ cup sugar	1½ cups raisins
1 tablespoon baking powder	3 slightly beaten egg whites
1 teaspoon baking soda	1½ cups low fat buttermilk
	3 tablespoons vegetable oil

Sift the flour, sugar, baking powder, soda, and salt together into a mixing bowl. Add the raisins and mix lightly.

Combine the egg whites, buttermilk, and oil, and add them to the flour mixture. Mix the batter lightly — only until all flour is moistened. Pour the batter into a greased round iron frying pan and bake it in a preheated moderate oven (350°F) for 1 hour. Cool for 10 minutes before removing bread from the frying pan.

Cornish pasties

Serves 4

1 recipe for a 2-crust pastry	2 ounces frozen peas
¾ pound beef or veal round steak	¼ cup concentrated cream of mushroom soup
½ cup cubed potatoes	1 teaspoon salt
½ cup cubed carrots	⅛ teaspoon pepper
¼ cup chopped onions	

Prepare the pastry for a double crust pie according to recipe in Chapter XI, Pies and Puddings. Roll out the pastry into four 8-inch circles.

Remove all the visible fat from the meat with a sharp knife and cut the meat into bite-sized pieces. Place equal amounts of the round steak, potatoes, carrots, onions, peas, and mushroom soup on one half of each circle. Add the salt and pepper and fold the remaining half of the pastry circle over the top like a turnover. Crimp the sides together and bake in a preheated hot oven (400°F) about 45 minutes or until pastry is well browned.

Welsh cookies

Yields about 2½ dozen 3-inch cookies

3 cups all purpose flour	2 tablespoons instant dry milk
1 tablespoon baking powder	

¾ cup sugar
½ teaspoon salt
1 teaspoon ground nutmeg
1 cup currants

¾ cup (1½ sticks) margarine
2 slightly beaten egg whites
½ cup water

Sift the flour, baking powder, sugar, salt, nutmeg, and instant dry milk together into a mixing bowl. Cut the margarine into the flour mixture as though you were preparing a pie crust. Add the egg whites, water, and currants, and mix to form a soft dough, about the consistency of sugar cookies. Roll the dough about ¼ inch thick on a lightly floured board. Cut the cookies with a floured 3-inch cookie cutter and bake on an ungreased cookie sheet in a preheated moderate oven (375°F) for 20 to 25 minutes or until the cookies are lightly browned on top. Remove the cookies from the cookie sheets while warm onto a wire rack.

Danish cabbage with wine

Serves 6

1 large head cabbage
¼ cup grated onions
½ cup finely chopped apples
2 tablespoons margarine

2 tablespoons brown sugar
1 teaspoon celery seed
1 teaspoon salt
1 cup dry white wine

Clean the cabbage, remove the core, and shred the cabbage. Add the onions and apples to the cabbage and sauté them in the margarine in a heavy saucepan over a low heat until the vegetables are limp, stirring occasionally to prevent scorching. Add the sugar, celery seed, salt, and wine to the cabbage. Reduce the heat and simmer for about 15 minutes.

salmon and vegetable salad

Serves 4

1 1-pound can of salmon	1 teaspoon sugar
1½ cups tomato wedges	2 teaspoons lemon juice
1 sliced cucumber	½ teaspoon salt
1 cup cooked frozen peas	¼ teaspoon white pepper
½ cup diced celery	½ cup L C mayonnaise

Drain the salmon, remove its skin and bones, and break it into bite size pieces. Combine the tomatoes, cucumbers, peas, and celery. Combine the sugar, lemon juice, salt, and pepper, and mix lightly with the vegetables. Add the salmon and mayonnaise, mix lightly, and chill before serving.

strawberry and rhubarb compote

Serves 6 to 8

1 quart fresh strawberries	4½ cups sugar
2 pounds fresh rhubarb	2 teaspoons cornstarch
2 cups water	2 tablespoons cold water

Clean and wash the strawberries and rhubarb. Detach the stems from the strawberries and cut the rhubarb into about 1-inch pieces.

Combine the rhubarb, water, and sugar, and cook over a low heat until the rhubarb is soft. Lift the rhubarb out of the juice with a slotted spoon and put the strawberries in the juice. Cook the berries over a low heat for about 2 minutes. Take the strawberries out of the juice with a slotted spoon. Arrange the strawberries and rhubarb in layers in a glass bowl.

Combine the cornstarch and water and stir until smooth. Stir the cornstarch into the hot juice and let it cook 2 minutes over low heat, stirring constantly. Pour the sauce over the fruit. Chill the compote in the refrigerator.

Serve with whipped instant dry or evaporated skim milk.

These are a popular item for buffets or they are good for a family dinner. The gravy is not generally thickened for a smorgasbord but it is if you want to serve them with noodles. The size of the meatballs will depend upon how you plan to use them.

Swedish meatballs

¼ cup finely chopped onions	2 tablespoons instant dry milk
1 tablespoon vegetable oil	
⅓ cup dry bread crumbs	½ teaspoon nutmeg
1 cup water	2 slightly beaten egg whites
½ pound ground round of beef	1½ teaspoons salt
	¼ teaspoon pepper
½ pound ground round of veal	¼ cup vegetable oil

Sauté the onions in 1 tablespoon oil until golden. Combine the onions, bread crumbs, water, meat, instant dry milk, nutmeg, egg whites, salt, and pepper, and mix until smooth.

Shape the meat mixture into balls with two spoons dipped in water or with a small ice cream dipper, and fry them in oil until evenly browned, frying only a few at a time. Use as much of the oil as necessary and add a little bit as you need it. Shake the pan while you are frying the meatballs to make them move around and brown on all sides.

If you prefer, you can put the meatballs on a greased cookie sheet and bake them in a preheated moderate oven (350° F) until browned. The length of time will depend upon the size of the meatballs.

spicy chicken

Serves 4 to 6

2½ pounds chicken breasts and thighs	½ teaspoon ground cumin
3 tablespoons oil	1 teaspoon ground paprika
2 cups chopped onions	¼ teaspoon ground ginger
⅛ teaspoon ground cloves	1 teaspoon garlic powder
½ teaspoon pepper	½ cup tomato puree
⅛ teaspoon ground cinnamon	¾ cup water
½ teaspoon monosodium glutamate (MSG)	2 tablespoons cornstarch
	½ cup water

Wash the chicken, drain and remove all the fat and skin with a sharp knife. Sauté the chicken in oil in a heavy frying pan until lightly browned. Remove the chicken to a 2-quart oven proof casserole. Sauté the onions in the remaining oil until well browned. Add the spices, tomato puree, and ¾ cup water to the onions and simmer for 5 minutes. Pour the onion mixture over the chicken, cover the casserole, and bake it covered in a preheated moderate oven (350°F) for 1 hour. Remove the chicken from the casserole to a hot platter. Combine the cornstarch and ½ cup water and stir into the sauce. Bring the sauce to a boil and cook for 1 minute, stirring constantly. Pour the hot sauce over the chicken and serve.

index